PORTFOLIO ACTIVIST

PORTFOLIO ACTIVIST

Babu Jagjivan Ram's Pursuit of Social Justice

ANIL KUMAR SARKAR

MANOHAR
2026

First published 2026
First eBook edition 2026

ISBN 978-93-6080-142-7 (hardbound)
ISBN 978-93-6080-549-4 (eBook)

Published by
Ajay Kumar Jain *for*
Manohar Publishers & Distributors
4753/23 Ansari Road, Daryaganj
New Delhi 110002

Typeset by Ravi Shanker, Delhi 110095

Cover design by Kamal Purna Jammual

Printed and bound in India

Contents

Acknowledgements 7

1. Introduction 9

2. The Broken Thread: Jagjivan Ram between 'Dalit' and 'Bahujan' Politics 31

3. 'The Cure-all for Everything': Babu Jagjivan Ram's Baptism in Politics 71

4. The Portfolio Activist: Jagjivan Ram as Parliamentarian 94

5. The Ministry of Arbitration: Jagjivan Ram, the Labour Ministry, and the Liberal Reforms 119

6. The Lonely Harijan: Jagjivan Ram's Politics for the Depressed Classes 155

7. The Repentant Politician: Jagjivan Ram, Caste Politics, and His Departure 197

8. Conclusion 215

Annexure
Caste Challenge in India: Jagjivan Ram 219

Bibliography 233

Index 245

Acknowledgements

The book aims to offer a fresh perspective on the life and achievements of Jagjivan Ram, focusing on his efforts to uplift the disadvantaged and marginalized in Indian politics. Titled *Portfolio Activist: Babu Jagjivan Ram's Pursuit of Social Justice*, this work was made possible through my appointment as Babu Jagjivan Ram Chair Professor at Calcutta University.

I am grateful to Meira Kumar, the daughter of Babu Jagjivan Ram and former Hon'ble Speaker of Lok Sabha, for providing the initial outline and inspiration for this project. Her valuable suggestions and words of encouragement motivated me to complete this work on time. I extend my sincere thanks to Professor Sonali Chakravarti Banerjee, the former Vice-Chancellor, for her consistent guidance and advice throughout the writing process. Her unwavering support was crucial in completing this book. Special thanks to Shri Arun Haldar, former Chairman of the National Commission for Scheduled Castes, for his inspirational words and encouragement to write about leaders who have made significant contributions to the upliftment of Dalits in our society.

I also acknowledge the continuous administrative support provided by Professor Debasis Das, Registrar of the University of Calcutta. I have received encouragement from Professor Sachindra Nath Bhattacharya, former professor of the Department of Museology at Calcutta University. I am grateful to the members of the Bengal Provincial Depressed Classes League, especially President Rabindra Nath Das, Vice President, Secretary, and other portfolio members, for their support and encouragement. I express my gratitude to Professor Ananda Gopal Ghosh, Emeritus Professor at North Bengal

University, and Professor Chittabrata Palit for their valuable suggestions and words of inspiration. Special thanks to my colleagues at Kalyani University and Calcutta University for their support. I appreciate the assistance of Aryama Ghosh, Partha Mukherjee, Kinshuk Bhattacharya, in providing source material and bringing this book to fruition. I also thank Sukanta Majumdar, A.K. Biswas, Akhil Sarkar, Ajit Kr. Das, Subhadip Das, Alok Kora and others for their support. My wife, Dipanwita Das, deserves special thanks for her constant help.

I am grateful to all my well-wishers who inspired me in this endeavour. Lastly, I thank Ananya Jain of Manohar Publishers and Distributors, New Delhi, for their role in publishing this book.

Garia, Kolkata ANIL KUMAR SARKAR

1

Introduction

In the words of Patrick K. O'Brien, political biographies have been called 'a serious enough genre', who has made a crucial point about whether or not, a litany of academic historians should pay attention to them. According to O'Brien, the majority of historians believe that political biographers make the mistake of either glorifying their subjects as 'superhuman' or showing them as 'ordinary people', whose behaviour and traits are used to generalize about the governments of that time. He further contends that political biographies fail to adequately inform historians about the fundamental goals of their field, which are to gain a correct comprehension of changing political systems and processes, and to recognize the enduring impact of notable persons involved in these processes. This is despite the fact that political biographies are driven by admirable intentions to educate, and entertain their readers. Possibly, when illuminating data is discovered as a by-product of biographical writing, lives—no matter how exemplary or captivating, are not very beneficial for such goals and could possibly be a diversion.[1]

It would be foolish, though, to completely ignore political biography as a tool for piecing together the past. 'The impact on recent world events of individuals like Churchill, Stalin, Gandhi, Hitler, and Roosevelt make it abundantly clear that the influence of the "great man", for good or evil, must not be underestimated,' as stated by Gardner Murphy, a prominent American psychologist who in 1950, urged a thorough examination of the character traits of world leaders in politics.[2] Even more frequently, political biographies appear to have been really helpful in gaining a comprehensive picture of a particular political atmosphere. According to Lewis J. Edinger, political biographers seem to aim for a careful equilibrium between being descriptively objective and artistically creative, between focusing on the person and the setting of one's political actions.[3]

The amount of emphasiz placed on the subject's personality and his sociopolitical milieu are two characteriztics that Edinger notes as a defining distinct types of political biographies. Purely descriptive biographies work under the premise that readers can be enlightened by 'facts' alone. Using this method, it has occasionally resulted in a massive chronological compendia. A concealed bias has often been incorporated into such kinds of research due to the data selection process and the sources' nature. Information about the lives of unsuccessful leaders is often far scarcer than that of their more successful competitors, and they are, thus, more likely to be the targets of snubs.[4] India has consistently possessed a plethora of political leaders and statesmen throughout its history. Numerous politicians showed a greater preoccupation with acquiring fortune, power, or celebrity status while displaying minimal inclination towards fulfilling their duty of serving the populace. Nevertheless, only a limited number of individuals have been able to leave a lasting impact through their visionary perspectives and exceptional leadership abilities. No matter how successful a national leader is, there are instances when critical biographies of him are lacking. Babu Jagjivan Ram is a prime example of this facet.

Babu Jagjivan Ram (fondly remembered as Babuji) has been largely ignored in the canon of modern Indian history books, despite his impressive political career. Despite representing an alternative Dalit politics to Ambedkar's, Jagjivan Ram has been either utterly disregarded or severely marginalized in the dominant Dalit historiography because of his tight and difficult relationship with the mainstream Congress Party. A character who held substantial portfolios, and used his position to improve their lifestyle is, however, crucial to understanding the framework of the alternative Dalit movement and postcolonial labour challenges.

The work, *Portfolio Activist: Babu Jagjivan Ram's Pursuit of Social Justice*, is a critical biography written on Jagjivan Ram. Being an experienced statesman, he possessed a comprehensive perspective and a strong practical judgement. He emerged as an undisputed and intrepid figurehead for the entirety of India, particularly for the marginalized and oppressed segments of society. We must always remember that Jagjivan Ram was a politician, with all the necessary requisites of politicking in an emerging nation, a cause due for which he has been criticized now and then. For instance, he was a man with different faces in different scenarios. The man acted judiciously while holding different portfolios, he never left politicking at different levels to keep up his prominence, a tendency which has often has been criticized as opportunism. For example, he acted very judiciously under Indira Gandhi's regime, but once the Emergency period came into action, he utilized every opportunity to assert his political prominence. In Bihar, he and his group tussled with L.N. Mishra's group and the Indira faction's preferred Chief Minister Abdul Ghafur.[5] His defection to Janata Dal and his tries to bring all the Congressmen to his side as a political plan was often criticized in contemporary news.[6] However, the pragmatism of politics and politics of progress, had a fine balance within Jagjivan Ram's working framework and larger credo. In that sense, this work of biography would try to do justice to this aspect. Facts were merged with a subjunctive mood through which the personality of a politician has been viewed in a kaleidoscopic approach.

In the preface of a commemorative publication dedicated to Jagjivan Ram, Somnath Chatterjee, a former Speaker of the Lok Sabha, articulated his perspectives. He holds a unique and notable position in the annals of contemporary Indian history. The individual in question possessed a notable background as a seasoned advocate for freedom, displaying exceptional skills in organization and public speaking. Furthermore, he showed an unwavering dedication to social and political causes, actively participating in trade union leadership and advocating for the advancement of marginalized groups. Additionally, his contributions as a recognized lawmaker, commitment to democratic principles, and adeptness in administrative matters further solidify their reputation. Jagjivan Ram exhibited a diverse range of qualities and attributes.[7] While he did possess certain idealistic tendencies, his predominant disposition was that of a realist who harboured a distinct vision for the future of India in its entirety, with a particular focus on the marginalized untouchable community. The individual in question did not exhibit a singular motivation rooted primarily in idealism; rather, their approach was characterized by a pragmatic blend of practicality and idealistic principles.

Over the course of his five-decade-long tenure in Indian politics, Jagjivan Ram emerged as a major proponent for the emancipation of his country and the empowerment of marginalized segments of society. K.L. Chanchreek, a widely acclaimed writer, drew a parallel between him and Marx in Western discourse, highlighting their shared commitment to the emancipation of the working class. Babu Jagjivan Ram was internationally revered for his advocacy and activism on behalf of the historically marginalized untouchable population and exploited individuals in India and other regions. He played a crucial role in connecting Indian labourers with their counterparts in foreign nations, and his bravery, perseverance, and commitment to duty remain a source of inspiration and guidance for India's advancement.[8]

Babu Jagjivan Ram emerged as a prominent leader whose contributions were crucial in effecting positive changes in the socio-economic and political landscape for marginalized communities, specifically untouchables, backward classes, and labourers. One of his most remarkable contributions to India's independence struggle was his amicable and proficient method of tackling the issue of untouchables. The individual's leadership played a crucial role in the protracted and arduous endeavour to secure the emancipation of the untouchable castes, demonstrating unwavering loyalty to Mahatma Gandhi. Jagjivan Ram's eminence and standing beyond the lofty positions he occupied was appreciable. He achieved prestigious positions by virtue of his talent, commitment, and fervour for promoting social justice and effecting social change.

According to the former Prime Minister, Dr Manmohan Singh, Jagjivan Ram was an exemplary leader of our country. Despite originating from a socio-economically challenged family, his exceptional talent and unwavering commitment enabled him to achieve remarkable success in his professional endeavours. In his role as a freedom warrior, he exemplified a commitment to public service, and his fervour for promoting social equity and transformation was apparent in the numerous policy choices he enacted and legislative proposals. Ram amalgamated the principles of Mahatma Gandhi and

Pandit Jawaharlal Nehru, establishing himself as a forward-thinking and proficient leader. The enduring significance of his vision for a society devoid of caste divisions and his emphasiz on the necessity of a cognitive transformation to eradicate caste biases, are evident in the contemporary times.[9] Jagjivan Ram devoted his professional life to championing the rights and welfare of marginalized individuals. The extraordinary nature of the guy in question can be attributed to his honesty, simplicity, and unwavering dedication to his purpose. The individual's honesty was seen as above reproach, even by those who opposed him, as they held great admiration for his dynamic and complex character. He exhibited a combination of compassion and strong self-control, embodying the qualities of an exemplary and energetic individual, really earning the title of greatness in every aspect.

Madhu Dandavate recounted an illustrative incident concerning Jagjivan Ram's endeavours to bring attention to the inequities experienced by Harijans in the region of Pipra. He orchestrated a scholarly discourse centred around a specific subject matter, wherein, he actively engaged and contributed by articulating his perspectives. During the debate, Jagjivan Ram articulated his position on the matter, stating, 'I am often referred to as a national leader and a national unifier. However, when I visited Varanasi to unveil the statue of my esteemed colleague, Shri Sampurnanand, and subsequently returned, as several self-proclaimed holy Brahmins poured the sacred water of the Ganges onto Sampurnanand's statue. This act was likely motivated by my untouchable status, potentially compromising the statue's sanctity and dignity. The intention behind this action was to purify the statue by using water from the Ganges.'[10] Following this incident, one of the organizers expressed, 'I am prepared to inquire about your concerns.' However, in response, Babuji exclaimed, '*Maraypaeritnesastenahinitein*.'[11] His comments caused others to experience feelings of humiliation.

The Hindu *shastras* have exerted a significant influence on our societal structure, characterized by a hierarchical organization based on caste, and upheld by those belonging to the caste Hindu community. The aforementioned circumstances have given rise to a particular mentality that impacts individuals, such as Jagjivan Ram. He originated from a family belonging to the untouchable caste and experienced adverse consequences as a result of this societal structure. Despite achieving renown, his intrinsic identity remained the most prominent aspect of his existence. He held the belief that the continuation of dynasty governance resulted in the perpetuation of a societal structure, wherein individuals belonging to a specific caste were compelled to endure their hardships without any acknowledgement or redress. Hence, Jagjivan Ram devoted his life to combating and eradicating this biased system.

Babu Jagjivan Ram fervently argued for the adoption of an ideology that is congruent with the cultural values and traditions of India, as opposed to the importation of political ideas or philosophies from foreign nations. He acted as a source of inspiration for marginalized communities and embodies a symbol of resilience for individuals across society, as he spearheaded the efforts towards establishing a robust, forward-thinking, inclusive, and fair society. Nau Nihal Singh, a former member of the Rajya Sabha, conducted an analysis of his political philosophy, encapsulating it in the following assertion: 'Jagjivan Ram exhibited exceptional qualities of intellect and emotion, embodying a profound sense of patriotism, unwavering commitment to democratic principles, and a deep-rooted nationalism.' The individual expressed strong opposition against the negative aspects of casteism, orthodoxy within the Hindu social structure, and the practice of untouchability.

Furthermore, he advocated for equality in social interactions. He advocated for the implementation of social justice and equal chances for the vast population belonging to the marginalized and disadvantaged groups. Over a span of around forty years, he provided guidance and protection for the Dalits, while demonstrating unwavering commitment as a progressive leader in their pursuit of social advancement. His efforts were primarily directed towards improving the conditions of the untouchables, the marginalized, and the impoverished, as well as addressing the needs of the severely overlooked working class.[12]

Jagjivan Ram espoused the perspective that the mere existence of political democracy falls short in its ability to effectively promote societal equality and adequately solve the challenges faced by marginalized and disadvantaged individuals. He conceptualized an egalitarian society that advocates for equal opportunities and freedoms devoid of prejudice, a perspective that was also endorsed by Ambedkar. Despite the attainment of political independence, persistent disparities continue to exist in Indian society across social and economic domains. Thus, addressing social and economic inequality is itself a crucial obligation that falls upon us.

Throughout his lifetime, he dedicated himself to the promotion and support of social justice, so establishing himself as a genuine advocate and an ardent champion of the aforementioned cause. His primary attention was directed towards advocating for the concept of social justice, which served as the fundamental motivation underlying his philosophical framework. The individuals in question did not actively pursue acknowledgement or public roles, but instead dedicated their efforts towards advocating for social justice in India. Specifically, their focus was on addressing the historical marginalization experienced by certain parts of society inside the country, particularly those affected by the caste system. The individual's pursuit of social justice was notable and warrants acknowledgement. Understanding the notion of social justice, which has experienced a surge in popularity in contemporary society, holds significant importance. Nevertheless, it is of equal significance to take into account the societal willingness to adopt it, alongside the response of the governing authorities.

The concept of social justice is multifaceted, and subject to diverse interpretations depending on the specific environment and circumstances. Numerous scholars have conducted analyses of the subject matter from various angles. An illustration of this concept can be found in the work of John Rawls, who formulated the notion of social justice as the guarantee of equitable availability of liberties, rights, and opportunities, coupled with the provision of assistance to individuals, who, are most marginalized within a given society. Consequently, the moral evaluation of an action is contingent upon its facilitation or obstruction of individuals' access to civil liberties, human rights, and possibilities for a gratifying existence, as well as its equitable distribution of advantages among the most disadvantaged.

Rawls's positions is that the establishment of social justice is achieved by means of a social contract. This suggests that individuals willingly provide their agreement to adhere to specific regulations that provide collective benefits, rather than just prioritizing their personal interests. According to Rawls, individuals who are rational and autonomous would endorse these norms in a fair and just context. The agreement plays a vital role in ensuring social fairness as it necessitates public support for the implementation of these policies. The aforementioned norms or principles delineate the fundamental rights and obligations that are to be allocated by the primary political and social institutions. They also govern the distribution of advantages resulting from social collaboration and assign the required costs to uphold it.[13]

Edmund Cahn's scholarly analysis mostly centres on the concept of justice, wherein he presents a critical perspective and advances his arguments. The issue of justice should be examined and understood primarily through its negative aspects rather than its positive aspects. The individual has a preference for prioritizing the perception of unfairness, as it is inherent in the human biological makeup, allowing for clear differentiation between instances of injustice and justice. Injustice is characterized by dynamic and emotive qualities that elicit outrage and wrath. Hence, the concept of justice fundamentally entails the act of rectifying or averting any circumstances that would elicit a feeling of unfairness.[14]

He held the belief that the act of religious conversion would neither effectively address the prevailing injustices experienced by the Harijans, nor would it lead to an amelioration of their social standing. Jagjivan Ram advocated for individuals to improve their social and economic status, assimilate into the dominant culture of the nation, and actively contribute to its advancement. He expressed the belief that the collective development of the country is intricately linked to the personal development of its citizens and that their liberation is intertwined with the liberation of the nation as a whole.[15]

Like Mahatma Gandhi, Jagjivan Ram, attributed his significance to authentic spirituality in his personal life, concurrently engaging in the struggle against the prevalent social injustices and societal vices. His unwavering conviction in authentic religious practises served as a catalyst for his subsequent actions. The individual exhibited a firm stance against casteism and rigidity prevalent in Hindu society, yet refraining from outright condemnation of Hinduism as its whole. He was a prominent advocate for social justice and a perceptive leader. In 1935, he assumed a pivotal role in the establishment of the All India Depressed Classes League with the aim of advocating for parity and advancement for the marginalized segments of society, known as the Untouchables. In his capacity, as a member of the Constitution Assembly, he subsequently advocated for the implementation of affirmative action policies to ensure the representation of Dalits in elected bodies and government services.

Jagjivan Ram prioritized the challenges encountered by the Dalit community. Enhancing their societal and economic standing constituted the primary objective of his activist endeavours. He assumed a prominent position in the execution of welfare programmes designed to empower the Dalit population. The individual, in question, garnered public interest through his statement, asserting that a comprehensive resolution to the issues faced by the Scheduled Castes and Tribes necessitates a fundamental restructuring of the socio-economic system.[16] However, the execution of welfare initiatives has been inadequate, falling short of expectations and leaving room for improvement. As the socio-economic situations of these communities ameliorate, it is inherent for its inhabitants to aspire towards a dignified existence. While individuals become increasingly cognizant of their entitlements, it is anticipated that they will exhibit a propensity to reject instances of unjust treatment. Nevertheless, it is worth noting that in some rural regions where this phenomenon has manifested, there has been a notable return of oppressive practices and instances of harassment.

Only a limited number of literary works provide insight into the significant contributions made by Jagjivan Ram to Indian politics. The literary work in question is titled, *Caste Challenges in India*, and has been authored by the said politician himself.[17] This literary work explores his ideological perspectives regarding the caste system prevalent in India. The subject matter encompasses a range of subjects, such as the historical genesis of caste, inter-group social tensions, and cultural challenges. He expresses his perspectives on: social transformation, Mahatma Gandhi, Scheduled Castes, the concept of a society without caste distinctions, the implementation of a fifth reservation, and the potential of religious conversion as a means of resolving societal issues. The book examines the rise of Scheduled Castes and their endeavours to combat the injustices and atrocities inflicted against them. Ultimately, he contemplates the enduring presence of caste-based prejudice in India, notwithstanding the progress made in the realms of science and technology. The author highlights that individuals who identify as reformers themselves contribute to the perpetuation of the concept of untouchability, as they endorse the notion of segregated advancement in several domains such as social, political, economic, and educational spheres. He proposes the implementation of mixed-house colonies as a potential solution to foster amicable coexistence among individuals from diverse socio-economic backgrounds.

The edited volume by A.C. Sinha, titled, *Struggles and Achievements: Babu Jagjivan Ram Commemoration Volume,* is a remarkable undertaking.[18] Its objective is to honour the multifaceted and inspiring life of him. The book has been partitioned into distinct sections. The initial segment comprises expressions of goodwill from notable individuals, both domestic and international, who have observed his accomplishments over an extended duration. Subsequent to the aforementioned correspondences, a concise biographical account is presented, encapsulating the key events and milestones of his existence. The subsequent segment presents a scholarly article authored by K.L. Chanchreek. The research paper examines the significant historical events in his life, with a particular emphasiz on his contributions to the field of K.L. Chanchreek. It incorporates a comprehensive analysis of categorized literature, consisting of his works and speeches. This paper is accompanied by two correspondences from Mahatma to Babuji. The book contains additional essays that cover many facets of his life and accomplishments. These articles are authored by individuals from various professional backgrounds, including diplomats, educationalists, political figures with divergent political ideologies, and the heads of state. The aforementioned articles have been authored by Nau Nihal Singh, Frank Moraes, Prakashvir Shastri, K.K. Shah, A.K. Jain, Tushar Kanti Ghosh, and Bimal Prasad. The individuals in question exhibit either a strong personal connection to the Dalit leader or possess a profound comprehension of his contributions and accomplishments. The book additionally incorporates interviews conducted by him with the international press and television units regarding the Indo-Pak War, as well as his engagements and responsibilities inside different ministries. An interview of significant interest and intellectual stimulation was conducted by the editor of said volume. In this discourse, Sinha examines his social philosophy. In conclusion, this publication will serve as a valuable resource for future scholarly investigations.

The commemorative volume titled, *Babu Jagjivan Ram in Parliament* was issued by the Secretariat of Lok Sabha.[19] The book is structured into four distinct sections. The initial section provides a full exposition of the life of Jagjivan Ram, encompassing his multifaceted engagements, both personal and public, as well as the challenges of a social and political nature that he confronted. The text also examines the political and legislative contributions of the individual in question, both prior to and subsequent to the India's independence. This serves to offer readers a comprehensive understanding of the individual's multifaceted persona, the obstacles faced, and the achievements attained. The second section has writings authored by individuals who were intimately associated with him and were contemporaries, including his daughter and the former Lok Sabha Speaker, Meira Kumar, the late former President of India Pranab Mukherjee, Sharad Pawar, T.N. Chaturvedi, Bali Ram Bhagat, Mohan Singh, Mohan Dharia, K.C. Pant, Sarojini Mahishi, and Avtar Singh Rikhy. The third half of this document comprises a collection of speeches delivered by Jagjivan Ram on the parliament floor, presented in English, Hindi, and multilingual versions. The aforementioned remarks serve as evidence of his profound expertise across several subjects and his genuine commitment to advocating for marginalized populations. The original language of the talks has been preserved, with the exception of necessary modifications to provide cohesion. The fourth section of the document comprises of testimonials provided by eminent individuals, intimate acquaintances, and colleagues, as presented in both the Upper and Lower Houses of Parliament. Additionally, the Parliament House witnessed the delivery of speeches by esteemed individuals during the ceremonial unveiling of his statue. The book provides a thorough examination of his political trajectory, while his profile succinctly encapsulates everything. The ten pieces offer a comprehensive portrayal of the individual's struggles and achievements, emphasizing their multifaceted leadership, viewpoints, and concepts. The selected remarks delivered by the individual in question inside the parliamentary setting, serve, as a testament to their esteemed attributes as a seasoned member of parliament and a highly regarded statesperson. Ultimately, the sincere expressions of admiration and respect presented in the tributes serve to highlight many facets of his personality.

The *Milestones: A Memoir*, penned by Indrani Jagjivan Ram,[20] narrates a vivid account of the life of the author, who happens to be the leader's spouse. The narrative encompasses the formative years of the individual, including her early life experiences, educational pursuits, and the active participation of her family in the struggle for liberation amidst the sociopolitical upheaval of the 1920s. The book additionally delves into the personal and professional trajectory of Jagjivan Ram, encompassing his formative years and the adversities encountered by his family. Indrani Devi offers a complete portrayal of his multidimensional character, encompassing all the events and advancements in both his private and public spheres. The book highlights the author's significant involvement in the liberation movement, his incarceration experiences, and the influential connections he established with leaders such as Rajendra Prasad and Jayaprakash Narayan, which played a pivotal role in fostering a renewed sense of purpose. The text also examines the individual's involvement in securing the nation's triumph in the Indo-Pak conflict while serving as the Minister of Defence, emphasizing their significant contribution to the success of V.V. Giri, who assumed the role of the President of the nation. Ultimately, the book offers an extensive portrayal of his accomplishments throughout his tenure as a clergyman.

Ramesh Chandra and Sangha Mitra, in their book titled, *Jagjivan Ram and His Times*, explored the lived experiences of those belonging to the marginalized social group during the era of his times.[21] The enduring and endearing remembrance of Babu Jagjivan Ram's influence throughout this pivotal era in Indian history is undeniable. Despite facing numerous challenges in his political trajectory subsequent to the 1960s, he had shown unwavering determination and resilience. In 1969, the individual in question had a notable setback in his pursuit of the most esteemed non-military position, primarily as a result of conventional factors. Despite receiving significant support for his views, he ultimately departed from the Congress party and established his own political party, referred to as Congress for Democracy, as a result of his services to Indira Gandhi. He exerted much effort in order to promote social justice within the realm of politics. The book additionally emphasizes the Dalit leader's formative years, his engagements with Mahatma Gandhiji and the former Indian President Rajendra Prasad, his ascent as a prominent figure, his participation in the struggle for independence, his political astuteness, his role as a catalyst for societal change, his enduring contributions as a cabinet minister during the pre- and post-independence era, and the genesis and amalgamation of Congress for Democracy with the Janata Party.

The book, *Babu Jagjivan Ram: A Nation Builder*, edited by K.L. Chanchreek, is a significant academic work comprising of two volumes.[22] This book holds great importance as it contains a total of 21 articles written by renowned scholars and experts in the field. These articles are thoughtfully organized into three distinct portions, enhancing the overall structure and coherence of the book. This literary work undertakes an analysis of Jagjivan Ram's accomplishments and contributions to the process of nation-building while shedding light on his perspectives concerning untouchability and his arduous endeavour to eliminate it. This analysis explores the multifaceted nature of his personality and his perspectives on the caste system, using a compilation of his speeches and writings to gain insights into his social philosophy and democratic ideals. Despite providing considerable coverage of these themes, the text falls short in identifying the precise political leadership of the individual in question. The second book, which consists of 32 pieces, offers an additional understanding of the multidimensional nature of Ram's personality. This analysis delves into the pivotal role played by the individual in question, as, a saviour of the Congress Party during a period of significant upheavals. Additionally, it examines the individual's notable accomplishments as a proficient politician and minister. Additionally, it encompasses his proficiency in administrative tasks and his educational ideology. Nevertheless, it fails to precisely identify the specific factors that led to his decision to resign from the Congress Party.

The literary work, *Babu Jagjivan Ram: Builder of Modern India* by Om Prakash Maurya, and translated by Rupali Kishore[23] comprises a collection of speeches delivered by Babu Jagjivan Ram, wherein he expounds upon his perspectives pertaining to social philosophy, the issue of untouchability, and a range of other subjects. The book provides a comprehensive examination of the author's familial origins, educational pursuits, and formative years. The text encompasses his participation in the liberation movement, his endeavours to ameliorate the marginalized, and his leadership of the recently established Congress Party subsequent to its division. The book additionally illuminates his contributions to the nation's progress. Furthermore, it underscores his arduous endeavour to build parity and foster a culture characterized by equal opportunities and fairness.

Jagjivan Ram: The Harijan Leader by S.R. Bakshi chronicles Jagjivan Ram's life trajectory of encompassing his political endeavours and his notable contributions to the Indian struggle for independence, as well as his efforts towards ameliorating the conditions of marginalized communities.[24] The book provides an account of Jagjivan Ram's adoption of Gandhi's principles, including the promotion of Swadeshi, and an active involvement in constructive endeavours, not just within the region of Bihar, but, also across the entirety of India. This study also delves into the emergence of Jagjivan Ram as a prominent figure among the Harijans, highlighting his adeptness in the sphere of organizing, his widespread appeal as a leader of the masses, and his esteemed standing as a lawmaker. The book explores the author's worldview, his involvement in the improvement of rural communities, and his aptitude for administration.

The primary objective of the book is to examine and engage with significant philosophical concerns that have adverse effects on the development and manifestation of the human personality. The text accomplishes this by situating the topic inside a conversational framework that prioritizes the significance of dialogue and encourages introspection. Regrettably, the Indian caste society has embraced an ideology characterized by violence and injury, which propagates animosity towards those who deviate from societal norms. The advent of casteism through the Vedas has resulted in the emergence of caste rigidities targeting marginalized populations. The collective memory of past atrocities and the ongoing instances of degradation and social ostracism shape our collective consciousness. All these developments grant a sense of invulnerability to acts of physical violence perpetrated against marginalized individuals, such as labourers, domestic workers, office attendants, agricultural workers, orphaned children, and beggars on the outskirts of temples. These individuals are subjected to widespread disdain within the contemporary Indian society. New justifications have been uncovered to undermine the value of individuals belonging to the marginalized segments of society.[25]

Jagjivan Ram posited that the establishment of democratic, socialist, and secular principles in India necessitates substantial advancements in social, economic, political, and educational domains. The individual identified the obstacles associated with attaining these objectives and articulated their apprehensions. It is regrettable that despite the presence of leaders of remarkable stature, dedication, and competence, as well as a substantial organizational structure, India has not achieved its desired objectives. There is a growing inquiry into the trajectory of the nation and whether the absence of a well-defined framework and the presence of conflicting ideologies and goals inside the Congress Party, are responsible for this situation. During the pre-independence era, the Congress organization lacked a clearly defined objective of achieving political independence. However, resolutions adopted during different Congress sessions demonstrated advancements in the formulation of independence goals, the integration of Western industrialization with traditional cottage industries, and the pursuit of a harmonious balance between scientific thinking and Gandhian thought.

During a public address in Anantapur City in the year 1968, Jagjivan Ram espoused the establishment of democracy, secularism, and socialism as fundamental principles in the Indian context. The speaker implored individuals to ready themselves for emancipation from the confines of enslavement and to demonstrate a willingness to bear the associated costs, which would not prove excessively burdensome if a substantial number were prepared to make the ultimate sacrifice. He underscored the movement's overarching mission of instilling elevated human values inside the Indian society, with democracy and socialism serving as important aims. Nevertheless, he argued that the coexistence of caste and democracy is untenable, as only one can prevail within a given community. The speaker underscored the significance of eliminating the caste system in order to render socialism meaningful, as the coexistence of the two is inherently incompatible. The establishment of human values in society is likely to present a formidable challenge until the country has firmly established both the tenets of democracy and socialism.[26] He was an advocate and implementer of secularism in its most authentic manifestation. The individual held the belief that the establishment of a secular state was the sole means by which the elimination of caste and untouchability could be achieved. Although he held a deep appreciation for Hinduism, he did not shy away from criticizing its unfavourable facets.

Jagjivan Ram's perspective on secularism can be succinctly encapsulated by his statement: 'Gandhiji's most significant contribution to social theory and praxis lies in his emphasiz on the veracity that the path of existence is intertwined with the path of affection.'[27] According to him, secularism encompassed more than just non-communalism or equal regard for all religions, rather, it constituted a comprehensive ideology rooted in truth and non-violence. Similar to Buddha and other esteemed wise individuals, Ram was profoundly disturbed by the widespread affliction endured by people globally. The individual's overarching objective was to alleviate the suffering of all individuals by eradicating any cause for distress. He held the belief that non-violence constituted the inherent principle governing our species, whereas violence was characteriztic of the brute. The ideals of non-violence, truth, love, and compassion were not just applicable to people but also extended to encompass groups, countries and nations. He acknowledged the imperative of initiating change at the individual level prior to its dissemination to others. On certain occasions, Ram employed linguistic terms and metaphors derived from sacred writings, which occasionally led to perplexity due to his individual circumstances. When examining his theory of trusteeship, he posited that the possession of surplus property bore a resemblance to the possession of unlawfully acquired items. He espoused the idea of relinquishing the said property and, in the meanwhile, utilizing it as a custodian for our personal gratification. In essence, his steadfast dedication to the ideals of secularism, truth, and non-violence transcended mere rhetoric, becoming guiding principles that shaped his life and finally led to his demise.

Jagjivan Ram underscored the imperative of converting Panchayats into genuine catalysts of transformation, enabling them to effectively embody the collective aspirations of the populace. Nevertheless, the existing framework, constitution, roles, and authorities of Panchayats exhibit significant disparities among different regions, thereby compromising the democratic principles underlying the concept of Panchayati Raj. The effectiveness of Panchayats in rural areas, where a significant proportion of the population resides below the subsistence level, is deemed impractical. Although Panchayats may have been effective in previous eras, those periods were characterized by a socio-economic context in which impoverished and famished individuals were relatively satisfied with their circumstances and acknowledged the privileged and prosperous as their natural overlords.[28] In the context of the contemporary society, the principle of equality is widely upheld, positing that all persons possess the same inherent worth and should be treated accordingly. Consequently, the notion of collaboration is contingent upon the presence of egalitarianism among individuals. Regrettably, achieving equality between individuals experiencing poverty and hunger and those who possess privilege and affluence is unattainable.

Jagjivan Ram has advocated for a comprehensive societal transformation in India through the implementation of a social revolution. The individual has the viewpoint that communalism is a detrimental mindset that necessitates restraint. In order to address and mitigate caste, regional, and language issues, it is imperative to undertake a process of cultural reform. According to him, a significant number of his previous associates expressed apprehension towards communalism. However, he argues that casteism is a more formidable challenge as it pervades our societal structure, influencing attitudes, beliefs, and behaviour at a profound level. The underlying nature of intercaste and interreligious antagonism is essentially identical. While the condemnation of communal tension is widespread, it is important to acknowledge that there are other forms of tensions that are equally deserving of condemnation. The emergence of these tensions might be attributed to a deficiency in the acceptance and adherence to principles, such as personal autonomy, logical decision-making, and reverence for the dignity of individuals. These origins can be traced back to a feeling of affiliation with a communal entity.

Jagjivan Ram exhibited a staunch commitment to the promotion and protection of the rights of Dalits. The protagonist's dedication to the advancement of their community was a central focus of his endeavours. He was a pioneering figure in implementing initiatives aimed at enhancing the well-being of the Dalit community. The speaker underscored the necessity of a comprehensive restructuring of the socio-economic framework in order to effectively tackle the prevailing challenges. Although some advancement has been achieved, there remains a significant scope for improvement in the execution of welfare initiatives. As the Dalit community experiences an increasing level of consciousness regarding their entitlements, they are increasingly inclined to reject any form of abuse. Regrettably, the aforementioned circumstance has resulted in a resurgence of oppression and harassment inside rural regions, perpetuated by upper castes that have not experienced substantial transformation. The persistent discourse about compassion and the inclination to provide assistance to these groups falls short in terms of efficacy. The fundamental attitudes which they hold, are, indistinguishable from those prevalent in the broader society.

The objective of this discourse is to examine the statesmanship of Jagjivan Ram and his endeavours to bolster democracy in accordance with the principles of socialism and secularism. It is a widely held belief that while not all politicians exhibit statesmanlike qualities, all individuals who possess statesmanlike qualities, are politicians. The differentiation between a politician and a statesman resides in their respective emphasiz and priorities. While it is well observed that politicians are frequently motivated by personal gain, statesmen, on the other hand, have a distinct inclination towards prioritizing the welfare of society, embodying a noble cause, and displaying unwavering dedication to the nation and its citizens. Hence, a statesman prioritizes the welfare of the nation and its citizens, before personal interests. As per the esteemed economist, V.K.R.V. Rao, who previously served as a cabinet colleague, the individual in issue consistently demonstrated attentiveness and has extensive expertise across many portfolios. The individuals in question demonstrated a rapid comprehension of the fundamental nature of each issue they addressed and were able to provide significant insights whenever they participated in cabinet deliberations. The individuals in question were held in high regard by the bureaucracy across various portfolios, leaving no room for uncertainty regarding their authoritative position.[29]

Jagjivan Ram has shown unwavering determination in his campaign, making a substantial impact not only on the struggle for independence, but, also on the establishment and a subsequent strengthening of liberated governance. His disappearance would have posed significant challenges in the endeavour to abolish caste boundaries and creating a national unity. Had it not been for his staunch opposition to the influential forces advocating for the divisive ideology of conversion during Gandhi's era, Gandhi's efforts may have been rendered futile. Ram effectively persuaded the Dalit community that pursuing improved social standing by religious conversion, would not effectively address the systemic injustices they encountered. Instead, he advocated for their self-improvement via diligent efforts and active participation in the nation's advancement. The advancement we make is interconnected with the development of our nation, and our state of welfare is intricately connected to the conservation of our nation. In a similar vein, the interdependence between our individual freedom and the emancipation of our nation is evident. This connection was emphasized during the Lucknow Conference of the All-India Depressed Classes League in 1936, wherein, the President delivered a speech passionately advocating for the recognition of Babuji's revolutionary endeavours. Thus, highlighting the potential injustice that would ensue if such recognition was withheld.

Babuji's activism in favour of Dalit rights was not characterized by hostility, rather, it was driven by a commitment to fostering national unity and promoting the formation of democratic and socialist principles in India.[30] His possessed a profound understanding and extensive expertise in diverse domains. He distinguished himself among his peers in the political sphere due to his persistent endeavours to remain abreast of the most recent advancements in human understanding. When engaging in discussions pertaining to caste and class, he exhibited a profound understanding and asserted that where as class can be fluid and subject to change, caste remains a much more rigid and an immutable entity. The integration of individuals from lower socio-economic backgrounds into higher social strata, is, contingent upon their improved financial circumstances. However, this process is considerably more challenging within a caste-based societal framework. The caste system is determined by one's birth, while social class is contingent upon one's societal standing. Nevertheless, the class hierarchy is comparatively less detrimental than the caste system. I believe that the implementation of mandatory intercaste marriages could effectively eradicate this societal ill. It would be advantageous if individuals belonging to the caste of Hindus were to relinquish the use of their caste names.[31]

Jagjivan Ram articulated apprehensions on social inequities within the Indian society. The speaker placed a significant emphasiz on the teachings of Mahatma Gandhi, the visionary ideals of Jawaharlal Nehru, the resolutions put out by the Congress, and the objectives of the planning process. Despite the advancements made in the domains of infrastructure, agriculture, and industrial production, there are a number of unresolved difficulties that necessitate attention and resolution. There has been a noticeable increase in social tensions and instances of violence, with a particular concern about caste conflicts in rural areas, which possess the capacity to escalate into volatile circumstances. The resurgence of communalism has brought out a notable dichotomy between ostentatious consumerism and extreme destitution. Casual labourers and individuals employed in unstructured sectors are also experiencing significant challenges. Despite significant advancements in the field of agriculture, it is evident that the overall increase in wealth has not correspondingly translated into a well delienated greater well-being for individuals.

NOTES

1. Patrick K. O'Brien, 'Political Biography: A Polemical Review of the Genre', *Biography,* vol. 21, no. 1, 1998, pp. 50-1.
2. Gardner Murphy, 'Tensions Affecting International Understanding: A

Survey of Research', *Social Science Research Council Bulletin*, vol. IV, 1950, p. 12.
3. Lewis J. Edinger, 'Political Science and Political Biography: Reflections on the Study of Leadership (I)', *The Journal of Politics*, vol. 26, no. 2, 1964, p. 425.
4. Ibid., p. 424.
5. 'Pray sab Rajyei Bidrahi Goshthir Abirbhab', *Darpan*, Friday, 31 May 1974, p. 7.
6. Banghidhar Bandopadhyay, 'Bhatare Sthitishil Sarkar Sarrbagrgonya', *Biplobi Bangla*, vol. 9, 1980, p. 11.
7. *Babu Jagjivan Ram in Parliament- A Commemorative Volume*, Foreword by Somnath Chatterjee, Lok Sabha Secretariat, New Delhi, March 2005.
8. K.L. Chanchreek, *Babu Jagjivan Ram: A Nation Builder*, vol. I, Shree Publication, New Delhi, 2006, p. 8.
9. Dr. Manmohan Singh, Former Prime Minister, in his message for a Monograph titled, *Babu Jagjivan Ram in Parliament: A Commemorative Volume*, Lok Sabha Secretariat, New Delhi, 2005.
10. *Babu Jagjivan Ram in Parliament*, op. cit., p. 569.
11. Ibid.
12. Chanchreek, *Babu Jagjivan Ram: A Nation Builder*, op. cit., p. 179.
13. https//:www.concept of social justicegov.in—Rawls, 2023, pp. 27-8. Accessed on 14 December 2022.
14. Lohit Naikar, *Basava and Human Rights*, Basava Samiti, Bengaluru, 2012, p. 18.
15. *Babu Jagjivan Ram in Parliament*, op. cit., p. 10.
16. S.R. Bakshi, *Jagjivan Ram: The Harijan Leader*, Anmol Publications, New Delhi, 1992, pp. 33-4.
17. Jagjivan Ram, *Caste Challenge in India*, Vision Books, New Delhi, 1980.
18. A.C. Sinha (ed.), *Struggles and Achievements: Babu Jagjivan Ram Commemoration Volume*, Alka Prakashan, Delhi, 1973.
19. *Babu Jagjivan Ram in Parliament*, op. cit.
20. Indrani Jagjivan Ram, *Milestones: A Memoir*, Penguin Viking, New Delhi, 2010.
21. Ramesh Chandra and Sangha Mitra, *Jagjivan Ram and His Times*, Commonwealth Publishers, New Delhi, 2012.
22. Chanchreek (ed.), *Babu Jagjivan Ram: A Nation Builder*, 2 vols., op. cit.
23. Om Prakash Maurya, *Babu Jagjivan Ram: Builder of Modern India*, Ministry of Information and Broadcasting, Government of India, 2010.
24. S.R. Bakshi, *Jagjivan Ram: The Harijan Leader,* Anmol Publications, New Delhi, 1992.

25. Suraj Yengde, *Caste Matters,* Penguin Viking, Gurgaon, 2009.
26. Bakshi, op. cit., p. 16.
27. B.M. Turadagi, 'Dr. Jagjivan Ram's Life and Achievements: A Critical Analysis', unpublished PhD thesis, Department of Political Science, Karnataka University, 2018, p. 82.
28. Ibid., p. 90.
29. Bakshi, op. cit., p. 57.
30. Sanjay Paswan and Paramanshi Jaideva (eds.), *Encyclopaedia of Dalits in India*, vol. 11, Kalpaz Publications, 2002, p. 118.
31. Ibid., p. 124.

2

The Broken Thread

Jagjivan Ram between 'Dalit' and 'Bahujan' Politics

The article titled, 'Where does Jagjivan Ram belong?' authored by Badri Narayan has been published in the national daily, *The Indian Express*. In that paper, Narayan asserts that monetary resources, political influence, populist policies, and patronage politics collectively exert significant influence in the realm of electoral politics. One further factor that holds significant influence, sometimes overlooked by political observers, is the development of novel symbols that draw upon established ones, rooted in the collective recollection of esteemed figures. I focus my attention on a certain matter pertaining to the 2014 elections. The emergence of Jagjivan Ram as a prominent icon in Dalit politics is ironic, considering his perceived irrelevance during his latter days. The emergence of Ambedkarite politics in the 1980s inside the Hindi heartland resulted in Dr B.R. Ambedkar being marginalized and relegated to a minor position in historical narratives, particularly following his passing. Jagjivan Ram's political ideology was portrayed as being opposed to Ambedkar, resulting in a negative perception of him.[1] This sentiment is supported by a news article published in *Amar Ujala*, titled, 'Congress Ko Dalit Virodhi Batane Ki Muhim Chalayegi Baspa,' which reports that the Bahujan Samaj Party (BSP) directed its coordinators in Lucknow to initiate a campaign in Uttar Pradesh to expose the Congress Party's discriminatory stance towards the Dalit community. BSP officials would engage in a series of village-to-village marches, whereby, they would assert that the Congress Party can be characterized as being anti-Dalit due to its perceived failure in facilitating the ascension of Jagjivan Ram to the position of Prime Minister, as well as its purported role in impeding the progress devised by Ambedkar.[2]

According to Ajoy Bose, the narrative of Jagjivan Ram's ascent and decline serves as a poignant example of the harsh conclusion faced by one of India's prominent Dalit leaders at the hands of the political elite, a story that has mostly faded from memory. There is a notable absence of commemoration and respect for an individual who was positioned by the leadership of the Congress Party as a competitor to Ambedkar during the period of India's war for independence. The radicalism exhibited by Ambedkar, together with his unwavering unwillingness to conform to the established norms, generated significant animosity during his lifetime. However, these actions also propelled him to become a lasting symbol of inspiration for his community. However, he serves as a significant illustration for prospective Dalit politicians regarding the potential risks associated with adopting a subservient role. This is evident despite his extensive tenure in parliament and numerous high-ranking positions within the cabinet.[3]

Throughout the twentieth century, a significant number of Dalit politicians exhibited scepticism about the social justice goal of the Congress Party. Nevertheless, Jagjivan Ram emerged as a notable anomaly, always aligning himself with the majority position of the Congress Party. The acts undertaken by him, a minister in a postcolonial state, exerted a notable influence on the social mobility of the poor. In his pursuit to replicate Gandhi's vision of interclass collaboration, Ram endeavoured to transcend caste or class-based boundaries within the lower strata of society. He distinguished himself from the working class and Dalit/Harijan activists of his era with his distinctive approach to advocating for social justice.

During the twentieth century, three prominent figures in India emphasized the significance of caste equality. Apart from Jagjivan Ram, the individuals who assumed leadership roles were Ambedkar and Kanshiram; all three individuals sprang from families belonging to the untouchable caste, and shared the common objective of eradicating the caste system and fostering a societal structure founded on principles of human equality. However, contemporary scholars do not consistently acknowledge Jagjivan Ram as a prominent figure or advocate for the Dalit community. Nevertheless, it is crucial to recognize his significance as a Dalit leader, given that he was the sole individual to assume a ministerial position and actively advocate for the marginalized communities till his demise. The legitimacy of his leadership role within the Dalit community should not be subject to scrutiny due to his efforts in promoting the well-being of marginalized socio-economic groups and his distinct approach to advocating for social justice within Indian Dalit politics. His endeavours mostly revolved around challenging the caste system and combating untouchability, which were often overlooked or inadequately addressed by mainstream political parties. He strongly adhered to the principles of Gandhian ideology. It is widely acknowledged that he hailed from a socially privileged background and dedicated his efforts towards advocating for the advancement of the Dalit community. He held a stance in opposition to the caste system.

According to Meena Charanda, Jagjivan Ram possessed a remarkable charisma and exceptional capabilities. He was regarded as a figure embodying the principles of social justice and social equality. The individual experienced a rapid ascent in the realm of public influence, ultimately establishing himself as a highly esteemed and well-supported political figure. Throughout his career, he dedicated himself to the advancement and well-being of the nation and its citizens. He is recognized as an advocate for individuals belonging to the marginalized and socio-economically disadvantaged groups.[4] Chanchreek views that Jagjivan Ram possessed a vision characterized by the aspiration for a Hindu society that is both casteless and democratic. He consistently endeavoured to implement democratic measures that would yield advantages for the entire populace. Ram, in his capacity as a member of the Constituent Assembly of India, played a pivotal role in ensuring the incorporation of principles of social justice within the framework of the Constitution.[5] Meena Charanda, in her statement, highlights notable contribution to his nation as a dedicated member of the Indian National Congress for a span exceeding four decades. He established a standard of excellence in each department in which he was employed. In his capacity as the Minister of Defence, he played a pivotal role in the establishment of

Bangladesh. The individual's notable contributions to the Green Revolution, as, the union agricultural minister continued to be highly regarded, while their lasting impact as the labour minister is well acknowledged. Despite witnessing the horrors inflicted upon the Dalit community, he steadfastly dedicated himself to the pursuit of societal equality. His unwavering commitment to peace and harmony served as the guiding principle in his efforts to uplift the marginalized group. The commemoration of his birth as *Samta Diwas* is attributed to his steadfast commitment to principles of equality, human dignity, and individual freedom.[6] In this context, I shall endeavour to explore Jagjivan Ram's role as a leader representing the *Harijan* or Depressed Class during his time. Prior to delving into the subject matter, it is imperative to conduct an analysis of the circumstances behind the emergence of the Dalit issue and the underlying philosophy of Ambedkar's Dalit politics, as well as Kanshi Ram's Bahujan politics.

It is widely acknowledged that the caste system has been ingrained in the Indian society since ancient times. However, it is clear that the Dalit community is progressively becoming more aware of their entitlements and recognizing their inherent humanity. In the eighteenth century, European researchers initiated an exploration of India's historical background. Their reliance on Brahmin sources of information, was, nearly exclusive, as these sources claimed to possess exclusive knowledge of the Sanskrit writings that retained the old traditions of the region.[7] Both scholars and administrators perceived Indian society as characterized by *varna*, distinctions, hierarchy, and social stratification based on Brahmanical perceptions. The perspectives of the upper castes shaped their understanding of the lower castes.[8] According to G.S. Ghurye, the British colonial rulers in India did not prioritize the issue of caste in a significant manner. The British administrators, particularly during the time of Warren Hastings, acknowledged the teachings of Manu due to practical factors. The British administration regarded the *Dharmasastras* as a form of law, with the intention of utilizing them as the foundation for the Indian legal system, regardless of their actual application within India at that time. Jurists employed the utilization of Manu.[9] The reluctance of British officials to intervene in caste-related affairs and their refusal to entertain caste-related inquiries inside the government courts, resulted in a limited judicial adjudication of numerous caste concerns. Within the realm of *varna* classification, *jati* offices, and inter-*jati* connections, several cases have been identified. Nevertheless, in the majority of cases, government legislation just establishes specific boundaries for societal behaviour. Within these expansive boundaries, the government either refrained from attempting to encroach or was effectively barred from doing so.[10]

The operations of the state were conducted with the caste system as the central focus. The existence and significance of the caste system in the everyday lives of ordinary individuals were augmented due to its institutional support and validation by authoritative entities. The caste system did not receive significant attention until it was officially acknowledged by the British. The estimation of the British in local traditional laws underwent a lengthy process of being shown incorrect, afterwards leading to challenges over its correctness. By the year 1853, there was growing criticism against the governing mechanisms in place, as they were seen as perpetuating the British dependence on the *Law Code of Manu*, which primarily revolved around the establishment of a caste system in India.[11] The colonial rulers implemented a formal system of categorizing castes in order to consolidate their imperial authority, marking the first instance of allocating resources towards this endeavour. There is a prevailing belief that the ideology underpinning the caste system held certain connections with Brahman, yet it is important to note that British colonial control did not contribute to any significant improvement in relation to the caste system. The process of formalizing, stratifying, and perpetuating political dynamics within the caste system has resulted in persistent disputes within the Indian society.

S. Bayly observed that the British Raj placed significant emphasiz on caste and its associated norms, actively promoting and perpetuating the use of caste languages. This colonial administration also portrayed caste as the sole means of attaining power and influence within society. Sumit Guha states that the contemporary manifestation of the caste system's political philosophy can be attributed only to the influence of the British Raj. The British colonial administration deliberately fostered the development and preservation of indigenous customs and cultural practices. Prior to the British conquest, the caste system was the prevailing social structure, characterized by a certain degree of flexibility and mobility. Nevertheless, subsequent to the invasion, the British implemented measures to strengthen and render the situation more stationary. The British colonial rule in Britain influenced individuals to conform to their conduct based on caste, transcending various societal divisions such as religion, faith, and economic standing. The concept of caste in India cannot be comprehensively elucidated solely through the lens of purity and impurity, as it underwent a significant redefinition throughout the period of colonial control. According to S.R. Rao, the inclusion of Brahmins in British courts proved to be highly advantageous for them due to their extensive theological knowledge, which enabled them to provide valuable assistance and cooperation to the British. As a result, they obtained significant positions of influence, financial gain, and, notably, the confidence of the British. The culmination of these factors ultimately resulted in the infusion of Brahmanical ideology within British India. The colonial rulers implemented a formalized hierarchical structure to classify castes, with the aim of consolidating their imperial authority. This marked the initial allocation of resources towards this endeavour. There is a prevailing belief that the ideology behind the caste system in India held some connection with Brahmanical principles. However, it is argued that the period of the British colonial administration did not yield any significant improvements in relation to the caste system. The process of formalizing, stratifying, and perpetuating political structures within the caste system has resulted in persistent disputes within the Indian society.

Bayly argued that the British Raj placed significant emphasiz on caste and its associated norms, actively promoting and perpetuating the use of caste languages. This colonial administration portrayed caste as the sole means of attaining power and influence within society. According to Sumit Guha, the contemporary manifestation of the caste system's political philosophy can be attributed only to the influence of the British Raj. The British colonial administration intentionally fostered the development of indigenous norms and culture. Prior to the British invasion, the caste system was prevalent, albeit characterized by a certain degree of flexibility and mobility. Nevertheless, subsequent to the invasion, the British implemented measures to enhance its stability and restrict its mobility. The British colonial rule in Britain influenced individuals to conform to their conduct based on caste, transcending many social, religious, and economic divisions. The concept of caste in India cannot be fully comprehended solely through the lens of purity and impurity, as it underwent a significant redefinition throughout the period of the colonial control.

As per the analysis conducted by Ishita Banerjee-Dube, the book titled, *Caste in History*, aims to rectify the existing disparity by examining the multifaceted and varied trajectory of caste across various social groups and geographical areas in India spanning from the seventeenth century to the twentieth century. This study aims to comprehend the multifaceted nature of caste as an institutional, ideological, imaginative, and practical construct, by examining its diverse historical paths and evolving characteriztics.[12] The author additionally asserted that the discrete conceptualizations and evolving delineations of caste within various communities, such as the Saraswat Brahmans in Maharashtra, and the Namasudras in Bengal, the Meos in Rajasthan and the Mukkuvars in Kanyakumari, were examined. The author analysed how unique understandings and deliberate self-representations of caste, influence, the behaviours and engagements of privileged caste, lower caste, and untouchable groups.[13] The British authorities introduced the practice of conducting decennial census starting from 1871 to 1872, which played a significant role in shaping the social hierarchy among various caste groups. These censuses included the recording of caste statistics, providing a valuable point of reference. However, it is worth noting that the compilation of caste data in both the 1871-2 and 1881 censuses was incomplete. Consequently, ethnographic surveys were conducted in the following decades to gather and on one hand, the census provided a comprehensive overview of the caste situation across India. On the other hand, its motivated various caste groups to compete for better status positions within the census classifications.[14] Examining the historical context of Dalit and Bahujan communities and the role of Jagjivan Ram within this paradigm is of significant importance.

The historical presence of caste-based conflicts in Maharashtra has been well-documented, with instances of caste groups displacing one another within the social hierarchy being a recurring phenomenon. Nevertheless, these disagreements did not challenge the fundamental principles that upheld the community.[15] The era of social reform was undoubtedly prevalent during the nineteenth century. The influence of Western education, the proselytizing endeavours of Christian missionaries, and the transformative impact of technological advancements, collectively served as catalysts for a diverse range of reform movements in India. During this period, the world of mind experienced the initial effects of significant changes. The attention was increasingly being directed towards the challenges faced by women and marginalized castes. The aforementioned organizations were established in different regions of India, including Brahma Samaj in 1828, Paramhansa in 1848, Prarthana Samaj in 1867, Arya Samaj in 1875, and Satyashodhak Samaj in 1873.

Swami Vivekananda corresponded with Haripada articulating his concerns on the hierarchical stratification of castes and the marginalization experienced by the untouchable communities. According to Vivekananda, individuals born into a lower caste in our nation face a bleak future with no prospects for advancement. What is the rationale behind this request? The prevailing circumstances exhibit characteriztics of a tyrannical nature. In our nation, each individual is presented with a range of potentialities, prospects, and optimism. Presently, he finds himself in a state of financial disadvantage, but, it is plausible that in the future he may attain wealth, knowledge, and admiration from others. There is a prevalent eagerness among individuals to provide an assistance to those who are economically disadvantaged. In India, there is a prevalent discourse highlighting the widespread poverty, although it is vital to inquire about the extent of philanthropic organizations dedicated to the welfare of the impoverished population. To what extent do individuals' express genuine empathy towards the pains and hardships endured by the impoverished population in India? Are we human beings of the male gender? What measures are being taken to enhance their means of subsistence and promote their overall well-being? We refrain from physical contact with them and consciously avoid their presence. Are we human males? What contributions do the numerous Brahmins make for the betterment of the marginalized and disadvantaged populations in India? The sole sentence that resonates on their lips is 'Do not touch!'

The current state of our eternal religion has been characterized by a significant degree of meanness and degradation as a result of external influences. In what state does our faith currently reside? The concept of 'Don't-touchism' is exclusively applicable within a specific context and not applicable elsewhere.[16] It is widely acknowledged that the Paramhansa Sabha was established in Bombay in 1848, spearheaded by Dadoba Pandurang. During the gatherings of this Sabha, it has been alleged that the members consumed European cuisine and disregarded caste regulations.

Following the conclusion of their discourse, the participants proceeded to engage in the recitation of hymns derived from the *Ratnamala*, subsequently partaking in a communal repast. Notably, the culinary provisions for this meal were meticulously prepared by an individual belonging to a lower social stratum. Membership was contingent upon an individual's willingness to consume bread prepared by a Christian, and partake in water provided by a Muslim.[17] During the eighteenth century, Jyotirao Phule emerged as a significant force challenging Hindu orthodoxy in Western India. Phule expressed criticism towards the Hindu religion, asserting that mythology and sacred texts serve as primary tools for the oppression of the Sudra caste. In 1869, *Brahmanance Kasab* authored a work that mostly examined the exploitation of the Shudra community by the Brahmins. Another significant publication by the author was *Gulamgiri*, in which he expounded his perspectives on Indian history and provided an examination of Brahmanical hegemony. Phule additionally disseminated the scholarly article titled, *Dinabandhu* to advocate for the rights and aspirations of the untouchable community. Phule advocated for the advancement of marginalized castes in the realm of education, specifically focusing on the Mahars, Mangs, Chambhars, and other low castes who constituted a significant portion of the population. Recognizing their profound state of ignorance and suffering, Phule felt compelled to address their plight through educational initiatives. In this regard, he prioritized the establishment of female schools, as he came to realize that they were even more imperative than male schools. Phule believed that the foundation of education lay in the crucial role that mothers play in shaping the character and development of children between the ages of two and three.[18] Jyotirao Phule holds the distinction of being the pioneer in establishing educational institutions for the marginalized sections of Indian society, including the Untouchables, as well as a ladies' school in the region of Maharashtra.

The individual sought to eradicate the lack of knowledge and irrational beliefs prevalent among the Shudras, Atishudras, and Indian women, in particular, with an aim of liberating them from the oppressive conditions they experienced. He courageously facilitated access to education for individuals from lower socio-economic backgrounds, especially Indian women. The individual in question endeavoured to re-establish the societal structure with a foundation rooted in principles of social equality, fairness, and rationality. Devi Chatterjee astutely observed that Phule deserves recognition as the initial advocate for the marginalized castes, emerging as their representative in the modern era. Phule exemplified the principles of the Enlightenment and showed a keen awareness of social inequity.[19] Gail Omvedt has highlighted the significance of violence, conquest, and state power in Phule's examination of the history of exploitation. Omvedt suggests that a valuable parallel can be drawn between Phule's emphasiz on these factors and Marx's emphasiz on primitive accumulation, which occurs before and outside the realm of factory production. This parallel is particularly relevant to the experiences of the majority of the peasantry in the Third World, where violence plays a crucial role in shaping historical developments.[20]

During the early twentieth century, Ambedkar emerged as a prominent figure advocating for the rights of Dalits and assumed the role of a significant critic and adversary of the caste system within the national context of India. He originated from a household belonging to the untouchable caste, wherein he endured considerable suffering due to his birth in a low-caste community. However, instead of losing his confidence, he actually enhanced it, equipping himself with intellectual sophistry and a heightened personal sensation of agony. Ambedkar's ideas evolved through a comprehensive amalgamation of Western liberal thought with Indian philosophical concepts, resulting in a nuanced comprehension of Indian society that surpasses superficial knowledge. The individual's extensive understanding of Hindu philosophy, acquired from a lifelong practise of reciting Hindu scriptures during childhood and further enriched by studying the teachings of Kabir and Buddha, allowed for a comprehensive exploration of the multifaceted nature of the Indian civilization. He perceived Western liberal philosophy as a potential solution to the pervasive social issues within his caste-stratified society, in which he himself endured significant adversity. The individual's emphasiz and the recognition of human dignity had a profound impression on him. Ambedkar's intellectual development was significantly shaped by prominent Western figures, including John Dewey, Edwin Robert Anderson Seligman, Goldenweiser, Edwin Cannan, John Maynard Keynes, Bertrand Russel, and others.[21]

Ambedkar's foray into Indian politics commenced in 1919 when he received an invitation from the Southborough Committee to express his perspectives on the Montague-Chelmsford Reforms. The major objective of the Committee was to gather pertinent information in order to ascertain the voting rights pertaining to the reforms. Lord Dufferin astutely observed and accurately depicted the prevailing conditions in India. The population is characterized by a significant diversity of nationalities, including a wide range of religious beliefs, engaging in numerous cultural practices, and speaking different languages. Additionally, a considerable portion of the population. Moreover, individuals are increasingly distanced from each other due to divergent biases, contradictory linguistic conventions, and even conflicting economic motivations. However, one prominent feature of Indian society is its clear separation into two powerful political communities that are vastly different from each other. On the one hand, there are the Hindus, who have a complex system of caste distinctions. On the other hand, there are Muslims, who prioritize social equality. In addition to the aforementioned groups, there exists a multitude of minor nationalities, many of which have populations numbering in the millions. These groups exhibited significant ethnological and political distinctions, comparable to the differentiation between Hindus and Muslims. Notable examples include the Sikhs, known for their martial traditions, and fervent religious beliefs, and the Rohillas, Pathans, Assamese, Baluchis, and other tribes residing on our frontiers, characterized by their wild and martial nature. Furthermore, there are the hillmen residing in the folds of the Himalayas, the Burmese population, who, are of Mongol descent and follow the Buddhist faith, and the non-Aryan communities, such as the Gonds, Mhars, Bheels, predominantly located in the central and southern regions of India. Lastly, the enterprising Parsees, known for their rapidly developing manufacturing sector and commercial interests, also contribute to the diverse fabric of our nation. Once more, inside these different settlements, one may observe simultaneously the diverse stages of civilization that humanity has traversed from the prehistoric eras to the present era.[22]

During his testimony before the Southborough Committee, Ambedkar argued that the social distinctions in India were not primarily based on religious affiliations such as Hinduism, Islam, Christianity, Parsi, Judaism, and others. Instead, he emphasized that these divisions were rooted in the categorizations of individuals as touchable Hindus, untouchable Hindus, Muslims, and so forth, based on their perceived social status. He emphasized the necessity of providing communal representation for the untouchables, whom he referred to as slaves, dehumanized, and conditioned to refrain from expressing grievances. This is because untouchability encompasses a distinct set of interests that only the untouchable community can effectively advocate for.[23] In order to develop a robust policy framework within a democratic system, it is imperative to acknowledge and address the prevailing differences that exist. This entails understanding the mechanisms by which social forces are disseminated among constituencies and franchises in order to enable the representation of individuals. In order to accomplish this objective, it is imperative to analyse the potential emergence of conflicts among heterogeneous groups in the context of electoral processes. Failure to consider these factors can hinder the efficacy of democratic governance.[24] The primary emphasiz of this argument lies in the depiction of Hindus as a collective entity, together with a particular concentration on the portrayal of untouchable Hindus. To initiate the discourse on the portrayal of Hindus, let us commence with a quotation that encapsulates the contemporary transformation in awareness within many Hindu communities. Ambedkar articulated that a community's assertion of representation is contingent upon the presence of distinct interests that necessitate safeguarding. In the context of India, there exist three primary categories of interests: those that stem from religious animosities, which are notably prevalent in the country; those that originate due to the educational underdevelopment of some communities; and those that result from socio-religious disadvantages faced by specific communities. Within the context of Hindu communities, there exist specific groups that not only experience significant socio-economic disadvantages but also endure severe social oppression. It is imperative that the marginalized social groups possess representatives within the Council Hall who can advocate for the resolution of their complaints. The non-Brahmin community, as a whole, experiences social and intellectual subjugation under the influence of the Brahmin priesthood. Consequently, they are justified in advocating for distinct representation.[25]

Ambedkar advocated for the allocation of nine MPs for the untouchables within the proposed hundred-member Legislative Council of Bombay presidency. However, only one representation was ultimately provided for the Depressed Classes. Despite this limited outcome, Ambedkar's endeavours significantly contributed to raising awareness and attention towards the issue of the Depressed Classes.[26] In 1920, Ambedkar initiated the publication of the periodical titled, *Mook Nayak* and assumed the position of leadership within the community known as the Depressed Class. The primary aim of this newspaper was to disseminate news pertaining to the marginalized communities and provide strategies to address the injustices faced by the Depressed Classes, as well as engage in discussions on initiatives for their social advancement.[27] In 1927, he commenced the publication of a biweekly periodical titled *Bahiskrit Bharat*, albeit its longevity was limited.[28] However, these magazines served as a means to disseminate information regarding the Depressed Classes.

Ambedkar held the conviction that mainstream media were disinclined to publish news pertaining to the Depressed Classes, therefore necessitating the existence of these papers. He progressively became involved in the mass movement, recognizing the imperative of fostering a collective awareness among his compatriots in order to crystallized societal upliftment. On 9 March 1924, a gathering was organized by an individual at the Damodar Hall in Bombay. The purpose of this assembly was to deliberate on the feasibility of forming a central institution that would address the challenges faced by the untouchable community and advocate for their grievances to be presented before the government. After extensive deliberation and discourse, a resolution was reached to establish an institution known as the *Bahishkrit Hitkarini Sabha.* Consequently, on 20 July in 1924, the aforementioned institution was officially founded, with its guiding principles centred around the notions of education, organization, and agitation. The primary objectives of this Sabha were to facilitate the proliferation of education within the Depressed Class through the establishment of hostels or the implementation of other necessary and desirable measures. Additionally, the Sabha aimed to foster cultural development among the Depressed Class through the establishment of study circles, enhance the economic conditions of this marginalized group by initiating Industrial and Agricultural schools, and advocate for the redressal of grievances faced by the Depressed Classes.[29]

In 1927, Ambedkar, under his guidance, staged the Mahad Satyagraha (or Conference). This event marked a significant struggle for the untouchable community's right to use water from the *Chawdar* tank. Access to this water tank was limited exclusively to individuals belonging to the untouchable caste. Ambedkar, a prominent figure symbolizing the awakened consciousness of the Untouchable Hindus, was proceeding towards the tank shared by Muslims, Christians, and the so-called touchable Hindus. However, despite their unwavering adherence to the Hindu faith throughout history, the Untouchable Hindus, who worship the Hindu Gods, were unjustly denied access to this vital resource, leaving them suffering from severe thirst. Consequently, under the guidance of a prominent leader from their own community, the Untouchables embarked on a historic march aimed at asserting their rights. All individuals exhibited qualities of discipline, energy, and excitement. The procession proceeded through the thoroughfares of Mahad and concluded at the *Chawdar* tank. Ambedkar found himself positioned at the precipice of the tank. The individual in question, possessing a profound level of enlightenment comparable to the most erudite individuals worldwide, identifies as a Hindu with lofty aspirations. However, it is disheartening to note that this individual is unable to partake in basic activities such as accessing water from a public watercourse or utilizing a public library within Hindustan, the nation of their birth and religious affiliation. This circumstance serves as a stark reminder of the prevailing arrogance exhibited by those in power, as well as the inherent injustice faced by individuals who share the same religious beliefs but are treated with greater disdain than even animals. Ambedkar fetched water from the reservoir and consumed it.[30] A significant number of individuals conformed to this pattern and successfully defended their entitlements. The battle has been described as the inaugural 'untouchable liberation movement'.[31]

The act of Ambedkar and his followers, wherein they set fire to the *Manusmriti* on 25 December 1927, foreshadowed the current era. When discussing the bonfire of *Manusmriti*, Ambedkar expressed his views during an interview with T.V. Parvate. In 1938, T.V. Parvate made a deliberate effort to set fire to the *Manusmriti*. The bonfire was ignited as a symbolic act in response to the perceived historical oppression and injustice that has been endured over the course of several centuries. Due to the educational influence it exerted, we have endured severe impoverishment, prompting us to engage in a confrontation, risking everything and embarking on a daring endeavour.[32] Following the Mahad Satyagrah and *Manusmriti Dahan,* Ambedkar, an undisputed leader of the Mahar community and the untouchable movement, found a renewed purpose in combating the issues of caste and caste-related inquiries.

In 1928, during the visit of the Simon Commission to Bombay, Ambedkar relinquished his position on the Committee in order to provide testimony from the witness stand. Ambedkar asserted the notion that the Depressed Classes were not to be considered as an integral component of Hindu society, but rather as an entirely distinct category. The individual strongly advocated for the Committee to grant political acknowledgement to the Depressed Classes and presented a formal declaration to the Commission. One initial assertion he would have liked to put up is the contention that they ought to be regarded as a discrete minority group, apart from the Hindu mainstream. The presence of our minority character has, thus, far been obscured by their assimilation within the Hindu community.

However, it is important to acknowledge that there is indeed no inherent connection between the marginalized groups and the Hindu population. One crucial topic that he would have liked to emphasize prior to the Conference was the need for them to be recognized as a unique and autonomous minority. Furthermore, it is imperative to assert that the marginalized class minority in British India necessitates significantly heightened political safeguarding compared to other minority groups. This is primarily due to its substantial educational disadvantage, economic impoverishment, social subjugation, and the presence of severe political disadvantages that are unparalleled among any other community. Ambedkar would argue that, 'in order to ensure our political safeguarding, it is imperative that we assert our right to representation on equal terms with the Mahomedan minority.'[33]

Ambedkar primarily emphasized two key aspects. Firstly, he advocated for the recognition of the Depressed Classes as a minority community, advocating for their separation from the Hindu community. Secondly, he advocated for their political empowerment, highlighting their significant social, economic, educational, and political disadvantages, which are unparalleled in comparison to any other community. The Second Round Table Conference took place in London with the objective of resolving the matter concerning the provision of separate electorates for the Depressed Classes. It is evident that Mahatma Gandhi participated in the boycott of the First Round Table Conference. The inclusion of Gandhi in the Second Round Table Conference was facilitated by the British Government, which was achieved through the implementation of the Gandhi-Irwin Pact. Ambedkar and Rao Bahadur Srinivasan were notable representatives of the Depressed Classes. Gandhi served as the representative of the Indian National Congress.

Ambedkar expressed that it is frequently emphasized that the issue of the Depressed Classes is a matter of social concern and that its resolution should be sought outside the realm of politics. However, we strongly disagree with this perspective. It is our contention that the issue pertaining to the Depressed Classes shall remain unresolved till they attain political empowerment. If the aforementioned statement holds true, and I find it difficult to argue against its validity, then it becomes evident that the issue concerning the Depressed Classes is fundamentally a political matter that necessitates an approach aligned with political considerations. It is evident that there is a transfer of political power from the British to individuals who possess a significant influence over our economic, social, and religious spheres. There is a collective willingness among individuals to consider the possibility of Swaraj, while the concept evokes memories of past tyrannies, oppressions, and injustices, leading to apprehension regarding their potential reoccurrence under the Swaraj. We are willing to accept the unavoidable danger associated with the current circumstances, with the expectation that we will be established as political leaders of the nation, alongside our fellow citizens, in a suitable manner. However, we are willing to agree to this under the condition that the resolution of our issues is not solely reliant on the passage of time. There is concern that the Depressed Classes have experienced a prolonged wait for the transformative effects of time to materialize. The British Government consistently excluded the Depressed Classes while it progressively expanded the reach of representative government.[34]

Ambedkar advocated for the inclusion of the Depressed Classes in various public services, specifically emphasizing the need to extend recruitment opportunities to them in the police and military, sectors that have historically excluded them.[35] The resolution was officially adopted. Additionally, he discussed his proposal for implementing political measures to protect the Depressed Classes under the prospective Constitution of India. He insisted that under the forthcoming constitution, people should be guaranteed a fundamental right that would render 'untouchability' illegal for all public purposes. He subsequently advocated for the equitable inclusion of the Depressed Classes inside the legislative body.[36] He advocated for the implementation of separate electorates for the Depressed Classes, expressing a distinct and unequivocal position on the matter.[37] The Depressed Classes expressed their demand for comprehensive segregation from the Hindu community, as reported in the *Indian Daily Mail* on 21 July 1931. They assert that while they have been politically labelled as Hindus, they have not been socially recognized as equals by the Hindu population. Ambedkar's presence at the Round

Table Conference yielded significant influence, with his address during the first session being regarded as a prime example of exceptional oratory throughout the conference.[38]

In his book, *The Tragedy of Gandhi*, Glorney Bolton provided a comment regarding the Round Table Conference. According to Bolton, Mr. Gandhi's state of being lost in London led to a decline in his previous sense of assurance and tenacity. Continuously, within the conference that he had grown to strongly dislike, he encountered delegates from the Islamic faith who remained steadfast in their refusal to compromise on any of their requests. Ambedkar's prominence increased with each passing day. The speaker advocated on behalf of the Untouchables, and any discourse concerning the well-being of India, regardless of political affiliation, invariably incorporated allusions to the distressing circumstances faced by the Untouchables. The worry was more romantic in nature rather than practical. Ambedkar's actions have effectively dismantled Mr Gandhi's platform, which previously garnered widespread praise and support from several influential figures in England, particularly in relation to his representation of the Untouchables. Furthermore, he expressed his opposition towards the revered Mahatma, resulting in the public perceiving the Conference as being primarily influenced by both Gandhi and Ambedkar. The statement in question could not have been more distant from reality. Firstly, it might be argued that Mr Gandhi's level of dominance at the Conference was insufficient.[39]

According to Gandhi, the issue of untouchability was not primarily a political matter, but, rather a social concern that required the Hindu community to address it from within. The Round Table Conference failed to effectively address the issue of separate electorates for the Depressed Classes. Ambedkar was constrained to acquiesce to the Poona Pact, a compromise agreement in the year 1932. Consequently, Ambedkar expressed discontent with the Poona Pact, leading to a subsequent escalation of animosity towards Mr Gandhi and the Congress. While the Poona Pact brought about an emotional triumph, it did not yield significant political gains. Indeed, subsequent to the aforementioned Pact, Dr Ambedkar emerged as the undisputed leader of the Depressed Classes. Over time, Gandhi successfully solidified his position as the leader of the whole Indian population, encompassing the Depressed Classes as well. Gandhi directed his focus on the matter of untouchability, establishing the *Harijan Sevak Sangha* and initiating the publication of the periodical *Harijan*.

Prior to 1930, Ambedkar's concept of the Dalit movement was primarily focused on a non-Brahmin movement. The Adi Dharma Movement, derived from Phule, encompassed the awareness and upliftment of Dalits. The thrust areas of the Dalit movement were observed to be diverse in both economic and social aspects. Efforts were made to acquire land for the Dalit community, with the aim of securing their emancipation from the *begaar*, a system of labour imposed based on caste. Additionally, active engagement in working-class mobilization was undertaken, particularly in urban areas such as Nagpur and Bombay, where Dalits were employed in textile mills. Additionally, they advocated for the advancement of education and endeavoured to promote internal social reform, such as advocating for inter-caste marriages and addressing issues related to devadasi-type prostitution.[40]

Ambedkar consistently contemplated the societal conditions of the Depressed Classes and their potential for upliftment. He held the belief that power plays a crucial role in enabling the community to make autonomous decisions. Therefore, it is imperative for the Dalits to establish themselves as a governing society. During the Round Table Conference in the 1930s, Ambedkar expressed his perspective that the issue concerning the Depressed Classes should not be solely considered a social problem, but rather one that extends beyond the realm of politics. This viewpoint challenges the notion that the resolution to this matter resides outside the realm of political action. Ambedkar asserted that the issue pertaining to the Depressed Classes will remain unresolved unless they acquire political authority within their own control. If the aforementioned statement is indeed accurate, then it can be asserted that the issue concerning the Depressed Classes is primarily a political matter and should be approached and addressed accordingly. It is evident that the transfer of political power is occurring from the British authorities to individuals who possess significant economic, social, and religious influence over our society. There is a willingness among us for the possibility of Swaraj, yet the concept evokes memories of the tyrannies, oppressions, and injustices that were inflicted upon us in the past, leading to concerns about their potential reoccurrence under Swaraj.[41]

It is evident that Ambedkar effectively communicated his stance on the matter of independence. The author stated that the Untouchable community, above all other societal groups, required emancipation from the British colonial rule. The rationale behind this assertion was that only with the attainment of swaraj, or self-governance, would they be afforded an opportunity to partake in positions of authority, which was seen as essential for their liberation.[42] He pioneered a distinctive leadership approach characterized by engaging with socio-religious matters at the grassroots level, coupled with strategic political initiatives at a broader scale.[43] The inquiry emerges on the means to get power, and Ambedkar's political approach is evidently discernible. Ambedkar recollected that the Congress Party was characterized by ideological alignment with or dominance by the Brahmin caste and the bourgeoisie, and advocated for the emancipation of Dalits from its influence. However, the task of forming a political party solely composed of Dalits, which aims to unite peasants, workers, Dalits, and the Bahujan Samaj, poses significant challenges. He made attempts to establish a political party with the aim of attaining political power, which led to the establishment of the Independent Labour Party in 1936.

The Independent Labour Party released election campaigns opposing the Mahar woman and their exploitation under the *Khoti*[44] system. In 1938, the party expressed opposition towards the legislation known as the 'black bill', which was perceived as detrimental to the interests of the working class. In the same year, tenants belonging to the Mahar and Kunbi communities collectively orchestrated a significant protest against the anti-*Khoti* movement, culminating in a gathering at the Bombay Legislative Council. The Kishan Sabha, a farmers' organization, orchestrated a significant walkout among textile workers, which was instigated by Ambedkar in collaboration with leaders from both the communist and moderate trade unions. Ambedkar advocated for non-Brahmin politicians in Maharashtra to refrain from aligning with the Congress Party and instead focus on fostering divisions between the peasantry and the working class. He holds a strong conviction that peasants and workers possess distinct political parties of their own. Ambedkar did not endeavour to establish unity with *Harijan* leaders, including Jagjivan Ram, during a period when the latter was organizing the formation of a Bihar agricultural labourers league in opposition to the dominant Kishan Sabha, which was predominantly composed of caste-Hindus and upper-tenants. Ambedkar made a comment regarding the issue of self-governance among certain individuals, questioning those who oppose the fair treatment of Backward Classes in their pursuit of entering the Public Services. He inquired whether it is not within the rights of the Backward Classes to make similar allegations against the Brahmins and related social groups, as previously done by the late Mr Gokhale on behalf of the Indian people against foreign influences. Can it not be argued that the exclusion of certain individuals from Public Services results in a form of diminishment or hindered growth? Is it not possible for individuals to express discontent with the fact that their exclusion necessitates their perpetual existence within an environment characterized by a sense of inferiority? Is it not possible for them to express regret regarding the inability to experience the moral upliftment that is felt by every self-governing population, and the progressive decline of their administrative abilities due to lack of practise, ultimately leading to their fixed role as manual labourers in their own nation?[45]

Ambedkar's strategic approach of pursuing a unified resistance against both Brahmanism and capitalism ultimately proved unsuccessful. Hence, it is imperative to analyse his political engagements throughout the 1940s within the context of this aforementioned setback. The Congress Party successfully rallied all segments of society, including workers, peasants, Dalits, and Shudras, under a unified strategic approach. The political group garnered widespread support from individuals belonging to many castes and origins, encompassing both *Harijans* and non-Brahmins. The Congress Party effectively utilized democratic mechanisms to garner electoral support and achieve victories. In this context, Jagjivan Ram may be observed actively interacting with individuals belonging to the lower caste.[46] As a leader belonging to the untouchable caste, he commanded significant respect and engendered confidence among the individuals he served.

In light of the prevailing circumstances of failure, Ambedkar founded the Scheduled Caste Federation (SCF) party with an exclusive emphasiz on the welfare and representation of the Dalit community. The main objective was to actively involve and instruct those belonging to the Dalit community with the benefits associated with political authority. Furthermore, the political party sought to segregate those belonging to the Scheduled Caste who were under the influence of the Congress Party. Its objective was to unite labourers, farmers, Dalits, and intermediate castes in order to campaign for reservation policies and develop distinct rural communities. The methodology employed by the individual in question entailed the establishment of interest groups within a system characterized by a wide range of diversity. During the process of drafting the Constitution, the individual in question adhered to a guiding principle and explicitly articulated it. It is evident that these three classifications possess inherent affinities. There are ample reasons for them to unite with the intention of dismantling the Hindu social hierarchy. However, they have not done so. Efforts have been made to combine them. The political organization known as the non-Brahmin party, which was active from 1919 until 1935, aimed to consolidate various non-Brahmin groups in order to challenge the prevailing supremacy of the Brahmins. The Brahmins, who had a pivotal role in shaping the Hindu Social Order, were also the primary benefactors of this system and thus remained its staunchest proponents.[47]

In his election manifesto for the SCF in 1951, Ambedkar placed the suggestion that the Backward Caste Federation may potentially dissolve itself if deemed viable. Following India's independence, Ambedkar went on to build the Republican Party of India and presented the idea of transforming the SCF into a Republican Party. According to Gail Omvedt, a significant step was taken towards inclusivity inside the party by incorporating people from lower castes and advocating for the empowerment of agricultural labourers, rural impoverished individuals, and other marginalized communities.[48] The Nehruvian state model revolved around the concept of 'four-*anna* socialism', which prioritized extensive industrialization through the implementation of public sector planning. The governance of the state was under the influence of a capitalist ruling class and a substantial bureaucracy that was predominantly composed of the Bania caste and the aristocratic Brahmin class. Ambedkar played a crucial role in ensuring the protection of the rights of Dalits within the framework of the Indian Constitution. The individual held a strong conviction that attaining political freedom subsequent to independence ought to pave the way for societal and economic emancipation, with the Constitution serving as the essential structure to facilitate such progress.

Kanshi Ram's primary objective revolved around the acquisition of political power. From its establishment in 1984 until the late 1990s, he played a pivotal role as the primary catalyst for the BSP's development and progress. At the outset, he displayed a reluctance to engage with the fundamental matter that has long preoccupied Bahujan intellectuals and scholars—namely, the enduring plight of socially marginalized Dalits and individuals belonging to the 'lower castes', characterized by their systematic subjugation and deprivation of self-esteem, resulting in profound and lasting effects on their personal identity. The early politics of the BSP revolved around Phule's ideology that opposes Brahmanical beliefs. This ideology entails an ongoing conflict between the Aryans, the invaders, the *Sanatanis*, the upper castes who propagate Brahmanical ideology, and the *moolnivasis*, the indigenous inhabitants, who are categorized as exploited by the exploiters. The early position of the BSP was that caste might serve as a 'political weapon' for the marginalized to challenge their oppressors, transforming a 'negative description' into a confrontational identity. This perspective can be seen as a contemporary interpretation of Phule's thesis on political struggle. Nevertheless, Kanshi Ram failed to thoroughly examine Phule's concepts within the context of the objective historical and social circumstances that shaped the struggles of impoverished and marginalized individuals.[49] Furthermore, the BSP leader failed to critically analyse the valid justifications for a specific type of political resistance, such as the promotion of Bahujan culture. This resistance does not necessarily involve glorification, as Phule proposed, but rather emphasizes the importance of granting political recognition to the egalitarian elements present in caste groups' customs and traditions. This stands in opposition to the dominant Brahmanical social and political ideologies, hierarchical social structures, and systems of political control.

During the early 1960s, Kanshi Ram was employed as a chemical assistant at the Explosive Defence Research Laboratory located in Pune. During this period, his intellectual development was significantly shaped by the influence of D.K. Khaparde, a prominent figure within the neo-Buddhist Mahar community, who gained recognition among government personnel belonging to the Scheduled Caste (SC) category in the Post and Telegraph, Defence, and Railways sectors of the region. While Kanshi Ram did not possess the academic prowess commonly associated with politicians like Ambedkar, he nonetheless sought to leverage Ambedkar's legacy for his own political gain. The individual's strategy entailed the deliberate avoidance of confrontations with fellow Ambedkarite politicians, namely the Republican Party of India (RPI) and Dalit Panthers (DP). These political factions had experienced internal discord, resulting in a diminished efficacy of Dalit movements following India's independence. In 1971, Kanshi Ram expressed his commitment to diligently establish a Bahujan Samaj, a collective representing marginalized communities, with the aim of influencing the political trajectory of the RPI in the state of Maharashtra. Subsequently, the individual recognized that the task of constructing a Bahujan Samaj proved to be more challenging in comparison to establishing a Bahujan political party. He came to the realization that the destiny of the marginalized individuals was contingent upon a distinct form of political structure in order to achieve their liberation.[50]

The formation of an organization took place in 1971, which subsequently evolved into a federation in 1973, extending its reach beyond the city of Pune. After a period of three years, Kanshi Ram departed from the town with the intention of initiating a novel social or political endeavour. The All-India Backward (SC, ST and OBC) and Minority Communities Employees Federation (BAMCEF) were founded by him on 6 December 1978. The primary objective of this organization was to mobilize the intellectual elite of the Bahujan Samaj, a group predominantly composed of wage earners who had qualified for reserved quotas.[51] The organization BAMCEF has the potential to rapidly develop traction and reach a critical threshold, primarily driven by the growing presence of educated individuals from the Scheduled Caste community among the administrative ranks.

The BSP was first established as a labour organization dedicated to advocating for the rights of government employees with a higher level of education. The party maintains its ongoing support for the concept of upward social mobility for Dalits, advocating for this through the avenues of formal education and government employment. This is achieved through providing support to educational institutions catering to the Dalit community, and striving to enhance the effective execution of reservation policies for individuals formerly classified as Untouchables in government employment. The political organization additionally pays tribute to the life and teachings of Ambedkar, who emphasized the pivotal role of formal education in fostering empowerment. The propagation of Ambedkarite ideology is facilitated via the establishment of various infrastructural developments, including parks, schools, hospitals, highways, and civic monuments that are specifically dedicated to the commemoration of Ambedkar. Furthermore, they coordinate and facilitate gatherings, processions, and cultural activities as a means of commemorating his legacy. The proliferation of Ambedkar sculptures dispersed over Uttar Pradesh serves as a potent representation of the embodiment of Dalit masculinity in a fitting manner. Nevertheless, the social programme implemented by the BSP primarily emphasizes the advancement of males in society, suggesting a discernible gender bias.[52] As articulated by Ambedkar, the caste system serves to not only stratify labour, but also engenders division within the labouring population. Kanshi Ram undertook the significant task of consolidating the subaltern castes and clans into a more cohesive entity.[53]

In the state of Uttar Pradesh, the Congress Party positioned itself as a non-ethnically affiliated entity that aimed to encompass all segments of society. However, it is evident that during the initial four decades following India's independence, the party primarily focused on addressing the interests and concerns of the upper castes. The political party incorporated individuals belonging to SC within their hierarchical structure, while the upper caste maintained power. While the party extended material assistance to the SCs, it did not grant them any leadership roles. The utilization of vote bank tactics enabled the party to amass support from the SC community, without providing them with any substantive policy benefits or adequate political representation. In 1960, Brass conducted a study in the state of Uttar Pradesh, and made the observation that the leadership and primary sources of support for the local Congress organizations, were, predominantly derived from the upper-caste former tenants of the *zamindars* and *talukdars*, as well as from the lower-ranking and middle-class ex-*zamindars*. In essence, these influential communities within the villages constituted the main base of support for the local Congress organizations. Brass posited that the control of land played a significant role in the political dynamics of the time.[54] He further contended that this control enabled the acquisition of support from subordinate castes that were economically reliant on the landowners. As a result, the Congress Party enjoyed a broad base of electoral support, extending beyond its leadership, with SCs being among the party's most dependable subaltern constituencies.[55]

During the mid-1960s, two distinct processes occurred within the state of Uttar Pradesh, which brought about notable shifts in power dynamics and subsequently had substantial implications for the Scheduled Castes. The Congress Party experienced a setback and brief slump subsequent to the 1967 elections. Furthermore, the middle and Backward Classes (BCs), who were politically organized by opposition groups like the Bharti Kranti Dal (BKD), became actively involved in the realm of politics. The mobilization observed during this period can be attributed to the changes that occurred in the countryside, namely those related to social class. This phenomenon has been extensively examined in Frankle's work, which focuses on electoral behaviour and the influence of the Green Revolution. The research revealed that the implementation of these changes primarily benefited medium to large-scale farmers belonging to the middle and backward castes in some regions of Uttar Pradesh. Conversely, Dalits, who were frequently characterized as petty tenants or landless agricultural labourers, had little advancement in their economic and political status.[56]

In 1969, the United States' Congress sought to enhance its public appeal by embracing a more progressive persona and implementing policies with a populist orientation, exemplified by initiatives like the

Garibi Hatao campaign and the 20-point programme.[57] Consequently, the Daliṭ population was incorporated into the party, resulting in integration. The independent and autonomous political activism of the Dalit population during this period did not yield beneficial outcomes. The Dalits demonstrated their most prominent assertion during the 1980s, a phenomenon that can be traced to the resurgence of caste-based mobilization in northern India sometimes referred to as the second wave. The initial wave of political mobilization in the mid-1960s witnessed the entry of Other Backward Classes (OBCs) into the realm of politics.

According to Jagpal Singh, there has been a significant increase in the awareness among the Dalits regarding the concepts and experiences of Ambedkar since the late 1970s. This phenomenon, for the purpose of conciseness, might be referred to as *Ambedkarisation.* Numerous committees, educational institutions, and libraries have been established in various rural communities, bearing the name of Ambedkar, accompanied by the installation of statues in his honour. The birthday of Ambedkar, observed on 14 April, is commemorated with great enthusiasm and jubilation. During this occasion, theatrical performances are organized to shed light on the discriminatory caste system, as well as the Hindu faith and culture. Furthermore, *Prabhat Pheries* and processions are conducted, accompanied by the singing of songs and the chanting of slogans in the admiration of Ambedkar. The proponents of the parade encourage individuals from the Dalit community to engage with Ambedkar literature, uphold their dignity without making concessions, and greet one another with the phrase *Jai Bhim* instead of *Ram-Ram* or, *Namaste*.[58]

Jagpal Singh further highlighted the discriminatory treatment experienced by Dalit leader, Ambedkar at the hands of prominent figures within the national movement, with a special emphasiz on Gandhi. The Poona Accord marked a significant divergence in perspectives between Ambedkar and Gandhi. Ambedkar perceived Gandhi's stance on the *varna* system as an endeavour to uphold the existing caste structure, hence viewing it as a source of humiliation. The name *Harijan* coined by Gandhi is widely seen as disparaging. The critique expressed by Mayawati, a prominent leader of the Bahujan Samaj Party (BSP), about Gandhi's usage of the term *Harijan*, as well as the act of vandalism that occurred at Rajghat (Gandhi's *samadhi*) in Delhi a few years ago, and the recent threat made by a BSP representative from Uttar Pradesh to boycott the 125th anniversary of Gandhi's birth, should be examined within the broader context. Certain members of the Dalit community lend credibility to the speculation that Ambedkar was subjected to poisoning allegedly orchestrated by his spouse, who belonged to the Brahmin caste.[59]

Following the establishment of BAMCEF by Kanshi Ram in 1981, another entity was subsequently formed. D-S4 refers to the acronym for *Dalit Shoshit Samaj Sangharsh Samiti*.[60] The BSP, a political party established by Kanshi Ram on 14 April 1984, is dedicated to the emancipation of the *Bahujans*, encompassing Dalits, backward communities, minorities, and other marginalized groups, through promoting the ideology of Ambedkar.[61] The party was originally founded on the support of Bahujan employees, serving as its fundamental base. The increasing political mobilization and knowledge among the marginalized population, along with the leadership of Kanshi Ram, have significantly contributed to the consolidation of minority groups and the impoverished.

In order to acquire a comprehensive understanding of the objectives, structure, beliefs, and methodology of the Bahujan Samaj Party (BSP), it is instructive to analyse it in relation to three key benchmarks: Reservation Policy Index (RPI), the Dalit movements across different parts of the country, and its affiliation with the Congress Party. According to Arun Kamble, a prominent activist and BSP leader, the collective representation of Dalits and backward minorities accounts for around 85 per cent of the population, establishing them as the prevailing majority. The proposition of establishing a distinct *Dalitisthan* is not desired; rather, the suggestion is for India to transform into a *Dalitisthan*.[62] The formation of Dalit-Shudra unity was observed to occur gradually during the 1980s. Under the guidance of Kanshi Ram, several personalities and organizations such as Kamble, V.T. Rajshekar of *Dalit Voice*, Sharad Patil, Satya Shodhak Communist Party, Dalit Sangharsh Samiti (DSS) of Karnataka, and Ryotu Sangh (RS) played significant roles.

According to Rajshekar, Dalits exhibit inherent Marxist tendencies from birth. Due to a lack of comprehension regarding the law of contradictions, individuals often encounter confusion, leading to erroneous conclusions. In the context of the Indian Revolution, Dalits assume a prominent role and bear the onus of avoiding any errors. It becomes imperative for us to persuade the Other Backward Classes (OBCs) that combating Brahmanism is equally essential to liberating themselves from the shackles of Shudra subjugation. The adversaries of OBCs do not consist of Dalits. Likewise, several Dalit organizations assert that Dalits are subjected to the oppressive system of Brahmanism. Consequently, the conflict between Dalits and OBCs can be characterized as non-antagonistic.[63]

Political scientist Christophe Jaffrelot conducted interviews with prominent politicians, analysed electoral data, and conducted historical research to assert that the emergence of Dalits in UP politics represents a significant transformation in the Indian political structure, which encompasses more than just symbolic modifications.[64] Varshney and Jaffrelot have underscored the importance of education and state-driven affirmative action in the Dalit political transition. The provision of reservations in educational institutions and government employment has provided opportunities for ambitious individuals from the Dalit community to attain economic wealth and acquire the necessary skills to effectively organize political campaigns.[65] According to Jaffrelot, there was a notable shift in the political landscape of rural UP due to the emergence of a new generation of Dalit leaders. This transformation resulted in a peaceful transfer of power from the upper castes to different marginalized groups.[66]

Kanshi Ram proposed the establishment of a society known as *Bahujan Samaj* to represent and uplift individuals from lower castes. This vision led to the formation of the BSP. The BSP has adopted a political approach referred to as 'patronage politics', as described by Kanchan Chandra (2004).[67] This strategy involves modifying or influencing the implementation of current government policies, rather than introducing new legislation. The BSP made efforts to alter the nature of the Indian bureaucracy by strategically assigning Dalits to influential posts within the governmental structure. Mayawati has implemented an extension of the Ambedkar Village Programme, wherein communities with significant Dalit populations are allocated additional monies for the purpose of infrastructural development.[68]

The endeavours undertaken by the Bahujan Samaj Party (BSP) to enhance the Dalit community's inclusion in positions of authority have coincided with the transformations within the official framework of local governance in India. It is imperative to acknowledge that subsequent to the implementation of the Mandal Commission, there was a progressive transformation in the prevailing circumstances. The leaders of the BSP called upon those belonging to the OBCs to unite in order to combat Brahmanical ideology. In a scholarly work focused on Phule and the topic of reservations, esteemed academic Gopal Guru made a notable observation. The potential impact of the Mandal Commission is to foster solidarity among non-Brahmin castes who have historically faced exploitation, thus weakening the influence of the exploitative castes. This process has the potential to undermine the existing caste structure rather than reinforce it. Additionally, the implementation of the Mandal Commission would significantly disrupt the Sanskritization process, which has played a role in upholding the hierarchical structure between pure Marathas (*shannavkuli*) and impure Marathas. This development aligns with Phule's concept of assimilating the so-called Maratha, representing the 'local great tradition', into the 'little tradition' that represents the larger Bahujan Samaj masses.[69]

Kanshi Ram and his BSP leaders effectively garnered support from the anti-caste movement. The politician's message targeted the Dalits, OBCs, and minority communities, encapsulated in his primary slogan: *Brahman bania thakur chor/ baki sab hain DS4* (Brahmans, banias, and Thakurs are thieves; the rest belong to us). The phrase (We possess the votes; your rule will no longer prevail) serves as a definitive declaration of the ambition for political dominance. The aforementioned slogan, *Vote se lenge PM/CM, arakshan se SP/DM*, effectively highlights the constrained scope of the pursuit of political authority.[70]

During a gathering in Karol Bagh, Delhi, Kanshi Ram enthusiastically directed attention to a political map of India. With his fingers tracing the boundaries of the Hindi heartland, he expressed unwavering confidence in the future dominance of his political party.[71] At the time, when the Congress Party held significant power, his statements appeared to be irrational and nonsensical. In retrospect, the aforementioned predictions bear resemblance to those made by the Delphic oracle. Mulayam Singh Yadav was the initial political figure to recognize the significance of the BSP as a valuable electoral ally. He participated in the 1993 UP Assembly elections as part of a coalition with the BSP. The coalition assumed authority, prevailing over both the Bharatiya Janata Party (BJP) and the Congress Party. At that time, Mayawati had established herself as a proactive advocate and the presumed successor to Kanshi Ram in the political arena. The mentor explicitly communicated to his alliance partner the intention of preparing the young woman for a significantly more prominent position in the realm of UP politics.

In the subsequent years, Kanshi Ram authored the following statement that he played a significant role in facilitating the ascension of Yadav to the position of Chief Minister of Uttar Pradesh in 1993. On 4 December, he underwent the administration of the oath of office and confidentiality. On 5 December, Kanshi Ram embarked on a journey to south India with the purpose of expanding the reach and influence of the BSP movement. Prior to departing from Delhi, he communicated to Yadav that Mayawati would assume the responsibility of facilitating effective governance and purposeful coordination within the alliance government.[72] Kanchan Chandra posits that the viability of the BSP's triumph hinges upon the advent of an erudite cohort of Scheduled Castes, which is a direct outcome of the government's affirmative action initiatives in the realms of education and employment. The establishment of BSP as a sustainable organization would not have been possible without the presence of this generation of educated employees. The observed correlation between compensating discrimination policies and the endorsement of an ethnic party, as identified in this context, possesses broader applicability beyond the specific instance of the Scheduled Castes.[73]

According to Vivek Kumar, the Congress Party, which once supported numerous Dalit leaders and held the highest number of reserved seats before the rise of the BJP and BSP, currently lacks any Dalit leader with significant national or regional influence. Though Jagjivan Ram, a prominent figure within the Congress Party, emerged as a significant Dalit icon during his time. The Congress Party, under his leadership, successfully secured a substantial number of reserved seats for Dalits and garnered significant support from the Dalit community, often without encountering any challenges. Currently, the political prowess of Mata Prasad and Mahavir Prasad in Uttar Pradesh is overshadowed by the formidable presence of Mayawati. Meira Kumar has recently relocated from Delhi to Bihar, where she is encountering the formidable presence of Ram Vilas Paswan. The states of Rajasthan, Madhya Pradesh, and Punjab lack representation from any Dalit Congress leader.[74] The aforementioned statement implies that the region commonly referred to as the 'Cow Belt', encompassing a total of 187 parliamentary constituencies in general, as well as 35 reserved constituencies, lacks enough representation for the Dalit community.

It is noteworthy that the BSP, mostly representing the Dalit community, achieved a majority in the 2007 Uttar Pradesh Legislative Assembly elections, a development that was unexpected after a span of twenty years. The implementation of this initiative was made feasible under the governance of Mayawati through her *Sarvajan* approach. The well-recognized slogan utilized throughout the electoral campaign was *Sarva Samaj Ke Samman Mein, Behenji Maidan Mein* (Mayawati's political ascendancy for the welfare and dignity of all societal segments).[75] Mayawati secured a majority mandate in order to establish governance. Kanshi Ram served as her tutor. The achievement she attained received prominent coverage on the front pages of numerous publications and newspapers. *India Today* noted that Mayawati's ability to attract the support of the upper castes demonstrates her skill as a strategic leader, potentially surpassing that of her mentor Kanshi Ram.[76] The magazine also highlighted the transformation of the party since its inception in 1984 by Kanshi Ram, which aimed to establish a political identity for Dalits through the provocative slogan *Tilak, tarazu aur talwar, inko maro joote chaar*, which was directed against the upper castes.[77]

Currently, there is a growing interest in Dalit studies within the realm of intellectual discourse. However, it is worth noting that Jagjivan Ram has presented an alternative perspective on this matter. However, there exists a research gap in the field of Dalit studies. The attainment of the correct objective necessitates the inclusion of him in our discourse. The study of Ambedkar is deemed necessary, as emphasized by him. He dedicated his final efforts towards the advancement of Dalits within the Hindu community. There is a clear consensus that Jagjivan Ram, following in the footsteps of Ambedkar, emerged as a prominent Dalit politician, often referred to as a representative of the Dalit community within the political sphere. Within the confines of Congress, he is not fully committed to achieving his goal. Indeed, it is accurate to assert that both Ambedkar and Jagjivan Ram actively advocated for the rights and welfare of Dalits. However, it is important to note that their approaches differed. Ambedkar said that the Dalit MPs in the Constituent Assembly only represented the interests of the Congress Party. He expressed his disagreement with the Cabinet Mission's assertion that the Congress Party had emerged victorious in the Dalit constituencies during the previous election. The author suggested that a thorough analysis of the electoral outcomes in the 1945 primaries would reveal the inadequate representation of Dalits inside the Congress Party. Dalits were granted a distinct electoral representation solely during the primary elections, as opposed to the general elections. The examination of the primary election outcomes revealed that the non-Congress Dalit parties secured a significant majority of 72 per cent of the total votes, while the Congress Party only managed to collect 28 per cent of the votes.[78] The evidence suggests that when Dalits are provided with the opportunity to use their voting rights as a distinct electorate, a significant proportion of them opt for candidates not affiliated with the Congress Party.

The response of Jagjivan Ram to the Mission's plan is intriguing, given his position as a prominent leader within the Congress Party. In relation to the triumph of Congress in the last election, the assertion was made that Dalits had declined the Ambedkarite political ideology advocating for separate electorates.[79] Nevertheless, he adopted a stance that diverged significantly from that of the Congress. The individual concurred with the notion that the Cabinet Mission had not adequately addressed the concerns of the Dalit community. Furthermore, they echoed the stance of the Dalit Community League (DCL) which advocated for proportional representation of *Harijans* in both the Constituent Assembly and the Legislative Assembly, aligning with their demographic size within a given province.[80] At a subsequent news conference, the individual elucidated the contrasting ideologies of his political party, the DCL, and the SCF. The DCL advocated for the safeguarding of the Dalit community without endorsing their segregation, whilst the SCF advocated for the separation of the Dalits.[81] The initial proposal for this request was put out by the DCL at its resolution on 18 August 1944, at the Nagpur session. The resolution expressed disappointment over the fact that both Gandhiji and Rajagopalachari's strategy for resolving the political gridlock failed to address the concerns of the untouchable community. The text underscored the imperative of safeguarding the interests of Harijans within the context of a political agreement involving the Congress, the Muslim League, and the British.[82] It is imperative to duly recognize that the resolution put forth by the Depressed Classes League signifies their initial divergence from the Congress Party.

Jagjivan Ram has been commonly perceived by historians as an 'agent' of the Congress Party, serving as an alternative to Ambedkar's leadership. This perspective demonstrates a lack of sensitivity towards the former's advocacy for the welfare of the Dalit community. The biographer, Nalin V. Sharma, highlights the predicament encountered by Jagjivan Ram during this particular juncture. He, due to his own beliefs, was unable to argue that the untouchables constituted a distinct country. Simultaneously, he was unable to entirely neglect the representation of the Untouchables' interests.[83] He recognized that in the absence of specific measures safeguarding the Dalit's rights, their circumstances would remain unaltered. According to his biographer, the predicament in question constituted a fundamental aspect of his cognitive framework. This assertion holds potential validity. I respectfully propose an alternative perspective, emphasizing the particularity of the 1940s. Jagjivan Ram developed an understanding of the significance of ongoing developments and subsequently re-evaluated his stance. He concurred with Lord Wavell's depiction of the Congress in 1944 as a political party predominantly representing the interests of the caste-Hindu community, due to this very rationale. During the period, when Gandhi expressed his opposition to Wavell's characterization of the Congress, Jagjivan Ram publicly endorsed Wavell's statement.[84] This matter holds considerable importance and should not be overlooked, particularly given the explicit contradiction made by the individual in question, who happens to be none other than Gandhi. The individual put forth the argument that the Poona Pact served as a distinct recognition of two distinct factions within the Hindu community, namely, 'the Harijan' and 'the non-Harijans' and 'Hindus'. The aforementioned radicalism exhibited by a prominent Congress Harijan leader serves as a significant indicator of the transformative shifts occurring during this period in the nature and disposition of Dalit politics. This statement also serves as a critique of the Congress Party's insufficient efforts in addressing the challenges faced by the Dalit community.

The Dalit community expressed universal disapproval of the proposed composition of the Interim Ministry outlined in the Cabinet Mission award. Ambedkar expressed his dissent at the inequitable and unjust configuration of the Ministry. According to his statement, the Dalits, who had made a request for three seats, were ultimately granted only one seat.[85] Jagjivan Ram further highlighted that, based on their population of 60 million; they were entitled to three seats.[86] He said that the allocation of three seats to Muslims, two seats to Sikhs, and only one seat to the Dalits is unjust and contradicts the objectives outlined in the Cabinet Mission Plan. Harijan leaders across Uttar Pradesh also expressed comparable criticisms. He advocated for the principles of *Swadeshi*, non-violence, Hindu-Muslim unity, and upliftment of *Harijans*, and *Swaraj* through various means such as speeches, writings, and a mass contact programme. His efforts extended beyond the borders of Bihar, as he conducted pioneering work in different regions of India.

The trajectory of Jagjivan Ram's political career, marked by both success and downfall, serves as a poignant example of the harsh conclusion faced by one of India's prominent Dalit leaders at the hands of the political establishment. Undoubtedly, there exists a notable dearth of commemoration and respect for an individual who was positioned by the leadership of the Congress Party as a competitor to Ambedkar during the period of India's war for independence. Ambedkar's extremism propelled him to become a lasting symbol for his community. However, Jagjivan Ram serves as a significant illustration for prospective Dalit politicians regarding the potential risks associated with adopting a subservient role. This is evident despite his extensive tenure in Parliament and numerous positions held inside the cabinet. The publication of Indrani Devi's memoir, first written in Hindi over 15 years ago but now accessible in English, was expected to offer valuable insights into the intricacies of Jagjivan Ram's career trajectory, potentially shedding light on the reasons for his inability to attain the status of a Dalit icon.

NOTES

1. Badri Narayan, 'Where does Jagjivan Ram belong? Both the BSP and BJP are trying to appropriate him as they compete for Dalit votes,' *The Indian Express*, 2013.
2. Ibid.
3. Ajoy Bose, 'The Unhappy Medium—Jagjivan Ram's High Point: Opposing the Emergency,' *Outlook*, 5 February 2022.
4. Meena Charanda, 'Jagjivan Ram', in Suratha Maik and Ankit Tomar (eds.), *Revisiting Modern Indian Thought: Themes and Perspectives*, Routledge, 2022, p. 127.
5. K.L. Chanchreek, *Jagjivan Ram's Crusade for Democracy*, Sultan Chand, New Delhi, 1978, p. 105.
6. Charanda, op. cit., p. 128.
7. Romila Thapar, *Early India: From the Origins to AD 1300*, Penguin, New Delhi, 2002, pp. 8-10.
8. Ibid.
9. G.S. Ghurye, 'Caste and British Rule', in Ishita Banerjee-Dube (ed.), *Caste in History*, Oxford University Press, London, 2008, pp. 44-5.
10. David G. Mandelbaum, *Society in India: Continuity and Change*, Popular Prakashan, Bombay, 1970, p. 449.
11. Rimsha Javed, 'The Caste System in India during British Raj (1872-1941)', *International Journal of Development Research*, vol. 11, issue 12, December 2021, pp. 526-79. Also see G. Campbell, *Modern India: A sketch of the system of civil government, with some account of the natives and native institutions*, J. Murray, 1853.
12. Ishita Banerjee-Dube (ed.), *Themes in Indian History: Caste in History*, Oxford University Press, New Delhi, 2010, p. xv.
13. Ibid., pp. xv-xvi.
14. Devi Chatterjee, *Ideas and Movements against Caste in India*, Abhijeet Publication, New Delhi, 2010, p. 12, also see Padmanabh Samarendra,

'Between Number and Knowledge: Career of Caste in Colonial Census', in Ishita Banerjee-Dube (ed.), op. cit., p. 47.
15. Ravinder Kumar, *Western India in the Nineteenth Century, A Study in the Social History of Maharashtra*, Routledge and Kegan Paul, London, 1968, pp. 319-20.
16. Swami Vivekananda wrote a letter to Haripada on 28 December 1893 from Chicago, America. *Complete Works of Swami Vivekananda*, vol. V, p. 32.
17. Devi Chatterjee, op. cit.,. p. 183.
18. Dhananjay Keer, *Mahatma Jotirao Phooley, Father of the Indian Social Revolution*, Popular Prakashan, Bombay, 1974, p. 190.
19. Chatterjee, op. cit., p. 198.
20. Gail Omvedt, 'The Anti-Caste Movement and the Discourse of Power,' *Race and Class*, vol. 33, issue 2, *Sage Journal*, 1991, p. 18.
21. K.N. Kadam (ed.), *Dr. Babasaheb Ambedkar and the Significance of His Movement, A Chronology*, Popular Prakashan, Bombay, 1991.
22. Vasant Moon (compiled), *Dr. Babasaheb Ambedkar: Writings and Speeches*, vol. 1, Dr. Ambedkar Foundation, Government of India, 2019, pp. 247-8.
23. Ibid., pp. 249-50.
24. Ibid., p. 250.
25. Ibid., pp. 252-3.
26. Chatterjee, op. cit., p. 216.
27. K.N. Kadam, op. cit., pp. 26-7.
28. Devi Chatterjee, op. cit., p. 216.
29. https://en.wikipedia.org/wiki/Bahishkrit_Hitakarini_Sabha, p. 1.
30. Hari Narake and Dr. M.L. Kasare, N.G. Kamble and Ashok Godghate (eds.), *Dr. Babasaheb Ambedkar: Writings and Speeches*, vol. 17, part I, Dr. Ambedkar Foundation, Government of India, 2020, p. 6.
31. Gail Omvedt, *Dalit Visions*, Orient Longman, New Delhi, 1995, p. 44.
32. Narake, Kasare, Kamble and Godghate (eds.), op. cit., p. 25.
33. Vasant Moon (compiled), *Dr. Babasaheb Ambedkar: Writings and Speeches*, vol. 2, Dr. Ambedkar Foundation, Government of India, 2019, p. 465.
34. Ibid., p. 506.
35. Ibid., p. 593.
36. Ibid., p. 533.
37. Ibid.
38. Chatterjee, op. cit., p. 221.

39. Glorney Bolton, *The Tragedy of Gandhi*, London: George Allen and Unwin Ltd, 1934, pp. 266-7.
40. Gail Omvedt, 'The Anti-Caste Movement and the Discourse of Power', *Race and Class*, vol. 33, issue 2, *Sage Journal*, 1991, pp. 18-19.
41. Moon, op. cit., p. 506.
42. Omvedt, op. cit., *Race and Class*, vol. 33, issue 2, *Sage Journal*, 1991, p. 19.
43. Christophe Jaffrelot, 'The Bahujan Samaj Party in North India: No Longer Just a Dalit Party?', *Comparative Studies of South Asia, Africa and the Middle East*, Duke University Press, vol. XVIII, no. 1, 1998, p. 35
44. In the Konkan region, there existed a revenue system known as the *Khoti* system. This system was under the control of *Khots*, who were landlords responsible for collecting revenue from their tenants. However, these *Khots* were also acting as agents for the British and often engaged in exploitative and oppressive practices against their tenants. For instance, they would require their tenants to perform unpaid labour, known as '*Begar*'.
45. Omvedt, op. cit., pp. 20-1.
46. Ibid.
47. *Dr. Babasaheb Ambedkar: Writings and Speeches*, compiled by Vasant Moon, vol. 5, Dr. Ambedkar Foundation, Government of India, p. 115.
48. Omvedt, op. cit., p. 21.
49. Jayabrata Sarkar, 'NMML Occasional Paper: Perspectives in Indian Development,' New Series 3, Nehru Memorial Museum and Library, 2012, p. 1.
50. Ibid., p. 3.
51. Jaffrelot, op. cit., p. 36.
52. Craig Jeffrey, Patricia Jeffery and Roger Jeffery, 'When schooling fails: Young men, education and low-caste politics in rural North India', *Contributions to Indian Sociology* (n.s.), 39, 1 (2005), Sage, p. 10.
53. Jaffrelot, op. cit., p. 36.
54. Sohini Guha, 'Ethnic Parties, Material Politics and the Ethnic Poor: The Bahujan Samaj Party in North India', unpublished PhD thesis, Department of Political Science, McGill University, Montreal, 2008, p. 74, also see Paul R. Brass, *Factional Politics in Indian State: The Congress Party in Uttar Pradesh*, Berkeley: University of California Press, 1965.
55. Ibid.
56. Ramiz Raja, 'Dalit Political Consciousness and the Emergence of Bahujan Samaj Party in Uttar Pradesh', Nityanand Tiwari (ed.), *Society*

and Politics, vol. 4, no. 1, January-June 2014, VL Media Solutions, p. 144.
57. Ibid.
58. Jagpal Singh, 'Ambedkarisation and Assertion of Dalit Identity: Socio-Cultural Protest in Meerut District of Western Uttar Pradesh', *Economic & Political Weekly*, vol. 33, issue 40, 3 October 1998, pp. 2611-12.
59. Ibid., p. 2612.
60. Bhaskar Roy, 'Paradoxes of Dalit Politics in Uttar Pradesh', *India International Centre Quarterly*, Monsoon 2002, vol. 29, no. 2, p. 111.
61. Ram Babu Mallavarapu, 'Transformation of Dalit Politics from Bahujan Samaj to Sarvajan Samaj in Uttar Pradesh State: A Successful Model to Achieve the Political Power by the Deprived Communities in India', *European Journal of Social Sciences,* vol. 6, no. 2, May 2008, p. 277.
62. Omvedt, op. cit., p. 24.
63. Ibid., also see V.T. Rajshekar, 'Dilemma of the Class and Caste in India', *Dalit Voice*, n.d., pp. 1-52.
64. Craig Jeffrey, Patricia Jeffery and Roger Jeffery, op. cit., p. 1372.
65. Ibid.
66. Ibid.
67. See also Kanchan Chandra, *Why Ethnic Parties Succeed: Patronage and Ethnic Head Counts in India*, Cambridge University Press, New York, 2004.
68. Ibid., p. 1370.
69. Omvedt, op. cit., p. 25. Also see Gopal Guru, 'Mahatma Jotirao Phule and Reservations', paper presented at the seminar on Phule at the Centre for Social Studies, Surat, 9-11 January 1991, p. 72.
70. Ibid., p. 25.
71. Roy, op. cit., p. 111.
72. Ibid., p. 112.
73. Kanchan Chandra, 'The Transformation of Ethnic Politics in India: The Decline of Congress and the Rise of the Bahujan Samaj Party in Hoshiarpur,' *The Journal of Asian Studies*, vol. 59, no. 1, 1 February 2000, p. 28.
74. Vivek Kumar, 'BSP and Dalit Aspirations', *Economic & Political Weekly*, vol. 39, issue 18, 1 May 2004, p. 1778.
75. Sudha Pai and Sajjan Kumar, *Maya, Modi, Azad: Dalit Politics in the Time of Hindutva*, HarperCollins Publishers India, New Delhi, 2023, p. 1.
76. Ibid., p. 4.

77. Ibid.
78. Moon, op. cit., vol. X, pp. 529-35.
79. Ramnarayan S. Rawat, 'Making Claims for Power: A New Agenda in Dalit Politics of Uttar Pradesh: 1946-48', *Modern Asian Studies*, vol. 37, issue 3 July 2003, Cambridge University Press, p. 596.
80. Ibid.
81. Ibid.
82. Nalin Vilochan Sharma, *Jagjivan Ram: A Biography*, Patna, p. 127. Also see Ramnarayan S. Rawat, op. cit., p. 596.
83. Ibid.
84. Ibid.
85. Ibid.
86. Ibid.

3

'The Cure-all for Everything'

Babu Jagjivan Ram's Baptism in Politics

> You can chain me, you can torture me, you can even destroy this body, but you will never imprison my mind.*
>
> –M.K. GANDHI

Jagjivan Ram was born and raised in a socio-economically disadvantaged family with a history associated with untouchability, wherein caste-based prejudice was prevalent in societal norms and practices. He consistently expressed his opposition to the presence of casteism and orthodoxy inside the Hindu social structure. Jawaharlal Nehru, the former Prime Minister of India, expressed the view that India encompasses both repugnant and admirable aspects, while also highlighting the detrimental impact of casteism on the fabric of our society. He vehemently fought the pernicious manifestations of casteism and orthodoxy within the Hindu social structure, and the deplorable practice of untouchability. In this journey, politics became his handmaiden. In 1932, when Babuji became a member of Arrah municipality and baptised into politics, it this time which acted as a lightning conductor between social duties and political interest. In 1935, he wrote a letter to his wife, Indrani Devi, in which he said,

> This municipal election! If anyone wants to experience a living hell on earth, he should take part in these municipal elections. I have also been a candidate

* This quote originally created by M.K. Gandhi but Jagjivan Ram used this quote number of times.

for this election, but, the bitter experiences of those three days will be with me all my life. . . . One's personal ambitions are cloaked under the garb of public service and benevolence. This is considered the cure-all for everything today.[1]

Jagjivan Ram, despite his early despair regarding politics, made a curious, pragmatic, but impossible amalgamation of both politics and social duties. He ardently advocated for equality in social interactions. He advocated passionately for social justice and equitable opportunities for the vast number of marginalized strata. For a span of around forty years, he provided guidance and protection to the Dalits, while demonstrating unwavering commitment as a radical leader in their quest for social upliftment. His efforts were primarily focused on addressing the plight of the untouchables, the marginalized and impoverished, as well as the severely neglected working class. He hailed from a modest familial lineage and belonged to a caste that faced societal discrimination. Despite his challenging circumstances, he was able to get a higher level of schooling. Since his early years, he cultivated his abilities in public speaking and actively engaged in debating competitions throughout his academic journey, spanning from the school to the college. The experience of facing discrimination based on caste throughout his time as a student served to enhance his determination to combat societal biases related to caste. He emerged as a prominent advocate for the marginalized classes in India. He held the belief that the caste system possesses a poisonous nature and exerts a pervasive influence, to the extent that marginalized populations choose to emulate the rituals and behaviours of the higher castes rather than actively challenging the constraints imposed by the system. He held the belief that such a cognitive framework is ill-suited for both the advancement of the community and the progress of democracy.

Jagjivan Ram was a prominent leader, who held a significant position in the broader political landscape, and was particularly known for his advocacy for the marginalized and oppressed sections of society. The inquiry arises regarding the attributes that facilitated his emergence as a leader. Numerous hypotheses and conceptions have been expounded by various scholars. According to Barnard Bass, leadership can be considered a universally observed and recognized phenomenon. Bass explains that leadership can be defined as a process in which two or more individuals within a group engage in interactions that frequently entail the organization or reorganization of the circumstances, as well as the shaping of the perceptions and expectations held by the group members. Leaders are individuals who possess the ability to bring about change, as their actions have a greater impact on others compared to the influence others have on them. Leadership is manifested when an individual within a group effectively influences and alters the motivation or competence of other group members. It is evident that under this comprehensive definition, each individual inside the group has the potential to demonstrate leadership qualities, and the degree to which they do so will differ among the members.[2] Jacobs and Jaques define leadership as the act of providing a meaningful direction to collective work and motivating individuals to devote their willing effort in order to attain a certain aim.[3] Chemers, however, has proposed a definition of leadership that enjoys broad acceptance among a significant proportion of scholars and researchers in the field. According to his perspective, leadership may be defined as a social process wherein an individual possesses the ability to effectively engage and garner the assistance and backing of others to achieve a shared objective.[4] Both Hogan and Kaiser assert that certain psychological traits, such as decisiveness, competence, honesty, vision, modesty, and persistence, play a significant role in determining the effectiveness and greatness of a leader.[5]

Jagjivan Ram exemplifies all of these attributes, albeit with certain limitations. The aforementioned qualities, such as self-confidence, decisiveness, resilience, energy, need for achievement, willingness to assume responsibility, flexibility, service mentality, personal integrity, emotional maturity, determination, sociability, and intelligence, have played a significant role in the individual's emergence as a leader and facilitated their ascent from a trade union leader to the position of deputy prime minister in the country. Indeed, the four prevailing theories of leadership, namely situational theory, trait theory, behavioural theory, and transformational theory, might be deemed suitable for analysing the leadership qualities of him.

Jagjivan Ram's birth took place on 5 April 1908, in the hamlet of Chandwa located in the Shahabad district of the Bihar state. Jagjivan Ram was the son of Sobhi Ram, a British Indian Army veteran. He acquired proficiency in the English language as a result of his familial customs and practises. Upon being stationed in Peshawar, Sobhi Ram made the decision to quit his position, and subsequently returned to his home village. There, he acquired land and established a permanent residence for himself and his family. Jagjivan Ram was enrolled in the village *pathshala* (school). During his formative years, he experienced the unfortunate loss of his father, which subsequently led to his family facing several social and economic challenges. However, his mother, Vasanti Devi, successfully navigated these difficulties, allowing Jagjivan Ram to pursue his education without interruption. Following the completion of his elementary schooling, he was enrolled at the Arrah Town High School in the year 1922. In this context, he encountered the phenomenon of caste-based discrimination and prejudice perpetrated by individuals belonging to higher castes, marking his initial exposure to such societal dynamics. He observed the presence of distinct earthen containers designated for the storage of water intended for individuals belonging to the caste Hindu community, as well as those considered Untouchables.

Jagjivan Ram demonstrated his unwillingness to endure the aforementioned insult by deliberately shattering the pitcher. Consequently, the governing body promptly procured a replacement, only to witness a recurrence of the same incident. As a result, the headmaster was driven to rescind this particular arrangement, and instead implement a communal clay pitcher for all pupils within the school.[6] He gleaned valuable insights from this particular episode, which instilled in him a resolute will to resist subjugation and effectively address the long-standing issue of discrimination. The individual had established a commendable standing as a resilient and morally upright individual who exhibited an unwavering aversion towards any manifestation of injustice. In light of the prevailing circumstances characterized by an inequitable social hierarchy, the individual in question showed an unwavering commitment to engage in a struggle, thereby achieving academic success by attaining a first division in his matriculation examination.

In 1926, Madan Mohan Malaviya and Muhammad Ali Jinnah visited Arrah with the purpose of addressing the local populace and raising awareness about the Khilafat Movement issue. The *Harijan* community residing in the Arrah region collectively selected Jagjivan Ram to deliver the welcome address, and he executed this responsibility with great proficiency. Malaviya was greatly impressed and invited him to sit next to him on the podium for the meeting. This occurrence enhanced Ram's standing as an adolescent male. The residents of Chandwa village had a sense of satisfaction and took pride in their accomplishments. This marked his initial encounter with prominent national figures, which served as a catalyst for his development as a leader. Malaviya extended an invitation to Jagjivan to enrol in the inter-scientific class, which pertains to the first-year scientific curriculum, at Banaras Hindu University (BHU).[7] Vasanti Devi, the mother of the individual in question, provided counsel for him to enrol at the BHU. During his tenure at BHU campus, he encountered the degrading experience of untouchability within the campus dormitories. The hostel staff member declined to perform the task of cleaning Ram's dishes on the basis of his membership in the Chamar caste. He expressed his opposition to the aforementioned matter, firmly stating his refusal to comply. In the typical scenario when meals are made for all students in the hostel mess and consumed collectively at a designated area adjacent to the kitchen, it is expected that an individual will partake in the communal dining experience, and will not be responsible for cleaning their own utensils.[8]

Due to his opposition to untouchability, there was a lack of food preparation for a day, as well as a subsequent shortage of meals for a couple of days. Consequently, the students made the collective decision to undertake the task of cleaning their own dishes. The individual arrived at the conclusion that the proposed solution was not pragmatic, prompting them to vacate the hostel premises and relocate to a leased residential property. The individual possessed an intrinsic leadership skill, which initially manifested in his opposition to the long-standing inhumane actions occurring within a hostel. This opposition ultimately led to the dismantling of the existing institution. The choice to relocate to a rented residence was authorized by Malaviya.

The occurrences involving the provision of separate pots for Untouchables at the school of Arrah town, the refusal of hostel servants in BHU to wash utensils used by Jagjivan Ram, and the denial of rental accommodation. Based on his caste, they have contributed to his rebellious nature and have served as a catalyst for the development of leadership qualities in his young mind. He experienced a subsequent distressing event that prompted him to adopt a rebellious stance, ultimately leading to the formation of an organization for the marginalized Untouchable community, with him assuming a leadership role. The barber would frequently engage in the act of trimming his hair. Upon learning about his caste, the barber declined to provide him with a shave and instead suggested he engage in self-help. He was profoundly affected by this response, experiencing a mixture of sadness and anger, which prompted him to undertake the organization of the Untouchable community. The conduct exhibited by the barber served as a catalyst for prompting a response. Jagjivan Ram contemplated the duration for which the Untouchable population can endure the perpetuation of upper-caste mistreatment and everyday humiliation. He made a commitment to advocate for the social and economic advancement of the Dalit community. He held the belief that the organization of the Untouchables would lead to a transformation in the conduct of the *savarna* Hindus. If not, it has the potential to be altered. While engrossed in his labour, he encountered Dev Nandan Singh Dixit, who subsequently emerged as a revolutionary figure. The individual's character appealed to the marginalized social group known as the Untouchables, while his persuasive reasoning left a lasting impression on them. In the end, the Untouchables made the decision to engage in a boycott of the barber. Following a period of six months characterized by a boycott, the barbers ultimately acquiesced and expressed remorse for their previous misconduct. The disagreement was resolved in a mutually agreeable manner.[9] The Untouchables had learnt under Jagjivan Ram's guidance, the value of the organization. He felt that destiny perhaps intended him to become a social reformer. The disabilities of the 'Dalits' filled his heart with anguish.

Jagjivan Ram possessed a robust physique and exhibited notable mental acuity. His appealing demeanour was enhanced by a round and radiant countenance. He expanded his intellectual horizons through extensive study of literary works authored by notable individuals, including Karl Marx's *The Communist Manifesto* and *Das Kapital*, Bankimchandra Chattopadhyaya's *Anand Math*, *Ramayana*, and the literary compositions such as, *Prem Sagar Sukh Sagar*, *Baital Pachisi*, *Chandrakanta* and *Santalis*. One further habit that he cultivated involved perusing contemporary newspapers and publications, such as *Bharat Mitra*, *Venkateshwara Samachar*, *Saraswati*, Gandhi's *Navjivan*, and *Tarun Bharat*. *The Statesman* newspaper of Calcutta would often arrive at Arrah railway station with the 6 a.m. train. So, he would routinely arrive at the station around 6 a.m. in order to procure a copy of it.[10] By engaging in an extensive study of diverse literary works, the individual acquired valuable knowledge, enabling them to effectively address a range of issues and internalize the principles of Democracy, Socialism, Secularism, and Communism. Furthermore, the skill of oratory was a notable characteriztic of his leadership. He possessed an exceptional oratory skills and showed effectiveness in his speeches. The orator delivered an impromptu address that was both compelling and skillfully executed.

During Jagjivan Ram's tenure, as a student at BHU, the institution boasted a distinguished group of literary figures, including Shyam Sunder Das, Ayodhya Singh Upadhyay 'Hari Oudh', Ram Chandra Shukla, and Lala Bhagwan Din. The prominent teachers associated with Hindi literature left a lasting impression on him. Additionally, he engaged in debating activities, which contributed to the development of his oratory skills. He actively participated in the mock parliament, engaging in debates on a regular basis. It was at this period that he acquired the foundational skills that would prove to be highly advantageous in his future endeavours. The potential for future leadership was inherent within him.[11]

Jagjivan Ram consistently contemplated the enduring adversity faced by the untouchables and harboured aspirations of emerging as a prominent figure in the realms of social and religious reform. Both the *Dadupanthi Sant* and the *Brahmachari* were ardent proponents of 'Pranayam' and they instilled their passion for it in the young Jagjivan Ram. However, his intention was to create societal transformation. During that era, the newspapers disseminated information pertaining to the endeavours of prominent national figures, such as Mahatma Gandhi, Motilal Nehru, Lajpat Rai, Bipin Chandra Pal, Sarojini Naidu, and various other individuals. He meticulously observed the prevailing national sentiment and developed a deep affection for *Swadeshi*. Malviya was an esteemed educationist who held strong Hindu beliefs.

Jagjivan Ram was profoundly impressed by the individual's eloquence and moral character, leading him to see the individual as a prominent figure of the era. It is noteworthy to acknowledge that during his final years as the leader of the Untouchables, he encountered disagreements with Malaviya. However, his love for him remained constant, and his respect and admiration for him never diminished. Arya Samaj and the Theosophical Society held a greater appeal for him compared to political assemblies, second only to his interest in engaging in discussions with *sants*, and other individuals involved in religious matters. He attended Annie Besant's compelling remarks. However, Mahatma Gandhi and a youthful Jawaharlal Nehru served as his exemplary leaders. Consequently, Banaras had progressively manifested his ambitions. Regardless of his eventual accomplishments or lack thereof, his primary dedication would be towards the service of the Untouchables. A clandestine oath has been surreptitiously undertaken, with minimal awareness on the part of the individual, devoid of any recognizable ceremonial procedures. A profound determination was established at the deepest core of the individual.[12] The individual in question observed the notable transformations and appearances of prominent figures, such as Gandhi, Subhas Chandra Bose, Motilal Nehru, C.R. Das, Jawaharlal Nehru, Rajendra Prasad, C. Rajagopalachari, Muhammad Ali, Shaukat Ali, Sardar Vallabhbhai Patel, Abul Kalam Azad, Bhagat Singh, and various other luminaries. He was greatly influenced by the ideas of Gandhi, Bhagat Singh, Khudiram Bose, and other prominent leaders fought for Swaraj, or self-rule, ultimately sacrificing their lives for the cause.. The events that unfolded at Jallianwala Bagh, Amritsar had a profound impact on him.

The concept of untouchability consistently perturbed his cognitive faculties, prompting him to engage in deep contemplation. Despite his persistent efforts, he was unable to discern any rationalization for the prevailing discriminatory practices inside Indian society. The individual embarked on a lifelong endeavour to investigate the genesis of discrimination and afterwards engaged in a persistent and arduous battle against it. Gandhi's inspirational impact is attributed to his initiation of the fight against untouchability. His primary aim was to eradicate untouchability and create a discrimination-free society in India. Jagjivan Ram adhered to Gandhi's non-violent approach in his struggle against the caste system. He advocated for the promotion of equality among individuals and strongly opposed the cultivation of animosity towards one another.[13]

The amelioration of socio-economic and political conditions of untouchables, backwards, and labourers may be attributed to the vision, courage, tact, dexterity, prudence, and statesmanship displayed by Jagjivan Ram. He successfully undertook a challenging and arduous endeavour. The individual's amicable and professional demeanour exhibited in addressing the issue of untouchability stands as a remarkable contribution to the advancement of nationalist India. The individual's leadership qualities were prominently demonstrated during the protracted and challenging endeavour aimed at securing the liberation of the untouchable caste.

Jagjivan Ram successfully completed his intermediate science exams in 1928, and afterwards pursued additional studies in Calcutta. He enrolled at the Vidyasagar College in Calcutta to pursue a Bachelor of Science degree. In Calcutta, he initiated the practice of donning *khadi* garments. The individual encountered a diverse array of leaders and participated in a meeting, actively participating in political and social endeavours. Subsequently, he orchestrated the Ravidas conference within the confines of Wellington Park. The seminar was attended by various senior Congress leaders from the Dalit Sudhar Sabha, an organization dedicated to the eradication of untouchability. The meeting had an approximate attendance of 10,000 individuals, a testament to the effective leadership of Jagjivan Ram. J.M. Sen Gupta, Subhas Chandra Bose, B.C. Roy and P.C. Ghose, observed and supported his endeavours.[14] Bose promised to help the economically and socially backward people and encouraged him to do this work. He formed Ravidas Sabha in various localities in Calcutta to create awareness.

According to B.M. Turadagi, Bose held a strong belief that the Dalits in society should cease accepting their deplorable condition as a primary step towards progress. The expression of irritation and discontent among individuals has the potential to ignite a significant social revolution, comparable to the eruption of a volcano. This auspicious revolution has the capacity to bring about transformative changes not only within Hindu society, but also propel the nation onto a new trajectory of progress. He engaged in profound contemplation and arrived at the conclusion that unless the Dalits voiced their dissent and ceased to acquiesce to their deplorable status within the Hindu culture, they would remain susceptible to exploitation by the upper-caste Hindus even in the post-Independence era. The regressive nature of their societal position will result in the exclusion of millions of Dalits from active participation in the political landscape of the nation. They would be devoid of agency. The attainment of political autonomy would not necessarily alleviate the suffering experienced by the Dalits, should they passively accept the mistreatment, marginalization, and derogation imposed upon them.[15]

Jagjivan Ram actively involved himself in labour and millworker advocacy in Calcutta, where he established connections with leaders and workers affiliated with the communist movement. During that period, communist literature was clandestinely imported from Moscow and necessitated covert consumption. The individual engaged with the literary works of Karl Marx, including *Das Kapital*, *The Communist Manifesto*, and other publications pertaining to the ideology of communism that were available in the English language. The individual was profoundly influenced by the underlying tenets of communism. He established contact with prominent revolutionary figures, such as Chandra Shekhar Azad, Manmath Nath Gupta, and various others.[16]

Jagjivan Ram spoke with prominent leaders of the Bengali Congress and many social workers and organizations in the region of Bengal. In numerous instances of conversations and talks pertaining to contemporary issues, the individual held the belief that political advancement could not be achieved in the absence of social advancement. Dalit leaders held the belief that a social revolution must precede a political revolution in India. He dedicated himself to the noble cause of mobilising the Dalit community, thereby establishing a formidable organization known as the Ravidas Sabhas.

Prior to his acquaintance with any significant Congressman from his native state of Bihar, he gained personal recognition as an emerging leader of the marginalized minority in Calcutta by several prominent figures within the Indian National Congress. The 1929 session of Congress took place on the banks of the River Ravi. A momentous proclamation was issued, expressing their aspiration for absolute autonomy or *purno swaraj*. Simultaneously and in the same location, he organized a seminar just for the *achhut*, or Untouchable community. The Dalit conference exhibited a high degree of success.

The *Sarva Dharma Sammelan,* a conference conducted in Arrah in 1932, extended invitations to both upper-caste Hindus and individuals belonging to the Untouchable caste. The convention saw the participation of the Pradeshik Hindu Mahasabha, Arya Samaj, and the Indian National Congress. Rajendra Prasad was bestowed with an honour. Jagjivan Ram engaged in interactions with individuals from all backgrounds. However, lectures delivered by upper-caste Hindus espoused the notion that Dalits should renounce the consumption of meat and alcohol. The individuals were encouraged to adopt a lifestyle characterized by cleanliness. Jagjivan Ram expressed his views with a strong sense of humour, asserting that Dalits are not in need of sermons or well-intentioned guidance. Rajendra Prasad had a reserved demeanour at first, but then reached out to Jagjivan Ram, urging him to focus his efforts on the state of Bihar. Jagjivan acquiesced to this counsel.[17] This was his political initiation. When he came to Bihar, he was made secretary of the All-India Anti-Untouchability League, which later became the Harijan Sevak Sangh.

Jagjivan Ram encountered Mahatma Gandhi for the first time during Gandhi's travel to Bihar, undertaken with the purpose of observing the individuals affected by the substantial earthquake in 1934. Simultaneously, Jagjivan undertook humanitarian efforts by actively participating in relief work. He assumed responsibility for ensuring that the varied dietary needs of the diverse population were adequately addressed. Additionally, he oversaw the publication of a bulletin to disseminate information regarding relief work progress to funders, sympathizers, and volunteers. The intimate association with Gandhi served as a catalyst for his early involvement in the war for independence and the upliftment of marginalized individuals, who were subjected to a lower quality of life due to the caste-based social structure.

As previously mentioned, Jagjivan Ram endeavoured to foster unity among marginalized individuals, thereby leading him to actively participate in many organizational endeavours. The inaugural gathering of the All-India Ravidas Mahasabha took place in 1934, specifically in the city of Calcutta. During this session, he engaged in discussions with leaders hailing from several provinces. The individual emphasized the necessity for Dalit leaders from various political parties to unite in order to enhance their effectiveness through the consolidation of their collective power. The organizers diligently prepared an appeal, which was then sent nationwide.[18] The second session of All-India Ravidas Mahasabha was held in Kanpur on 16-17 March 1935. At that meeting, he strongly stated that the Dalits were not making an impact all over India in political and social affairs. Dalits needed to keep pace with national activities and form an all-India organization.

Jagjivan Ram underscored the existence of distinct local caste organizations within the Depressed Classes, which, regrettably, did not garner significant support for Indian nationalism and remained primarily focused on social reforms. Merely implementing social reforms would not be sufficient. It is said that Dalits should refrain from isolating themselves from nationalist politics, as it is believed that social reform alone may not be sufficient. Instead, Dalits required a political platform to advocate for their rights and interests, which can only be achieved by the establishment of a cohesive forum. In the absence of governmental power, there would be a reliance on the high-caste Hindus. The establishment of a comprehensive and meticulously orchestrated Dalit movement on a national scale might be seen as a crucial historical imperative. The assembly aimed at fostering a robust sense of nationalism and facilitating the structuring of Hindu society, ultimately resulting in the establishment of the All India Depressed Classes League. Rasiklal Biswas was appointed as the Chairman, while P.N. Rajbhoj and Jagjivan Ram assumed the positions of Secretaries.[19] The organization witnessed the participation of various nationalist Dalit leaders, who subsequently initiated the establishment and operation of state units. Jagjivan Ram expeditiously established the Bihar section of the organization and was subsequently elected as its President. The organization had evolved into a representative entity for the Dalit community and made significant contributions in amplifying the voices of Dalits. He had a distinct strategy for addressing the issues faced by the Depressed classes, which diverged from the conventional nationalist perspective. The individual held the belief that a transformative economic and socio-psychological revolution was a necessary prerequisite for the empowerment and self-determination of the Depressed classes. Additionally, he regarded the attainment of national independence as the initial stride towards achieving that objective.[20]

It is widely acknowledged that the Government of India Act introduced a democratic element to the governance of India, necessitating the implementation of elections. Jagjivan Ram enthusiastically dedicated himself to the organization of the League. As expected, the elections played a significant role in the advancement of democracy in India. According to the author's perspective, the acquisition of electoral rights by Dalits alone was deemed insufficient. It is imperative for individuals to recognize the significance of their vote. It is imperative that Dalits received education in order to effectively exercise their rights for their own benefit as well as the advancement of the nation. With this objective in mind, he began to develop a profound fascination with the issues pertaining to the voting rights of *Harijans*. The speaker emphasized the meticulous efforts made to secure the inclusion of all eligible *Harijans* in the voting process, as well as the careful consideration given to the delimitation of double-member seats. The individual encountered the esteemed Mansfield, who held the position of Reforms Secretary inside the Bihar Government at the time. Subsequently, the individual provided testimony before the Hammond Commission. His astute political acumen played a pivotal role in expediting the implementation of constitutional amendments and advancing the trajectory towards enhanced civic engagement in electoral processes. On 20 November 1935, the individual in question corresponded with his spouse, Indrani Devi, expressing that his testimony in Ranchi has political significance, which may be challenging to comprehend solely through written communication. The deposition primarily focused on several key matters, namely, the delineation of constituencies for Dalits within the provincial legislative council of Bihar, the determination of voting and polling procedures, the implementation of measures to prevent acts of violence or bribery against Dalits by individuals belonging to higher castes during elections, and the proposal to lower the educational requirements for Dalits to exercise their right to vote from matriculation to middle school level. The draft pertaining to this matter has been prepared by the provincial government. The delegation originating from England sought to ascertain the populace's endorsement of the proposal, as well as any modifications requested by the populace. The researchers aimed to ascertain the public's reaction to it. Depositions were conducted with representatives from various groups, including labourers, Dalits, Christians, and Muslims. The commission had arrived only for the purpose of conducting an inquiry. The entity lacked the authority to make a judgement.

The study was scheduled to be presented before the British Parliament in January and February, with the subsequent assessment of its impact expected to occur several months thereafter. I expressed disapproval of the draught document that was developed by the state government. I successfully persuaded the commission that the draught was both perplexing and erroneous. However, the state government has a reluctance to acknowledge its errors. Let us observe the outcome.[21]

Jagjivan Ram believed that it was imperative to expedite the process of constitutional reform in order to facilitate the development of Indian democracy, to which he dedicated a significant portion of his life and made considerable sacrifices in the same connection. The enfranchisement of voting rights had a pivotal role in fostering the consolidation and expansion of democratic principles. The forty-ninth session of the Indian National Congress took place in Lucknow from 12 to 14 April 1936, with the notable presence of Mahatma Gandhi. Jawaharlal Nehru served as the president of the organization. According to Nehru, the issue of *Harijans* can be considered mostly theoretical or intellectual in nature. From a socialist perspective, this matter does not pose significant challenges, as socialism inherently eliminates any form of distinction or victimization. From an economic perspective, the group known as the *Harijans* has historically comprised the landless proletariat. An effective economic intervention would address the social hurdles that have been established by custom and tradition.[22] Jagjivan Ram also stated strongly that our rise is linked to the nation's rise. A free nation will free us too. The welfare of the nation is our welfare.

Jagjivan Ram's stature grew in his role as the leader of the Depressed Classes League, leading to his nomination as a Dalit representative in the Bihar Council in 1936. During the Bihar Legislative Assembly election in 1937, he fielded a total of 14 candidates representing the All-India Depressed Classes League for the purpose of contesting reserved seats in the state of Bihar. He ran as a candidate representing the Depressed Classes League and was elected without opposition to the Bihar Legislative Assembly from the East Central Shahabad (Rural) constituency. Through this resounding and uncontested triumph, Jagjivan rose as an influential figure capable of determining the outcome of political power. An electoral modification had taken place in the Congress pertaining to a single seat. The tireless efforts of the individual led to the victory of all the candidates from his party who ran on the ticket of the Congress. Subsequently, they became members of the Indian National Congress. Jagjivan Ram received significant acclaim among the Congress circles for his triumph. However, the Congress Party declined to establish administrations unless there was a guarantee that governors would cease their interference.[23] As the founder of the Dalit Varga Sangh, Jagjivan struggled for the rights of the Dalits he had become famous throughout the country.

Following the Poona Pact, Ambedkar issued a plea urging the *Harijans* to renounce Hinduism and embrace an alternative religious faith. However, Jagjivan Ram expressed opposition to this proposition, and subsequently, all the regional divisions of the League adhered to his stance. Jagjivan Ram, the leader of the League, expressed his regret about the departure of the esteemed individual, Ambedkar, from the Dalit Varga movement. However, he also conveyed satisfaction in the preservation of unity within the Hindu society.[24] He also expressed the viewpoint that caste discrimination was pervasive across Indian society. The Islamic theology and faith, in its core tenets, does not endorse the existence of caste distinctions. However, the practice of Islam in the Indian context has been influenced by the prevailing caste system. The individuals who transitioned from the occupation of manual scavenging to the Sikh faith were commonly referred to as Mazhabi Sikhs. The individuals belonging to the tanner community, known as Chamars, who had a religious conversion to Sikhism were commonly referred to as Ramdasias. Differences emerged within the converted population to Christianity based on the specific caste and social backgrounds from which they originated. Rather than undergoing conversions from Hinduism, Dalits ought to advocate for equitable rights within the framework of the Hindu religion.

The term 'conversion' in relation to Jagjivan Ram denotes an act characterized by a perceived display of cowardice and fleeing from a situation. The individual's perspective was that without a comprehensive transformation of Indian society, the situation at hand would remain unresolved. Ambedkar expressed his disagreement by suggesting that over time, possibly after a span of several generations, there could potentially be a shift in the prevailing attitudes towards individuals who had converted. He believed that individuals who had changed to a different religion several generations ago, continued to experience discriminatory treatment.[25] Jagjivan Ram made significant contributions to the Dalit Varga Sangh through diligent efforts. He issued a plea for solidarity, coordination, and mobilisation, actively engaging in door-to-door outreach to disseminate his ideology. During the All-India Ravidas Sammelan held in Monghyr on 18 February 1936, and subsequently, at a Dalit Varga Sammelan, the individual in question successfully advocated for the passage of a resolution asserting that religious conversion lacked intelligence and did not offer a viable answer to the challenges faced by the *Harijan* community.[26] Jagjivan Ram emerged as a prominent figure representing the dreams and aspirations of the marginalized 'Depressed Classes'. Jagjivan was appointed as a representative for the Haripura session of the Indian National Congress, convened on 19 February 1938. In addition, he was elected as a member of the All-India Congress Committee in 1940. Further-more, he participated in the elections for the position of Secretary of the Bihar Provincial Congress Committee and emerged victorious, holding the position until 1946.[27] He joined the Quit India Movement and was arrested.

In 1946, Jagjivan Ram, in his capacity as the head of the All-India Dalit League, presented himself before the Cabinet Mission. During the discussions with the Mission, Ram explicitly asserted that Dalits should be recognized as part of the Hindu community. He issued a memorandum containing the following statement: Dalits, from a religious and cultural perspective, are integrated into Hindu society, but they also possess a unique political identity. Given their social, economic, political, and scholastic disadvantages, individuals in such circumstances require specialized resources to safeguard their rights and interests. The provision of these specialized services should persist until those belonging to the Dalit community attain equal status with caste Hindus and achieve parity in all aspects of Hindu culture.[28]

Jagjivan Ram emerged as the unequivocal leader of the nationalist scheduled castes by effectively countering the objectives of separatist movements. On 16 June 1946, General Wavell corresponded with him and other individuals, attaching the written statement he had published earlier that day. This statement extended an invitation to Jagjivan Ram to join the Interim Government as a member.[29] The individual in question assumed the position of overseeing the labour portfolio starting on 3 September 1946, and continued in this role until the occurrence of the first general elections in May 1952. The individual's performance demonstrated a significant historical impact, positioning him as a revered figure among the working class due to his vital role in guiding substantial legislative measures. In the preceding chapter, I have discussed several significant enactments, including the Industrial Employment (Standing Orders) Act of 1946, the Mice Mines Labour Welfare Fund Act of 1947, the Industrial Disputes Act of 1947, the Dock Workers Act of 1948, the Factories Act of 1948, the Minimum Wages Act of 1948, the Employees' State Insurance Act of 1948, and the Coal Mines Provident Fund and Bonus Scheme Act of 1952, among others.[30] ESI Act, the country's first multidimensional social security scheme for workers in the organized sector, was introduced in India. All these laws brought tremendous change in the service conditions of the working class.

Jagjivan Ram always maintained a cordial relationship with all people belonging to all sections of the society. He was against any type of injustice, but on flip side was so kind-hearted. In any situation, he felt injustice to depressed and downtrodden people, he immediately raised his voice against it. Radheshyam Sharma stated one incident, when, Mohan Lal Pippal (a Lok Sabha MP) once commented on him that, 'why should he wear the same shirt? Last time, it had a torn shoulder and till now it has not been mended.'[31] He displayed a strong inclination towards the education of *Harijan* boys, demonstrated his commitment to providing medical assistance to the underprivileged and ill children, actively sought financial resources to aid those affected by the oppressive actions of *zamindars*, and initiated legal proceedings against those responsible for acts of repression. His compassion for the ordinary citizens was evident in his actions. The key facets of his character were his austere simplicity, his compassion for the oppressed, and his fervent enthusiasm for improvement. These qualities made him an ideal and a source of hope for millions of individuals who were marginalized and disadvantaged.[32] He had a genuine connection to his cultural roots and demonstrated a strong inclination towards addressing the issues that directly impact the general populace. He had a clear understanding of his intended actions and proceeded accordingly. The primary attributes that defined him were his ability to anticipate future events and his resolute determination to make choices. The attributes of patriotism, courage, and straightforwardness have been identified as the underlying factors contributing to his achievements.[33]

During Jagjivan Ram's tenure, as the Transport Minister, he showed an appreciation for the imperative to improve the transport infrastructure in post-Independence India, recognizing its significant benefits for both rural and urban populations. Additionally, he implemented a policy aimed at establishing post office facilities in close proximity to rural areas. The individual referred to as 'Babu' Jagjivan Ram implemented several significant measures to address the increasing demands of the nation. These initiatives included the procurement of new model aircraft, the establishment of additional aerodromes, the expansion of air services through the promotion of air-mindedness, the modernization of the postal system, the establishment of post offices in rural areas, the creation of rural public call offices, the introduction of automatic telex services, the enhancement and construction of national highways, and the nationalization and reorganization of civil aviation, among others.[34]

Jagjivan Ram made significant contributions to improve the state of food conditions during his tenure as the Minister of Food and Agriculture. He played a crucial part in facilitating the occurrence of the Green Revolution and in achieving food security inside the nation. In response to the food scarcity scenario, arising from the exceptional droughts of 1965 and 1966, Jagjivan Ram implemented a series of initiatives that effectively addressed the issue.[35] He was instrumental in the establishment of several initiatives, such as the Public Distribution System, fair-price shops, and domestic procurement of food grains. The individual in question showed a commitment to prioritizing the domain of Land Reforms, a strategic measure aimed at effecting a significant transformation in the rural economy by safeguarding the welfare of marginalized individuals. The individual in question participated in the Chief Ministers' Conference convened in 1976 with the aim of expediting the execution of land reform initiatives.[36] His leadership was proved as a saviour of the downtrodden.

During the Annual Convocation of the Agricultural University in Udaipur, held on 20 January 1968, Jagjivan Ram, the Union Minister of Food and Agriculture, made the following statement:

> Throughout the period of the East India Company's rule, a series of devastating famines took place in various regions. These famines occurred in the years 1770, 1784, 1802, 1824, and 1837. Subsequently, under the administration of the British Government in North-West India, famines were witnessed in 1860, followed by occurrences in Orissa in 1865, Rajasthan in 1868, Bihar in 1873, South India in 1876, and the entire country in 1896 and 1899. In the aftermath of the famine that occurred in 1876, a Famine Commission was duly created, and subsequently, the establishment of the Agriculture Department was undertaken in response to the findings and recommendations put out by the initial Famine Commission report. In the past, there has been intermittent scarcity of food grains due to a prolonged period of stagnation in our agricultural sector. Agricultural productivity continued to rely solely on natural forces. Significant transformations have taken place in the field of agriculture since the year 1947. The advancement

of irrigation infrastructure has led to a reduced reliance on monsoons within the agricultural sector. Efforts are being made to preserve and enhance soil fertility while simultaneously mitigating the detrimental impact of pests and diseases on crop production.[37]

During the Diamond Jubilee Celebration of the Poona Agricultural College on 2 January 1968, Jagjivan Ram expressed the notion that the nation's prosperity is contingent upon achieving self-sufficiency in food production. He expressed that it would be appropriate to schedule the Seminar during the Convocation Week of the Indian Agricultural Research Institute. This timing will effectively draw the attention of the graduating students towards the issues and potentialities associated with dry farming. It is vital that adequate attention be directed to regions characterized by poor rainfall and a want of irrigation. The issues at hand must be addressed from the perspectives of both the Agricultural Department and the broader human population.[39]

During his tenure as the President of the Indian National Congress in Bombay, Jagjivan Ram (1970-1) made the following statement:

> Over the course of several years, our reliance has been placed upon an administrative apparatus that was originally established with distinct objectives. The initial purpose of this entity was to serve the colonial agenda and ensure the continuation of British dominance. At that time, the civil services did not possess the widely publicized attribute of neutrality. The service in question had a strong dedication to upholding British authority, regardless of the associated expenses. During the period following Independence, the administrative machinery experienced certain modifications, yet, its' fundamental structure remained unchanged. The machinery in the upper echelons is being operated by highly skilled individuals who have graduated from prestigious Indian universities. These individuals adhere to and uphold British ideas and traditions. However, it might be argued that, at its most favourable, it can only be characterized as a feeble replication of its British equivalent.

The impartiality of public services in a nation characterized by significant socio-economic inequalities and where the privileged elite hold dominant positions of authority consistently resulted in preferential treatment for the wealthy and detrimental consequences for the underprivileged. Furthermore, in a nation that has experienced a prolonged stagnation over the course of many centuries and is now attempting to condense centuries of delayed progress into a mere decade, the need to expedite the speed of economic transformation becomes paramount. In this context, the ostensibly impartial administrative apparatus proves to be an obstacle rather than a facilitator. The relevance of the principle of a neutral bureaucracy to Indian settings is questionable. The civilization in which the thought arose and became institutionalized exhibited distinct characteriztics and possessed a unique historical context. Considering the aforementioned history, it is arguable that perceiving it as an inherent component of the democratic framework is not entirely defensible, nor essential. Does our bureaucracy, specifically at the lower levels, exhibit the same level of commitment to duty and a sense of pride in their work, as shown in its British counterpart? Does it possess the characteriztic of impartiality, which is synonymous with neutrality? Hence, it is imperative to possess an equipment endowed with intentionality and cognitive capabilities.

We require a service, that is dedicated to upholding the principles of democracy, socialism and secularism. The proposed change necessitates a significant paradigm shift in the mindset of the organizations, as well as in the administrative protocols, policies, and guidelines. The reorientation of the recruitment policy and the role of recruiting agencies is essential in order to ensure that the individuals responsible for administering various levels of government are capable of facilitating the necessary social and economic transformations required to establish a stable foundation for democracy, socialism, and secularism.[39]

Jagjivan Ram performed a pivotal role in the advancement of a significant portion of society who were compelled to endure a poor quality of life. He played a significant role in advocating for the rights of Dalits, making a noteworthy and innovative contribution towards improving the conditions of marginalized and disadvantaged social groups inside the nation. He played a crucial role in altering the destiny of the marginalized individuals. Through the implementation of meticulously devised strategies and initiatives, he attempted to establish a state of existence characterized by reverence and honour for the individuals involved. It might be said that the prevailing hardship of Dalits throughout his tenure played a significant role in the emergence of his leadership. The individual's determination to assume the role of advocating for marginalized individuals was fuelled by the mistreatment and verbal abuse he endured. The concerns pertaining to Dalits and marginalized communities have consistently occupied his thoughts. Intensive scrutiny of these issues prompted a profound transformation of his mindset, ultimately giving rise to the concept of leadership. The issue of untouchability consistently occupied his thoughts. The individual discovered a lack of rationale for the type of discrimination prevalent inside the Indian society. In his lifelong endeavour, he embarked upon a relentless campaign to eradicate this form of discrimination.

NOTES

1. Indrani Devi, *Milestones: A Memoir*, Penguin Books India, New Delhi, 2010, pp. 40-1.
2. Heather Lyne de Ver, *Conceptions of Leadership*, DLP, March 2009, pp. 3-4.
3. *International Encyclopedia of Social Sciences*, 2nd edn., p. 378.
4. Ibid.
5. R. Hogan and R.B. Kaiser, 'What we know about leadership', *Review of General Psychology*, vol. 9, pp. 169-80.
6. Sanjay Paswan and Pramanshi Jaideva (eds.), *Jagjivan Ram: Champion of Dalits* in *Encyclopaedia of Dalits in India: Leaders*, vol. 4, Kalpaz Publications, Delhi, 2004, p. 81.
7. K. Sadashiv, *Babu Jagjivan Ram: Jeevana Mattu Vyaktitva,* Priyadarshini Prakashan, Mysore, 2015, pp. 17-18.
8. Om Prakash Maurya, *Builders of Modern India: Babu Jagjivan Ram*, Publication Division, Ministry of Information and Broadcasting, Government of India, New Delhi, 2010, p. 12.
9. Sadashiv, op. cit., pp. 20-1.
10. K.L. Chanchreek, *Babu Jagjivan Ram: A Nation Builder*, vol. I, Shree Publication, New Delhi, 2006, p. 23.
11. Ibid., p. 32.
12. Ibid., p. 33.
13. S.R. Bakshi, *Jagjivan Ram: The Harijan Leader*, Anmol Prakashan, New Delhi, 1992, p. 6.

14. Ibid., p. 7.
15. B.M. Turadagi, *Dr. Jagjivan Ram's Life and Achievements: A Critical Analysis*, unpublished PhD thesis, Karnataka University, 2018, pp. 42-3.
16. Devi, op. cit., p. 39.
17. Turadagi, op. cit., p. 45.
18. Devi, op. cit., p. 49.
19. Ibid., p. 50.
20. Chanchreek, op. cit., p. 42.
21. Devi, op. cit., p. 51.
22. Chanchreek, op. cit., p. 47.
23. Turadagi, op. cit., p. 59.
24. Devi, op. cit., p. 51.
25. Ibid.
26. Ibid., p. 53.
27. Turadagi, op. cit., pp. 62-6.
28. Ibid., pp. 67-8.
29. Chanchreek, op. cit., p. 74.
30. A.C. Sinha, *Struggles and Achievements: Babu Jagjivan Ram Commemoration Volume*, Alka Prakashan, Delhi, 1973, pp. 140-1.
31. Radheshyam Sharma, *Who After Morarji?*, Pankaj Publications, New Delhi, 1978, p. 42.
32. Ibid., pp. 42-4.
33. Ramesh Chandra and Sangh Mitra, *Dalit Identity in the New Millennium*, Commonwealth Publishers, New Delhi, 2003, p. 62.
34. B.M Turadagi and Dr. M.B. Dalapati, 'A Paper on Babu Jagjivan Ram's Leadership and Modern India', published in *Sanshodhana Marga*, a peer reviewed journal under the *Journal of Social Science, Humanities and Language*, Institute of Praja Vikasa, Mysore, 2018, pp. 138-9.
35. *Babu Jagjivan Ram in Parliament,* Lok Sabha Secretariat, New Delhi, 2005, pp. 229-38.
36. Ibid.
37. Jagjivan Ram, *Four Decades of Jagjivan Ram's Parliamentary Career*, S.Chand, New Delhi, 1977, p. 163.
38. Ibid.
39. *Babu Jagjivan Ram in Parliament: A Commemorative Volume*, Lok Sabha Secretariat, New Delhi, 2010, pp. 45-6.

4

The Portfolio Activist

Jagjivan Ram as Parliamentarian

A Cabinet Minister navigates a delicate balance between two distinct realms: the executive branch, responsible for devising and implementing policies, and the legislative, which serves as a representative of citizens and ensures governmental transparency and responsibility. The presence of this dual role gives rise to a multifaceted ethical terrain. Let us discover the fundamental ethical standards that govern the behaviour of a Minister within the context of the Parliament. Ministers function within the framework of collective responsibility, wherein, the Cabinet collectively provides a cohesive stance on matters pertaining to government policy. Nevertheless, this does not exempt individual responsibility. Ministers are required to demonstrate readiness in justifying their judgements and policies to the Parliament, especially in cases when they deviate somewhat from the collective position. Ministers, although affiliated with a political party, also, serve as representatives of their constituency. Managing these allegiances can be challenging. In addition to endorsing party objectives, it is imperative for politicians to actively express the concerns of their constituency and advocate for their needs. Jagjivan Ram balanced himself between portfolios and his parliamentarian position.

An able administrator may not necessarily mean a skilled parliamentarian and vice versa, but as a Minister Jagjivan Ram's greatest asset, here, was his capacity to carry the House with him, which indeed speaks volumes about his personal qualities, his attitude towards the House and his equipment and standing as a Parliamentarian.

Unoffending by nature, soft-spoken and ever urbane and courteous in his dealing with others, he was a genial personality much loved in the House. Those who have sat for long years in Parliament would tell us how in his conduct in the House, he always gave the impression of one who has a genuine reverence for the parliamentary institution and was ever conscious of his obligations towards it. He knew the value of listening carefully and getting to know the other opinion. He was unruffled amid all the swirling passions in the House and with his abundant self-assurance was able to react to any criticism. And, when his turn came for reply, he was ready to meet them all with reason, telling arguments interlaced with his native wit and humour. A seasoned debater confident of his powers, he had no need to bend low to score victories over his adversaries on the legislative floor. He was sure of his ground, with his enviable grasp over facts, he was also never known to unduly lean on departmental briefs or allow himself to be cramped by them in his performance in the House. His interventions were cogent, to the point and full of facts, making part of constructive debates in the House.[1]

RAILWAY MINISTRY

When Jagjivan Ram took the charge as the Minister of Communications, he was also in-charge of Railway Ministry, which fell under the umbrella of communications. However, at that time, Railways was rushing towards a moribund phase. In terms of fleet strength, service, maintenance and industrial standards, the situation was somewhat bleak. Since 1952, under his tenure as the Railway Minister, a significant number of train accidents had occurred. During the period of 1957-8, there were a total of 30 collisions, and 200 derailed incidents involving passenger trains. In the preceding fiscal year of 1956-7, the frequency of occurrences was recorded as 23 and 197, respectively. During the period of 1955-6, there were a total of 36 crashes and 520 derailments recorded.[2] Upon a closer examination, it became evident that he made concerted efforts to improve the railway system, while facing obstacles, such as financial constraints. As a result, there was a notable and gradual decrease in rail accidents during his tenure. But, as the opposition continuously criticized the condition of railway, he patiently tried to balance his position for being accountable for his activities in one hand, both in Lok Sabha and Rajya Sabha, while keeping up the good works as minister.

Some of the severe criticisms that he had to face were related to not only the service and maintenance, but more importantly to the handling of employees. His stature as the face of labour class had already been established in the national stage, and it was discussed in this book as well. However, the criticisms concerned with railway workers need to be discussed as well. It will be a great display of balance that he showed as an activist, as well as a portfolio holder. In one such incident, that occurred on 8 March 1958, Rajendra Singh accused Jagjivan Ram of considering the coolies engaged with Railways to be 'sub-human'. Singh mentioned that, 'the Honourable Minister of Railways constantly voiced disapproval on the widespread allegations of victimization within the railway system.' Although, Jagjivan Ram wanted to assert that such disapprovals were false. He levied allegations against him and his government, asserting that they regarded the coolies as a subordinate species, inferior to street dogs, and expressed his desire to inform him of their mistreatment. During his visit to the Howrah Station, he learned that over twenty individuals, who were actively engaged in the union and had expressed their complaints, requests, and the distressing emotions of the workers, had been unjustly terminated without any rhyme or reason. He enquired that whether these actions constituted victimization or not. He stated that victimization does not follow a consistent pattern, but rather varies over time and in different locations. To provide an additional illustration of this scenario, the individual recounted the narrative of a dear companion of his, who, coincidentally held the position of a coolie. He asserted that his friend was terminated from railway employment only due to the investigation conducted by the CID, Bihar, which revealed that he had a concubine almost a decade ago.[3]

Jagjivan Ram did not lose his temper under such verbal bombardment. He maintained that the word 'victimization' had been used loosely by the labour activists, even when it did not cover all the scenarios. He strongly proposed that in the Railways department there were, and still are, rules and regulations for executing disciplinary actions against insubordinate employees, who derelict orders or decorum. However, there were proper channels for appeals and second appeals if one or a group of employees felt that they had been falsely accused, and on contacting the members, higher officials he meant, could initiate the process of appeals. Even if the employee is convinced that injustice had been perpetrated on a worker, he must contact the members, who could advice and at the same time initiate the procedures for appeal on the behalf of the workers. His prompt reply in this manner made Singh silent in this case, as all the things which he said were just and appropriate. He was well aware of such incidents, and knew exactly how the employees could deal with such circumstances, with proper legal channels created to help them.[4]

However, Singh was not ready to submit completely yet, albeit he had to turn down his violent accusations a bit. He presented the case of coolies, porters and casual labourers, and said that when the members of the Railway Board were enjoying greater privileges, those who were responsible for the smooth operations of the Railways were denied any privileges at all. He, therefore, asked him to take their case and provide the minimum necessities which they demanded.[5] Jagjivan Ram listened to his demand carefully and gave an articulate reply, based on facts rather than whimsical claims. He said that porters were not railway employees, but rather worked to provide facilities to the travelling public. They got their wages from the public as well. Therefore, they did not fall under the concerns of Railways. Moreover, in certain countries, those institutions did not exist at all, and if it was not the Indian way of life, they would have also remained absent, as he stated.[6] Secondly, as far as casual workers were concerned, they too did not fall under the employees of Railways. However, there were certain rules that if the casual workers had worked for more than six months, they would automatically get absorbed in the spectrum of Railways, giving them a permanent post. As to the engagement of such casual workers in Railways were concerned, he stated that it was necessary for any large enterprise, such as railways, to employ certain temporary workers for conducting day-to-day operations efficiently, particularly if work load increased suddenly. Here, he assured that the best they could do was to supervise if the contractors paid their casual workers serving in the railways justly. Although, he, or the railways for that matter, could not advice the contractors due to the Minimum Wages Act in different states.[7]

Jagjivan Ram said that wherever the casual labourers were employed, the Railway department consulted the District Magistrate to get the figures of minimum wages prescribed in the district. So, they were bound by the Minimum Wages Act was in force. However, certain state governments did not follow the Act and in such cases, Railways paid them wages prevailing in the locality. He also said that departmentalizing all the casual labourers was not practicable, even if it had been a matter of discussion. His pertinent answers finally made Singh to quit questioning.[8]

As far as the State Governments were concerned, Jagjivan Ram hands were tied. In the case of casual workers, we have seen this. Although, his development initiatives related to material domain, remained barred due to this problem as well. One incident can be mentioned in this regard. As a Railway Minister, he was concerned with the expansion of Railway connectivity in every nook and corner of the state. In that regard, he proposed a route from Barasat to Basirhat, two towns in West Bengal for greater connectivity. However, there was a massive problem in that, i.e., acquisition of land. The State Government in West Bengal failed to provide the Railway authority with the land needed for this, and allocations of budget every year for this cause could not be used due to this reason and rationale. Renu Chakravartty, representing the state government as well in that case, told Jagjivan Ram that the land would be delivered to them, as promised. She made a dubious suggestion that the railways should start constructing stations first. He patiently told her that even if the railways start constructing the stations, they would still require land to construct station buildings. The premises were heavily congested, and therefore, it would not be possible to construct anything unless the state government starts acquiring the land. However, Hon. Chakravartty thought these to be mere 'excuses' and lamented with a warm tone.[9] On the other hand, he kept his temper well under control and assured the house that they would take the matter to state government once again, without going into a direct conflict with Chakravartty.

There were plethora of such instances, where certain matters barred his vision of development. However, Jagjivan Ram never showed a slight tint of tiredness in his face. His development initiatives did not remain confined to material realm as well. He was interested to do a lot for the people too. It is with this sense, that he proposed the matter of SC/ST representations in the Railways. While answering Daljit Singh's comments on this facet, he stated that at that time, their representation in the Railways had been far from adequate. The government and the Railways had been taking specific measures over one or two years, prior to ensure that they fill the positions intended for them. Regarding the Scheduled Castes, he noted that the 1957 recruitment's outcomes had been largely good. Yet, it was still far from enough in the Scheduled Tribes instance. He confidently proposed that a few further actions would need to be undertaken. He told the House that they might discover that there would have been greater recruitment in 1957, if they continued to carry over open positions for an additional year. There were 4,321 total openings in the four commissions located in Allahabad, Bombay, Calcutta, and Madras that were designated for members of the Scheduled Castes, out of whom 5,454 were chosen. However, just 342 applicants were chosen for the 2,074 reserved slots in the Scheduled Tribes category. In the case of Scheduled Castes, in the lower category in Class IV, all the scavenging staff that was required came from among the Scheduled Castes and therefore, there also, perhaps, their number became slightly inflated. In order to ensure that the representation of Scheduled Castes and Scheduled Tribes increased to the quota set out for them, the government and the Railway Ministry were constantly monitoring this issue.[10]

Jagjivan Ram was aware that the expansion of Railways required more trained railway staff and for this reason, he was in the favour of creating new staff colleges, as well as increasing their training facilities. In order to answer a question raised by Thirumala Rao, Jagjivan Ram maintained that the Baroda Railway Staff College could then accommodate more students, thanks to the Railways. As a result, lengthier training sessions, sufficient refreshers, and specialized courses could be offered. The accommodation for the training schools at Chandausi, Sini, Udaipur, and Guwahati was extended from 1,050 seats to 1,750 seats at a time. The N.E. Railway Training School was being relocated to Muzaffarpur, with a capacity increase from 600 to 850. Additionally, other apprentice hostels had been established in Jhansi, Lallaguda, and Kharagpur, and 40-person training establishments for mechanical and electrical apprentices had been established in Lucknow, Ajmer, and Bangalore City. Moreover, he insisted that work was underway in Kharagpur to build a Central Training School that could accommodate 800 trade apprentices and 225 apprentice mechanics. In addition, three schools with a combined capacity of 600 men studying civil engineering had been constructed in Mhow, Shahjahanpur, and Madhupur. All in all, he guaranteed that the information was current and that the number of training facilities would rise from 21,000 to 53,000 in year 1955-6.[11] This rapid expansion was incomprehensible to many at that time, and those who said that the railways was a failing industry had to remain quiet. Jagjivan Ram wanted to make Railways as a means to nurture friendly relationship with the neighbouring countries as well. For example, in 1961, keeping in mind the good relation between India and Nepal, he remodelled the station of Raxaul, on the model of Pashupatinath temple, as a symbol of friendship and goodwill between those two countries.[12]

POSTS AND TELEGRAM SERVICES

Even though Railways were important for rearranging communications, Jagjivan Ram could not show intolerance to the postal services. These activities included the development of personnel working, as well as materially improving the postal and telegraph services. In the Lok Sabha, the issues were being constantly raised from 1953 onwards on both of these matters, and he had to address them with prowess and calm at the same time. Speaking on the development of personnel engaged, S.C. Samanta on 18 September 1953 raised concerns regarding the government initiatives to tackle the quality of the personnel of the Posts and Telegraph Department, in relation to the Planning Commission. He answered him in detail by stating that it remained a difficult matter due to the Partition and successive wars. However, on the steps taken by him, he added,

(i) The Department had stopped the recruitment of candidates by relaxing the prescribed educational and technical qualifications.
(ii) Those who joined in the service during War Years had been, generally, made to pass departmental examinations before attaining permanency in order to ensure their knowledge of rules and procedure.
(iii) Ex-state staff, who did not go through the training before their appointment were being given the prescribed training.
(iv) The Department was ensuring that certain arrangements were made to impart training to all new recruits before they had taken up any appointment.
(v) The Department had tightened the supervision and instructions were issued to the officers to maintain a healthy relationship with the staff and, in certain cases, to educate them about the need to efficiently serve the public
(vi) Initiatives were also being taken to provide improved facilities to the staff in the shape of accommodation and aids for work.[13]

D.C. Sharma asked if the quality and effectiveness of inspectors had improved, only to receive an answer from Jagjivan Ram that the inspectors are appointed from the clerical section, only of they stand well in the competitive examinations. However, at that time the Department was thinking about creating a separate examination by which graduates would be recruited directly for maximum efficiency and quality.[14] Moreover, on Sanganna's query regarding advance pay in flood affected, Jagjivan Ram stated that in flood affected areas of UP, Bihar, Assam, Madras and Bengal, the workers received advance pay for the strenuous service that they were providing.[15] His affection towards the working class, irrespective of their caste, religion or ethnicity, was proved once again with this statement.

Materially speaking, Jagjivan Ram envisioned and tried to expand rather multiple and palpably terrific concepts at that point of time. It was about the mobile post office, night post offices, Hindi Telegraph, Post Offices in rural areas and Hindi Posts &Telegraph Department. In a discussion in Lok Sabha with D.C. Sharma on 10 September 1953, Jagjivan Ram gave certain details in the direction of the mobile post offices. Sharma asked about the implementation of this idea, in Punjab, along with a number of post offices of that nature and new mobile post offices that were opened in the year 1953-4. He stated that the cities which had night air mail service would receive such post offices. Since, Punjab had no such cities at that time, the mobile post offices could not be established. At that point of time, there were only four cities in which such mobile post offices were established in India in cities like Delhi, Madras and Nagpur, with total kitty of five post offices. In the year mentioned above, none were constructed.[16] It must be kept in mind that at that point of time, the night mail service did not develop much, and the number of cities that could demand such mobile post-offices were lesser than what we have now.

On 2 December 1954, Sarangadhar Das, asked if the P&T Department was thinking about keeping the post offices open on Sundays in cities and facilitate the general public to transact their business on that day. It is in connection to these queries that Jagjivan Ram had proposed opening the night post offices which would remain open on Sundays as well. He was very convinced that it would help people in a place with commercial and industrial importance and foster growth on a larger scale. The service was designed to cater to five lakh population as well.[17] However, the problem in this case was the night mail service as well. As far as the Hindi telegram was concerned, while answering questions raised by L. Jogeswar Singh, he emphasized on the matter. He assured that the Hindi telegraph service was working well, and extra expenditure were being fuelled in the training of the operative staff to ensure maximized operationality. He had also given brief description of the means adopted to encourage Hindi telegram service. They were as follows:

(1) The service is being gradually extended into the interior of the country, such as District and Tehsil Headquarters.
(2) Telegraph outlets are earmarked exclusively for the transmission of Hindi telegrams where necessary for expeditious disposal.
(3) Teleprinters in the Nagari script have been and are being developed and provided for. Four such machines have actually been made over for trial to the news agencies on a nominal fee.[18]

To promote the Hindi in P&T Department, he, in 1962, issued orders to give free textbooks to the trainees in training classes and suggested cash prizes to the trainees by the Ministry of Home Affairs.

He assured Narayan Das that many administrative offices were implementing this. He was also adamant on recruiting teachers in the P&T Department for this purpose.[19] As far as rural post offices were concerned, it was during his tenure that post offices in the rural villages were being converted to combined post and telegraphs offices. Subodh Hasda's question regarding the conversion in the Midnapore district of West Bengal made him to give an assurance that such conversations were gradually taking place in the post offices under a police station.[20]

AIR CORPORATIONS BILL, 1953

Just like Railways, Jagjivan Ram embarked upon a prominent role in developing airline services in India. Under his leadership, the government implemented the nationalization of all prominent private airlines in India in 1953. Consequently, the establishment of aviation India and Indian Airlines ensued, serving as the official national aviation carriers of the nation. The aforementioned action was perceived as a vital measure in enhancing the civil aviation industry in India. The individual in question, serving as a Minister of Transport and Communications, encountered numerous challenges related to air traffic and transportation. Initially, there existed a limited number of active interior routes and two foregoing airlines, necessitating the need for expansion. Furthermore, the increased expenses associated with petrol necessitated the adoption of air transport as an alternate method for delivering mail and goods. Moreover, the utilization of the twin engine, domestically manufactured Dakota aircrafts was the exclusive method for such transportation, and their cost was substantial.[21]

Hence, the development of domestically manufactured aircraft and other essential advancements in aviation technologies, in addition to the aforementioned challenges, need collaborative efforts from both the government and private entities that were already in progress at that particular juncture. In this regard, he expressed support for the restructuring of civil air transport. The Air Corporation Bill, enacted in 1953, served as his approach to addressing this issue. The matter of fact is that the issue of civil airlines amidst declining quality of

Railways would have been a hardly convincing issue to be discussed in the Parliament. Jagjivan needed to balance the timely need with populist rhetoric in a harsh parliamentary atmosphere.

Jagjivan Ram posited that he would now provide a concise overview of the benefits associated with the implementation of a unified organizational structure. The optimal utilization of available resources, such as equipment, workshop capacity, and technical personnel, can be maximized. From a defence perspective, it is evident that a state organization, operating all air services would be the most preferable arrangement. This is because in an emergency, it would be simpler to make arrangement to meet the requirements of the defence services compared to if private airlines were responsible for operating the services.

The significance lies in the fact that air transport is a public utility and should be developed in the best interest of the nation, without being hindered by the primary objective of generating profit, which would be the dominant factor in private industry. A governmental entity would possess the capacity to strategize the future trajectory of the industry in a more holistic manner. Significant advancements are already occurring in the field of civil air transport, and it is only a State agency that possesses the necessary size and resources to effectively capitalize on these technological advancements.[22] Some members who support the nationalization of the industry have raised the question of whether now is the right time for it to be nationalized, and if it should be given priority over other urgent needs of the country. But, he dealt with the debates pertinently. One esteemed acquaintance expressed the viewpoint that due to the industry's declining performance and the government's awareness of its decline, it should not be subjected to nationalization. The aforementioned logic could potentially be applicable to an industry that is involved in the production of consumer items of lesser significance. However, its application to this industry is not feasible. It is not an industry that can be perceived as a passive observer gradually losing and ultimately succumbing to an ignominious defeat.

Jagjivan Ram, against all criticisms, argued that aviation service should not be viewed solely as a luxury for the aristocratic classes of the country. Instead, it should be viewed as a service that must be upheld for the defence of the country, the maintenance of law and order, and the provision of goods and services during emergencies and natural disasters.[23] Similarly, when Seth Govind Das raised the question pertaining to the matter of aviation and if it really deserved the priority which the Government is provided, Jagjivan Ram answered aptly.

It is very difficult, human nature as it is, to break away from a status quo. And, whenever any proposal comes, which wants to break away from the status quo, persons who are advanced in life, persons who are advanced in their way of thinking, persons, who have formed some sort of set ideas, it is very difficult for them willingly to fall in line with the change.[24]

When few others pointed out that the focus should be on making India's own aviation industry, being a very pragmatic minister, Jagjivan Ram balanced the need of the reality and the attendant developmental rhetoric. He expressed his belief that such would not be the more prudent course of action. He considered it the most advantageous moment for the government to replace India's planes. It was necessary for them to initiate the procurement process for the replacement of those aircraft. It was imperative for the administration to expeditiously make a judgement in this situation. India did not engage in the production of its own aircraft at that time. She would have great joy when they begin producing their own aircraft. However, this process would require a significant amount of time. In the current global context, it was observed that even if the government issued an order immediately, it would typically take several years for them to receive the aircraft. There was an absence of ambiguity regarding the importance in this matter, and if the members were to allocate a small portion of their attention, they would concur that it was imperative to promptly nationalize this industry, as any more delay would be unacceptable. He was astonished when his acquaintances from that faction inquired: Why not pursue a complete nationalization? He lamented that perhaps the individuals had become accustomed to relying solely on phrases. Moreover, he displayed an uncertainty about their understanding of the concept of nationalization.[25]

Some members, asked about why it should not act similarly to the Railway Board? Jagjivan Ram's prompt reply was concerned with the part of efficiency, as he stated that it was the members of the house who questioned the deteriorating honesty and efficiency of the Railways. Their suggestion therefore was found contradictory by him, perhaps. On the other hand, he pointed out in the direction of maintenance and safety. He said that any mode of transportation that operates on land has the ability to temporarily disregard the maintenance or overhaul of its machinery. However, any system that operates in the air could potentially neglect this task, posing risks not only to the passengers, but also to the people involved. Thus, assuming that the services or management would disregard the maintenance of the aircraft was assuming something that would surpass human nature. No individual expressed a willingness to jeopardize their own life, including our ground engineers and pilots, who, as previously mentioned by him, were a commendable group of individuals. They would refrain from operating equipments that had not undergone adequate maintenance, repair, or replacement of worn-out components. The individual expressed these sentiments due to the fact that, notwithstanding any potential leniency on the part of the management, the individuals directly responsible for operating the machinery would not tolerate any delay in the repairs or replacements. The comparison between railway, road transport, and river transport, was, not valid in that regard.[26] He constantly expressed his views that if the corporation faced any loss, as a public utility service, the corporation would pay for such loses being an earner in its own accord, as it would neither be a burden on public exchequer, nor on taxpayer. His pertinently replied that the sole purpose of the corporation was not to make money only, but also to provide great service, which showed his empathy for the people of India, as a minister.[27]

Jagjivan Ram's ministerial experience in the labour department perhaps made him closer to the problems that the class faces. When the questions of employees were on the table, he made certain statements that indeed showed his sympathy. He said that when the Corporation would assume control of these enterprises as ongoing operations on a designated date, it would ensure the continuity of service by assuming all the workers of those companies. Upon the Corporation's assumption of control from the companies, there would be no reduction in workforce. Upon assuming control, the Corporation would be required to undertake the integration of all the companies, including the integration of their respective staff. Upon the completion of this process, which he thought might span duration of six months, nine months, or potentially even longer, there would be possibilities that certain categories of staff might be deemed surplus in relation to the Corporation's requirements. In order for the Corporation to operate efficiently and maintain a decent cost of fare and goods, it was not advisable to continue having more staff than necessary. There were two options available according to him. Either the government would reduce the excess workforce to meet the Corporation's needs, or they explore alternative job opportunities for them. He expressed his intention to be the final individual to adopt the initial option. He expressed his primary focus on expanding the Corporation's activities to accommodate the surplus workers beyond the current routes.[28]

On 6 May 1953 the discussion regarding the Air Cor-porations Bill was brought forth again by Jagjivan Ram, particularly for discussing the changes the select committee had made. It is interesting to note that when he initiated the discussion, the other members, from the opposition it seems, started squabbles, so prominent that the speaker had to ask the undisciplined members to leave. However, he kept his calm and carried forward, keeping both the necessary serenity of a cabinet minister and an obedience towards the Parliamentary decorum, as an elected member. He laid down the suggestions that were made, and showed utmost satisfaction in those. Firstly, he appreciated that the select committee laid important conditions regarding 'disqualifications for members of the corpora-tions', which were not present in the original Bill. Secondly, he welcomed another change that had been implemented to facilitate the advancement of air transport within the nation, as well as in the global arena. While it was suggested that the Corporation would exert maximum effort to foster the growth of the sector, it was not explicitly stated. The select committee had ensured that the development of the industry was explicitly included as one of the objectives of the Corporation's programme. Thirdly, the Bill stipulated that all personnel who were employed by the current air firms prior to1 June 1952, and were now employed, would be transferred to the Corporation upon the acquisition of the airlines. There had been reports from specific sources indicating that upon the introduction of nationalization, certain individuals who were employed before to the specified date had been unlawfully terminated or subjected to mistreatment. In the event that the government determined that a certain employee had been unlawfully or unjustifiably terminated or fired from their employment with a corporation, it possessed the authority to instruct the Corporation to hire that employee. This change held significant importance in relation to the employees. Finally, it had been stipulated that within the Air Transport Council, an individual possessing expertise in labour affairs will be designated and employed by the Corporation. The Corporation's reports for the previous year and the overall programme forecast for the upcoming year would be presented to Parliament. All regulations established under this legislation must be presented to the legislative body.[29]

The suggestions pertaining to the bill was multifaceted, and there were strong criticisms lying underneath those. However, it was also one such day, when the sublime nature of Jagjivan Ram, as a Parliamentarian, became visible and apparent. As far as the primary concerns with the Bill were concerned, the other members proposed suggestions pertaining to administration, employment, labour and compensation. The first backlash came in the direction of the administration. The matter pertaining to the establishment of two organizations for international or external and internal, received tremendous opposition from the 'other' members of the parliament, something which he had to deal with at that point. However, he remained firm on his stand. He was quite aware of the economic burden that an extra organization might have on the general economy. Although, for him the efficiency and reputation of the international flights, and on the greater picture, the international prestige of his dear nation was more important. He could have gone forward with his stand, but his duties as a parliamentarian demanded answering, or rather presenting his cause in front of other members of the Parliament, irrespective of the backlashes. He stated,

> As I said on previous occasions—I do not want to repeat that in extension —the Air India International has established a reputation for itself. It is a fine organization. It is today regarded as one of the best, if not the best airlines in the world. We should not take any chance by which, in any

way, the reputation or efficiency of that fine service is affected in the least.[30]

Jagjivan Ram recognized the further cost that would arise from having two corporations instead of merely one. As he previously informed the House, it would result in an additional cost of around six lakhs of rupees annually. However, in the event that the service experienced any disruption, even if it amounted to a mere 10 per cent, it is probable that they would incur losses exceeding the said cost. Consequently, the government had to implement all necessary measures to ensure that the reputation of Air India International remained unaffected in any way.[31]

Shyama Prasad Mukherjee, as a MP of BJS from Calcutta South-East, surprisingly was in support of Jagjivan Ram's proposed bill. However, he was not in support of the entire control of the government but rather proposed a mixed administration. On administration itself, he wanted to have full time government employee in the Corporation for maximum efficiency and responsibility. They would advise the government in matters which needed their advice, or for that matter intervention. In this regard, he wanted a semi-independent organization. He was not satisfied with the explanation concerning two organizations rather than one. In this regard, he suggested that there should be one parent organization and under that two separate organizations, for internal and external purposes. Other suggestions pertaining to training, employment and compensations were made by him, which did not go hand in hand with what Jagjivan Ram had proposed. He attacked Jagjivan particularly by stating that his proposed policies regarding compensation and shares were actually to safeguard managing agents. Mukherjee proposed certain measures to safeguard the interests of poor and middle-class shareholders, and wished that they should not get trapped in the hands of managing agents, who could operate freely in the Memorandum of Association provided in the Bill.[32] Jagjivan Ram did not make a reply at that point of time. However, we shall see that later, he appreciated Mukherjee's suggestions and concerns, so much so that he was thinking about adopting it to some extent. This is a testimony of his character as a parliamentarian, where the constructive voices of the opposition were also important to him.

One of the most important concerns was raised by K. Ananda Nambiar, an MP of CPI from Mayiladuthurai and Tiruchirappalli. His questions regarding labour issues and the turbulence it caused in the Parliament proved to be a test for Jagjivan Ram's parliamentary as well as ministerial self. Nambiar raised the issue by using particularly wage and welfare as bases. His questions echoed Renu Chakravartty's concerns on labourers, which stated that under two organizations, there will be a disparity in labourers, as those who will be in the international section gain more wage and privilege than those working in the internal section. This would ultimately create a cleavage in the labour unity as such. Nambiar's questions and suggestions rather had a violent tint, which could easily boil the very nerves of the most veteran parliamentarians. In one such statement, he said that the whole idea of nationalization would be a shame if the labour voices were not heard well. However, Ram accepted his suggestions wholeheartedly and assured him that the labour issues and their dissent, would not remain unheard. He added that he would listen to the suggestions not because they were made by Nambiar, but on his own accord.[33]

Nambiar then turned his attention to the part of compensation. The opposition's concerns, he asserted, revolved around numerous topics rather than just one or two. Regarding the matter of compensation, if the Government had made an effort to provide fair and justifiable recompense, he would have comprehended it. He desired to prevent the ex-operators from being deprived of their rightful payments. However, despite numerous deductions, the sector was in a state of disintegration. Nambiar enquired whether Jagjivan Ram had considered this issue in the determination of the remuneration. He alleged that he lacked knowledge on this particular issue.

Despite the Government's unfavourable calculation rate for depreciation and the company's attempts to avoid income tax by allowing depreciation, he asserted that Jagjivan Ram was unwilling to accept the depreciation level recorded in these companies' books. A selection of Dakotas and machinery had been subjected to one rupee. However, he refused to accept this. Based on his comprehension, Jagjivan Ram must have acted for a different motive, and he stated that he must provide fair recompense. Furthermore, as per his statement, he had proposed a formula in the schedule that would require him to provide compensation for a period of 16 years. This compensation would be paid when the worth of the company's assets had been reduced or recorded as one rupee.

Nambiar sought clarification from him regarding the rationale behind the provision of a greater rate of pay. He alleged that his actions were motivated by a preference for the former operators, as he declined to accept the proposed formula. What he suggested was a fixed rate of compensation, in connection to the formation of the corporations. Furthermore, with adding the labour issue as well, the CPI affiliated MP even accused Jagjivan Ram vehemently on ignoring the interests of the nation.[34] Even after experiencing such demeaning behaviour from the minister, he remained composed enough to answer the queries. For him, and for any minister, it would be quite hard for fixing a compensation in a fixed rate. In that period, when these nation-building initiatives were in their cradle phase, such actions would have jeopardized the ordinary citizens, as well as company interests to the brink of deterioration.

The only breathing space was, in this tight situation, was provided by Ghamandi Lal Bansal. According to the latter, the select committee had proposed satisfactory methods to enhance the reliability of the Bill. However, the issue of compensation had generated divergent viewpoints. Bansal asserted that the select committee was perplexed by the compensation and that the previously suggested option appeared to be the sole viable one. Nevertheless, the recommendations put forth by S.P. Mukherjee also suggested the possibility of making amendments. Jagjivan Ram concurred that the formula proposed by him in the bill was not the exclusive one, and it was always open to receiving ideas. However, Mukherjee's advice necessitated his examination prior to its consideration. Furthermore, Jagjivan Ram requested Bansal to propose several suggestions pertaining to the aspect of compensation. Despite Nambiar's assault, Jagjivan Ram remained composed and displayed patience in attentively considering the constructive recommendations placed by his fellow House members. Simultaneously, he maintained a firm hold on the Bill, exuding a serene demeanour. Jagjivan Ram's understanding of the Bill became evident when he corrected an error made by Bansal while commenting on Clause 20(1) of the Bill, which deals with the terms and conditions of the service following the merger.[35]

Jagjivan Ram's attitude towards the suggestions was reflected in Matthen's comment. He said that the minister always had a smile while listening to the suggestions and accepted them in a sporting manner, for both pleasant and unpleasant ones. He said that he was among those individuals who vehemently opposed the two corporations. However, his statement indicated that he shared the same viewpoint as he articulated during the House proceedings. He encountered specific challenges in implementing this viewpoint at present. Nevertheless, he expressed his willingness to promptly deliberate on the matter after the domestic service was fully integrated. In response to this, Matthen expressed his support for him. He fully understood Ram's gratitude for the exceptional services provided by Air India International and its esteemed global reputation. However, he failed to see the rationale behind the government's endorsement of this nationalization, particularly its rapid pace. Consequently, he proposed that the government should allocate additional time to execute this decision. According to Matthen, he concurred with the majority of the members of the Select Committee regarding the usefulness of a unified Corporation, particularly during a subsequent phase. Why not let him depart for the moment? The individual referred to the esteemed Air India, which is under the management of the Tata family and holds a majority stake of 51 per cent. A firm in which an individual possesses a majority stake of 51 per cent exercises control over the company. In this regard, the payment of compensation would be much higher. There was no justification for Jagjivan Ram to nationalize it at that time. If the government were to nationalize the corporation at present, it would be necessary for them to make a payment of approximately two crores or more to the Tatas. If they possessed authority over the corporation and benefit from its services and efficiency, why not refrain from intervening and proceed with the nationalization of domestic services for the time being? Given the current financial constraints faced by our community initiatives and planning, it was questionable why the government should be rushing to address this matter of nationalization. He was unable to comprehend that, albeit had expressed his support for the Bill and continued to do so at the time of discussion.[36]

On 8 May, another session was called to discuss certain clauses in the Bill, particularly Clause 4. Nambiar also was in a mood to disrupt the activities that day, but due to the Speaker's involvement, it remained unnoticed. Two important figures became the flag bearers of criticism that day, namely Jaipal Singh and Damodar Menon. They questioned the Subclause 2 of Clause 4, and Menon started with his argument. He said that the Subclause pertained to individuals who had been engaged in employment with the company prior to July 1952, or, who had experienced harm as a result of their association with these companies. He requested an ample elucidation from the minister regarding those who had been hired subsequent to 1952. He said that the minister, in his speech, acknowledged the potential need for downsizing, which he duly acknowledged. Nevertheless, he expressed apprehension that it was conceivable that starting from July 1952, numerous individuals could have been hired in enterprises that the government intended to acquire, and then secure employment in their respective government departments. In such instances, it may have been imperative for the government to downsize certain individuals if they were deemed unproductive to the corporation or lacked the requisite qualifications. The government must take into an account all of these factors, he underlined. The government would evaluate the eases of those who are eligible to continue in the companies or who possess the necessary qualifications to do so in a compassionate manner. The individual made a prediction that in the event of government intervention in the companies; their own employees would be retained, while others would face unemployment. He had to be cautious about such a peril. He inquired what the measures undertaken by the government prior to implementing layoffs? He believed that the application of Subclause (2) to them was not entirely appropriate. Moreover, a provision was incorporated into the Bill pertaining to individuals who have experienced victimization. He desires the government to exert their influence on the corporation and ensure that these individuals who were victimized get re-employed. Menon asserted that it is likely that these individuals who were victimized had experienced prolonged periods of unemployment, and expediting their employment would be advantageous for all parties involved. He desired to witness their contentment. Furthermore, he proposed that following the designated period, the government may need to establish a committee to further investigate the issue of merger. He inquired whether the government was considering the possibility of issuing a directive to the corporation, specifically regarding the re-employment of all affected individuals, only after the Committee had addressed the issue of merging the air services.[37]

Jaipal Singh continued after this and followed the same line of enquiry. Singh was critical about the fixed date and how that could leave a large number of technical staffs unemployed. He was critical of the clause in this regard, and was not confident about Jagjivan Ram's assurance about changing the clause. He particularly emphasized on the point, which stated,

> . . . except a director, managing agent, manager or any other persons entitled to manage the whole or a substantial part of the business and affairs of the company under a special agreement.[38]

This portion also meant that those who would not be in the aforementioned posts would automatically be carried over by two corporations. If this was to remain, the persons who were engaged in both technical and managerial posts, would be left out of the clause, and if they lost their jobs, would not receive any covers from the government or corporation for that matter.[39] G.S. Singh, also raised an amendment, by taking reference from the earlier concern of Rohini Kumar Chaudhuri, on this matter of fixing a date. He said that employees in an air company (about to be undertaken) before 1 July 1952 shifts to another company after 1 July 1952, their employment in the corporation would be barred. This would indicate that only those who were continuously serving in the air companies should remain a part of the corporation. This point was crucial, as the employees in companies, who, were exercising pay cuts wanted to transfer to a better company. However, the amendment that was proposed would not only endanger their career, but, also would make them suffer, as the corporation was trying to keep the same 'terms and conditions' of the employment, with same privileges.[40]

Jagjivan Ram observed the amendments carefully and emphasized on the question of employment first. Towards Jaipal and indirectly Menon, he said that he might have not realized the implications of the amendment he had proposed, as they would inevitably lead to a conclusion that the employees, who were in service of an air company four years ago from the date of 1 July 1952 and had not been in touch with the company since will be covered, which would not be fruitful. He satisfied that those who were recruited before 1 July 1952 and were still in employment would be covered. Those who were discharged after that date would also be covered. The question was regarding those who were employed after that date and still in service. In their case, if the retrenchment affected the persons employed before 1952, then the provisions made by them would cover their case. He even stated that if the retrenchment affected those who were a bona fide employee of the air companies, and still working or discharged after the date fixed, their cases would also be covered by the government. In the later cases, they would have to be bona fide. His assurance made the questioners silent, as Jaipal Singh and G.S. Singh withdrew their amendments.[41] Much of the clauses raised for discussion that day were adopted, some even without suggestions for amendments, where the opposition were so satisfied with them, that they accepted them without opposition. This again shows the dedication and articulated thoughts that Jagjivan Ram had put in the Bill.

These criticisms, debates, and suggestions remained active for several sessions, but Jagjivan Ram never, for once, walked out in the face of such circumstances, turbulent as they were. He accepted the just suggestions and amendments, even if they came from the opposition. After all the actors were satisfied, the Bill was put forward to Rajya Sabha and subsequently became an Act. Thus, India, along with certain developed powers such as England and Australia, was able to get her own nationalized Air Corporation, which was quite a drastic step, for a country which obtained its independence just a few years back. It was a milestone, perhaps the first major one towards the national empowerment. It still serves with the same pride and reputation, as envisioned by Jagjivan Ram, in the hot summer of 1953.

CONCLUSION

Jagjivan Ram had a chequered, purposive, and remarkable career as a public man. He participated in the freedom movement, became a member of the Bihar Legislative Assembly and then the Central Legislative Assembly and from 1946 onwards, till almost his death, he served as a member of the Government under every Prime Minister from Jawaharlal Nehru to Morarji Desai. During this time, he made varied and lasting contributions to the political life of the nation and its economic and social development the likes of which we rarely see and are not likely to see easily in the future. He fought against caste prejudices all his life. He was keen for social solidarity and social progress and amity and for the removal of social inequity of every kind and complexion. He wanted, quite simply equality for all and harmony between everyone. Is it a wonder that his birth anniversary is observed throughout the country as Samta Diwas? Though profoundly concerned with the problems of the Scheduled Castes and other deprived sections in society, throughout his life, he transcended the narrow frontiers of caste, community, religion and region and rose to be a popular mass leader interested in the welfare, progress and future of all of his countrymen.

One particularly noticeable thing was the silent authority that he carried with him with ease while in office or out of it. Whether party workers, common people or officers, everyone will defer to him and try to gather around him and carryout his wishes as if he was one in office even when he had left the government under the Kamaraj Plan. It seemed quite natural that his equanimity, his habitual courtesy, his prodigious memory, and his capacity to explain in simple language the most difficult issue, would leave a mark on everyone around him. The brief or occasional opportunities that I have had to meet him would leave their mark on me.

NOTES

1. Sanjay Paswan and Paramanshi Jaideva, *Encyclopaedia of Dalits in India*, vol. 11, Kalpaz Publications, New Delhi, 2002, pp. 115-16.

2. 'Jagjivan Ramer Railpath', *Prabashi*, vol. 58, no. 1, September-October 1958, p. 1365.
3. Lok Sabha, Lok Sabha Debates, 8 March 1958, Lok Sabha Secretariat Press, p. 3879.
4. Ibid., p. 3895.
5. Ibid., p. 3879.
6. Ibid., p. 3897.
7. Ibid., p. 3898.
8. Ibid., p. 3899.
9. Ibid., pp. 3903-4.
10. Ibid., pp. 3901-2.
11. Ibid., p. 3902.
12. Shree Sudhir Brahma, 'Pasupatinather Deshe', *Bharatbarsha*, vol. 51, part 2, no. 4, March-April 1964, p. 543.
13. Lok Sabha, Lok Sabha Debates, 18 September 1953, Lok Sabha Secretariat Press, pp. 2170-1.
14. Ibid., p. 2172.
15. Ibid., pp. 2220-1.
16. Ibid., 10 September 1953, Lok Sabha Secretariat Press, p. 1827.
17. Ibid., 2 December 1954, Lok Sabha Secretariat Press, p. 841.
18. Ibid., p. 848.
19. Ibid., 8 May 1962, Lok Sabha Secretariat Press, pp. 3001-2.
20. Ibid., 14 March 1955, Lok Sabha Secretariat Press, p. 882.
21. Ibid., 20 April 1953, Lok Sabha Secretariat Press, pp. 4629-35.
22. Ibid., pp. 4635-6.
23. Ibid., 21 April 1953, Lok Sabha Secretariat Press, pp. 4787-8.
24. Ibid., p. 4788.
25. Ibid., 20 April 1953, p. 4655.
26. Ibid., 21 April 1953, pp. 4790-2.
27. Ibid., p. 4792.
28. Ibid., p. 4794.
29. Ibid., 6 May 1953, pp. 5888-92.
30. Ibid., p. 5890.
31. Ibid.
32. Ibid., pp. 5899-905.
33. Ibid., p. 5930.
34. Ibid., pp. 5932-4.
35. Ibid., p. 5943.
36. Ibid., pp. 5940-41.

37. Ibid., 8 May 1953, pp. 6097-8.
38. Ibid., p. 6098.
39. Ibid., pp. 6098-9.
40. Ibid., pp. 6099-100.
41. Ibid., pp. 6102-3.

5

The Ministry of Arbitration

Jagjivan Ram, the Labour Ministry, and the Liberal Reforms

Jagjivan Ram has often been called the 'messiah' of the labour class. We are attempting to comprehend the actual circumstances of the labour class and their issues under colonial authority before getting into details about him. The modern labour class in India first emerged in the nineteenth century. It was made feasible by the construction of contemporary industries, railroads, dockyards, tea, and coffee plantations, and other types of structures and roadways. The living and working circumstances for the labourers were exceedingly miserable at that time.

There was likely a 12- to 16-hour shift, poor pay scale, child labour, discrimination against women workers, unclean and subpar housing, severe levels of debt, and no insurance against accidents or illness. Consequently, the death rate among workers was unusually high. In 1881 and 1891, the British Government passed the Factory Acts, but these were executed only for women and children. Male adult labourers were exempt from the application of these acts. The machinery used to carry out various provisions of the Factory Act was less robust. The Factory Act of 1911 set the maximum working time for adult males at 12 hours daily, and it was further amended by the Act of 1922, which lowered the maximum working time to 11 hours per day. Although there had been a steady improvement in income growth and job security, workers were still unsatisfied, and the situation was not uniform across all industries and locations.

The social reformers emerged and expressed concern for the well-being of workers or labourers. The Brahmo social reformer approached the labourers to work with them. One of them, Sasipada Banerjee, founded the Workingmen's Club in 1870 to promote the advancement of the working class in the Bengal Province. Banerjee additionally released a journal called *Bharat Shramjeevi* to educate the working class. In Bombay, N.M. Lokhande published the Anglo-Marathi weekly newspaper *Deenbandhu* in 1880. Additionally, he founded the Bombay Millhands' Association in 1890. In addition, workers in Bombay founded the Kamgar Hitwardhak Sabha in 1909, and the Social Service League in 1911. To improve working conditions and maintain social programmes among them, they attempted to entice the British to discuss the working class in legislation. After 1885, the strategy of the freedom movement changed its direction though Congress did not take any favourable decision for the labour class. When the working class protested against such long hours, a nationalist paper, *Kalpataru,* wrote in September 1905, 'We have to build a nation and it matters not if all the mill hands are placed at the altar of martyrdom.'[1]

Gopal Ganesh Agarkar was a social reformer and educator who played a significant role in advocating for the upliftment of the lower castes and the promotion of education. While he may not be primarily known as a pro-labour reformer, his efforts in education and social reform were part of the broader movement for social justice. Bipin Chandra Pal was a prominent nationalist leader and one of the early leaders of the Indian freedom movement. He advocated for the rights of workers and peasants and was known for his fiery speeches and writings. He was part of the radical wing of the Indian National Congress and supported labour and social reforms as part of the struggle for India's Independence. Chittaranjan Das, also known as *deshbandhu*, was a lawyer, politician, and nationalist leader. He was a crucial figure in the Swadeshi Movement and advocated for the rights of workers and peasants. He played a significant role in his time's labour and political movements. G. Subramanian Iyer was a lawyer, journalist, and freedom fighter from south India. While he was not a well-known pro-labour reformer, his contributions to the freedom struggle and his work as a journalist helped raise awareness about various social issues, including labour rights. Regarding Dadabhai

Naoroji's statement in the second session of the Indian National Congress, he suggested that the Indian National Congress should primarily focus on issues that had a direct national impact, such as political and constitutional reforms related to India's self-governance under British rule. He proposed leaving social reforms and class-specific issues to be addressed by specialized organizations or class congresses. This viewpoint reflected the diversity of opinions within the Indian National Congress at the time, where leaders held differing perspectives on the scope and priorities of the Congress's activities.[2] John McLane argues that the Congress, in its initial phase, only concentrated on those demands for reform about which the vast majority of Indian nationalists could agree. The Congress also enjoyed bourgeois support, and thus, it could not adopt a pro-working-class position in its early years.[3]

Before 1905, the nationalist leadership focused heavily on legislative actions taken by the British Government to improve labourers' working conditions. After the First World War, the world situation radically changed particularly for workers. The mass nationalists came forward and attended the nationalist movement and raised their voices against economic distress. The Russian Revolution and the formation of the International Labour Organization (ILO) did have an impact on the labour movement and political landscape in various parts of the world, including India. The Russian Revolution of 1917, which led to the Bolshevik seizure of power, did inspire left-leaning movements and individuals in India also. The revolution was seen as a symbol of workers rising against oppression and seeking social and economic justice. The ILO was indeed established in 1919, as a specialized agency of the League of Nations (later the United Nations). Its purpose was to promote labour rights, improve working conditions, and address various labour-related issues on an international scale. While the ILO's formation was significant for international labour standards, it wasn't directly related to the Indian labour movement. Gandhi, returned to India in 1915. However, he wasn't initially associated with the INC or the labour movement upon his return. He became actively involved with the INC, and the broader freedom movement over the subsequent years.

The Indian labour movement was gaining momentum even before

Gandhi's return, partly due to socio-economic factors and the influence of the global labour movements. Workers in various industries began to organize and demand better working conditions, fair wages, and other labour rights. The formation of the All-India Trade Union Congress (AITUC) in 1920 was a significant step in unifying various labour organizations in India and advocating for the rights of workers. Gandhi's influence on the labour movement came later, as he recognized the importance of labour rights in the broader struggle for Indian independence. In the meantime, Congress played a vital role in uniting the various organizations and all individuals in favour of the national movement. The middle-class leadership was also interested in the matter of workers. So, the overall national movement deeply influenced the labour class. Rajnarayan Chandravarkar argues that nationalism provided the Indian working class with a new identity.[4]

Dipesh Chakraborty argues that Bhadralok trade union leaders maintained a distance from the workers. From a Hegelian perspective, Chakrabarty argues that the workers accepted the superiority of their masters at their own will. This is because, depending on the circumstances, they realized that sometimes choosing to serve would be the finest way for them to 'exercise their power'.[5]

This position came to be challenged by Manju Chattopadhyaya, Deepika Basu and others. Nirban Basu talks about the communist leaders, Deepika Basu deals with the trade unionists who readily mingled with the workers.

Jagjivan Ram too championed the cause of the labourers. In the traditional Marxist writings, the Gandhian movement has often been criticized as counter-revolutionary and Gandhi's *satyagraha* was termed as a tool to prevent the revolutionary aspirations of the workers. From Marxist leaders like Shapurji Saklatvala[6] to Marxist historians like Rajni Palme Dutt,[7] and Suniti Kumar Ghosh[8]—all of them have argued on the same line. However, Rakhahari Chatterji shows that while Gandhi was cynical regarding the violent revolutionary programme of the communist labour leaders, the labours of India appropriated the Gandhian cult to raise their voices. Thus, in the Second Annual Session of the AITUC, held at Jharia, the *pandal* was wrapped in *khadi* clothes.[9] Workers took part in their agitation to bring about Gandhi's *swaraj*.

Gandhi's realization of the oppressive nature of the colonial government was triggered by the Jallianwala Bagh massacre, which led him to launch the Non-Cooperation Movement—the first mass movement in the Indian freedom struggle. Alongside this movement, the Khilafat Movement was also initiated, which marked a romantic phase of Hindu-Muslim relations. At a time when both communities were discontented, Gandhi found a way out. His solution was to advocate for non-cooperation with the colonial rulers and support the Khilafat Movement. Though Jagjivan Ram was a high school student during this time, he was deeply impacted by these politics. Upon completing his ISC at Banaras University, he was influenced by Pandit Madan Mohan Malaviya. Principal Dhruba was another individual who had immensely influenced Jagjivan Ram. He had encouraged him to enrol in Banaras University in the hopes that one day he might be able to receive the Birla scholarship.[10] After that, in 1931, Jagjivan Ram earned his B.Sc. from Calcutta University. He always accorded priority to Calcutta because he began his political career in this place. Since Jagjivan Ram himself belonged to the Dalit community, he was well aware of the centuries-long caste-based atrocities. He was able to realize that under the colonial rule, the working class had been suffering from severe socio-economic oppression. We are all well aware that India is primarily an agriculture-based country. However, Jagjivan Ram understood that land would not be able to attain prosperity had it not respected the labourers. He believed that organizing the landless labourers would help them to improve their situation. '90 per cent of our population', according to Jagjivan Ram, 'were agricultural labourers, rather than agricultural serfs.'[11] To provide evidence of such slavery, he gave examples of the *halwahas*[12] of the rural areas. These *halwahas* pointed out that Jagjivan Ram was made to serve a *Kisan* on a meagre subsistence allowance and mortgage themselves to the *Kisan* in exchange for a few rupees. These individuals often come from the lower socio-economic classes and rely on agricultural work for their livelihoods. The *halwahas* received two and a half seers of coarse grains during the sowing season as compensation for their labour. This form of payment in kind was common in agrarian economies, where labourers might receive a portion of the crops they helped cultivate instead of cash wages. The mention of a high demand for labour during the sowing season suggests that there were specific periods in the agricultural calendar when additional labour was required. This could be due to the need to plant crops quickly or tend to other time-sensitive agricultural tasks. The description emphasizes the physically demanding nature of the work, often carried out under adverse weather conditions such as sweltering heat or heavy rain. This underscores the difficult and often harsh working conditions that farm labourers faced. The statement suggests that these farmworkers were not free to relocate to other villages for higher wages. This lack of mobility could be due to various factors, including social and economic constraints, lack of access to information, or a dependence on the local agricultural economy.[13]

Jagjivan Ram knew the socio-political realities of the Dalits. In his presidential address to the Second Session of the 1937 Bihar Provincial Depressed Classes Conference at Gopalganj, Jagjivan Ram prescribed organizing the agricultural labourers to carry on a constant agitation to ameliorate their plight. During his tour of the villages, he noticed seething discontent in the heart of the labourers. Jagjivan Ram raised the slogan, 'Land to the actual tiller of the soil.'[14] Additionally, he stated that there were limitations on Scheduled Castes purchasing agricultural land in rural sections of the nation. The most astounding aspect of this restriction was that such castes which played a crucial role in several agricultural operations were considered non-agriculturalists. After the Constitution went into effect, these restrictions were lifted; however, it has since come to light that even arable wastelands were not accessible to them. As a corollary, they were forced to earn their livings as agricultural labourers.[15] In 1937, Jagjivan Ram founded Khetihar Mazdoor Sabha, a farm labourer's organization in Bihar. The main objective of forming this organization was to protest against evil practices like *begar* labour (working without payment for the upper-castes), low wages, and carnages. Khetihar Mazdoor Sabha demonstrated against these evil customs (coming from generation to generation for a long time) before the Bihar Assembly. The Haripura Congress session saw demonstrations from this group's members as well. This was unpopular with the Gujarati population. This was also opposed by Sardar Patel. He feared that this would have an impact on the Kisan Sabha, his organization for farmers.

This, he claimed, would create a rift between farmers and farm workers. There were indeed differences between the interests of farmers and the labourers who worked for them, but at that time, Sardar Patel's Kisan Sabha was fighting the powerful *zamindars* and sought to abolish the *zamindari* system.[16] The Khetihar Mazdoor Sabha wanted proper wages and freedom from atrocities.

Jagjivan Ram was the chief architect, who provided hopes and aspirations to all. In 1938, during the Haripura Congress session, Jagjivan Ram became one of the most prominent Congress leaders and came to the forefront. Jagjivan Ram, a prominent Indian politician, indeed held the position of Secretary of the Bihar Provincial Congress Committee in 1940 and he continued to hold this post till 1946. He was a key figure in the Indian National Congress (INC) and played a significant role in the independence movement and post-Independence Indian politics. His election as the Secretary of the Bihar Provincial Congress Committee in 1940 reflected his active involvement in the INC's organizational and political activities at the provincial level. During his tenure in this position, he would have been responsible for coordinating and organizing the Congress Party's activities in Bihar, which was an important state in the struggle for India's Independence.

Jagjivan Ram gradually prepared the ground to fight for the *Harijans*, the working class, etc. M.C. Saksena precisely points out that though the role of Jagjivan Ram as a political leader is well known, he played a pivotal role as a Trade Union Leader as well. Under his direction, the working-class population in Bihar began their epic struggle. When he was elected vice-president of the Bihar Trade Union Congress in 1940, he gained immense respect as a labour leader. He always had a strong belief in Gandhian philosophy. As a result, he inspired the lower classes to fulfil their legitimate demands in a dignified manner, 'peculiar to the Indian traditions'.[17] During the Quit India Movement, on Mahatma's advice, the labour force in Bihar was organized and mobilized by Jagjivan Ram to support the national liberation struggle. Workers in Bihar came together under his guidance and joined the Quit India Movement. Along with other prominent Congressmen who took part in this movement and were involved in trade unionism, he was imprisoned. Jagjivan Ram successfully brought about certain improvements in the working conditions of the agricultural labourers of Bihar by storming the shackles of the feudal structure down.[18]

Jagjivan Ram realized the need for reorganizing society by ushering in qualitative transformations in the rural economy. He emphasized the reorganization of agriculture and the 'rural economy'.[19] The distribution process is determined by the production method. A new and unique method of production must be used to achieve an 'equalization of economic power' in the villages.[20] The substantial and middle farmers, Jagjivan Ram lamented, used to assert their leadership over the village affairs, while the small farmers and the landless labourers continued to be excluded. Old zamindars continued to exert their influence. The traditional upper-castes were still in-charge of village life. The village's caste and class system were reflected in the governmental apparatus, which supported, if not served, the maintenance of the status quo. Hence, to bring about complete transformation, he argued that reliable organizations must be established at the village level, and new leadership must develop. [21] These organizations need to be made up of committed locals who care about progress. All individuals with empty bellies, open hearts, little or no land, and no means of production must be included in such an agency. In this way, the agency must practically grow out of the village's soil.

Jawaharlal Nehru was deeply moved by the priceless contributions Jagjivan Ram provided to the Bihar working class. When an interim government was established in September 1946, Jawaharlal Nehru invited Jagjivan Ram to assume charge of the Ministry of Labour's portfolio. He retained his position up to 1952, even after the independence. He considered the peasantry and the workers as 'the backbones of the nation'. Hence, he said, 'real Swaraj lies in installing then a worker in the field and factory to his rightful place in society. Let us work for that and build the India of our dream.'[22]

Jagjivan Ram developed his special methods of achieving his objectives and always used his position of influence for the good of the populace as a whole and the oppressed in particular. His sole focus was on serving his people or country. Jagjivan Ram was primarily 'a man of the masses', Brindaban Das opines.[23] Regardless of his portfolio, he always placed forth the needs of the working class, farmers, and the underprivileged as his priority. Because of his extensive knowledge and experience of people and affairs, he was able to perform his role with remarkable success and distinction.[24] Since becoming the labour minister, he had implemented numerous progressive and historical policies that had proven to be a turning point in the lives of the Indian working class. As a labour minister, he enacted several labour-friendly laws to uplift the living standard of poor workers and to provide them with socio-economic security. Hence, he was aptly called the 'messiah' of the working class.

As the Labour Minister, Jagjivan Ram proposed that after the attainment of Independence, Congress had to invest its energy to accomplish the 'next great task', i.e. setting up 'real democracy' in India by ensuring 'social justice and equality'.[25] He raised his voice further to argue that large-scale industries had to be organized in such a way that the workers would not only be the 'co-sharers' of the profits, but they were gradually included in the managerial sectors of the industry.[26] Jagjivan Ram's conviction found reverberation in the speech of Jawaharlal Nehru at the Nagpur convocation, in which Nehru emphasized the need to uplift the standard of living of the millions of poverty-ridden Indians by providing them not only the bare necessities of life, but also several other opportunities and equalities which every human being must possess.[27] Its worth noting that he and Gandhi had a relationship characterized by mutual respect and shared values, particularly in their commitment to social justice and the welfare of marginalized communities. Throughout his political career, he was known for his advocacy for the rights and welfare of oppressed and marginalized groups, including the Dalits and labourers. His familiarity with the suffering of the poor workers and oppressed masses of India, made him, a suitable candidate for leadership roles within the Indian National Congress and other political organizations. Gandhi's blessing and instruction to his to take good care of neglected workers aligned with Gandhi's own principles of social justice and his emphasiz on the well-being of the weakest and most vulnerable members of society. Gandhi often emphasized the importance of social and economic equality in the broader struggle for Indian Independence.

Addressing representatives of the Rashtriya Mill Mazdoor Sevak Sangh, he exclaimed,

> ...the philosophy of Mahatma Gandhi, not Communist or Socialism, would lead us to the goal of a classless society. A certain section of the people in India who styled themselves as *radicals* and *revolutionaries*, exploited the sentiments of labour for their party ends by mere shouting of slogans. The Government of India on the other hand, are silently working for the establishment of a classless society under the inspiration of Gandhiji—a philosophy which put the rich and the poor, the labour and the capitalist in the same category—all working for the common good. Our guiding principle in all our activities is love and persuasion and not violence, hatred or fear.[28]

Jagjivan Ram's contributions to the welfare and empowerment of various segments of Indian society, including the working class, are indeed notable. His active involvement in founding associations and unions for landless labourers, village artisans, and depressed classes demonstrates his commitment to addressing the socio-economic challenges faced by these groups. While it is common to call leaders, who, have made substantial contributions to workers' rights and social justice 'saviours' and 'liberators' of the working class, it's important to recognize that the struggle for worker rights and social justice in India was a collective effort involving many individuals and movements. His work was aligned with the broader goals of social and economic justice that were central to the Indian Independence movement. His advocacy for labour rights, especially for those in marginalized and oppressed communities, played a significant role in shaping policies and legislation aimed at improving the conditions of workers in India. He was very much conscious of the welfare of the working class. He said that even though India achieved political Independence on 15 August 1947, she had yet to achieve economic liberation. Thus, freedom in a true sense could only be achieved through the eradication of poverty and illiteracy.

Financial liberation also implied providing adequate housing, a healthy environment, and at least two meals a day for the millions of country labourers. This could only be conceivable should millowners and labourers act like brothers, respect the struggles of the latter, and monitor the concentration of capital in a small number of hands.[29]

Jagjivan Ram refused to disregard the workers, who were unable to present their concerns and requests to industrialists, the general public, or the government. While there was a struggle between the working class and the capitalist class, the government must step up to support them, and take an action to enhance their living standard and working conditions. He specifically mentioned that there were a lot of labourers working in the country's mines, plantations, and villages. Given their illiteracy, ignorance, and helplessness, their conditions were rather appalling.[30] Jagjivan Ram was logically considering how to resolve any issues including disagreements between employers and employees through negotiations and agreements.

On 13 April 1947, *The Bombay Chronicle* published a report, headlined 'Better Working Conditions for all Categories of Labour'. This report showcased that as a Labour member, Jagjivan Ram clearly explained the policy of the Central Government. He assured that he would be introducing a bill in the Central Assembly to ameliorate the conditions of the commercial workers. Factory Amendment Bill would also be introduced for the welfare of the labours.[31]

THE INDUSTRIAL DISPUTE ACT, 1947

The Tripartite Indian Labour Conference was presided over by Jagjivan Ram, who noted that a wave of industrial unrest had been sweeping through the nation. This was a widespread industrial unrest issue, not just a peculiarly Indian problem. He argued that the laboured cause was legitimate and had a history. He always favoured open discussion to resolve any employer and labour issues.

On 14 February 1947, *The Bombay Chronicle* published a report, named—'Joshi's Amendments Thrown Out: Central Assembly Discusses Industrial Disputes Bill'. The report shows that the Defence Secretary, G.S. Bhalja, introduced in the Central Assembly that day a bill to enable duties in connection with vital services to be imposed in any emergency on the armed forces of the Crown. During the war, according to the Statement of Objects and Reasons, Defence of India, Rule 81(3) empowered the Central Government to direct the employment of persons subject to the Indian Army Act or the Indian Air Force Act in any undertaking essential to the life of the community.

The Defence of India Rules had now expired. This Bill provides that in any emergency, the Central Government may by notification declare that any specified service is a service of vital importance to the community and that commands to members of the armed forces about employment in that service shall then be lawful. The Bill includes a clause to make valid commands of this nature given under the orders of the Government between the expiry of the DIR, and the passing of this Bill.[32] The House resumed discussions clause by clause of the Bill. The Provision was open for Investigation and Settlement of Industrial Disputes and agreed to an amendment moved by Vadilal Lallubhai regarding the personnel of the Industrial Tribunal. The relevant clause in the Bill provided that every member of the Tribunal 'shall be an independent person who is or has been a Judge of a High Court or who possesses qualifications required for appointment as a Judge of a High Court'.[33] Vadilal's amendment prescribed that every member of the Tribunal should be a Judge of the High Court, or a District Judge or was qualified for appointment as a Judge of a High Court and further provided that in the absence of a Judge or District Judge, appointment to a Tribunal should be made in consultation with the High Court of the Province in which the tribunal was intended to have our usual place of sitting. The House rejected N.M. Joshi's amendment to the same clause when wanted that every member of the Tribunal should be paid the salary of a Judge of a High Court. The House discussed at length and rejected another amendment moved by N.M. Joshi, which wanted that an industrial dispute might be referred to a Tribunal for Adjudication 'on the joint application of the parties to an Industrial Dispute'.[34] Joshi was supported by Maniben Kara and opposed by the Labour Member, Jagjivan Ram, the Labour Commissioner, S.C. Joshi, Diwan Chamanlal, S.S. Sanyal, Cowasji Jehangir and Pandit Balkrishna Sharma. Joshi moved another amendment seeking to delete Subclause 3 of Clause X which says,

> Where an Industrial Dispute has been referred to a Board or Tribunal under this Section, the appropriate Government may by order prohibit the continuance of any strike or lock-out in connection with such dispute which may be in existence on the date of the reference.[35]

Jagjivan Ram maintained that this Act aimed to establish cordial relations between the workers and the industrialists. Regarding N.M. Joshi's critique, he argued that he never claimed himself as a revolutionary, nor did he claim his bill to be a revolutionary one. Jagjivan Ram refuted Joshi, as the latter thought only from the perspective of organized factory labour. He made it clear that the factory workers solely did not represent all the labour classes of India.[36]

The Industrial Disputes Act of 1947 was decided to be implemented all over India from 1 April 1947. This Act called for two ways of settlement of industrial disputes. The establishment of Work Committees and Industrial Tribunals as mechanisms for resolving labour disputes, with a particular focus on the emphasiz on voluntary negotiation. Jagjivan Ram's influence by Mahatma Gandhi's idea of class cooperation and his belief in the effectiveness of voluntary negotiation in resolving disputes, is highlighted. These were proposed mechanisms to resolve labour disputes in India. Work Committees typically consisted of representatives from both employers and employees and their primary role was to facilitate voluntary negotiations to reach a settlement. Industrial Tribunals, on the other hand, served as adjudicatory bodies and could make binding decisions to resolve disputes. Jagjivan Ram was influenced by Gandhi's ideas of class cooperation. Gandhi's philosophy of non-violence and his emphasiz on resolving conflicts through peaceful means had a profound impact on many leaders of the Indian independence movement, including those involved in labour issues. Jagjivan Ram believed that voluntary negotiation should be the primary and standard mode of settling disputes between employers and employees. This approach aligns with Gandhi's principles of peaceful resolution and cooperation between different classes and groups within society.

It is mentioned that adjudication, which involves making decisions through a formal legal process, was intended to be optional. This means that while Work Committees would actively encourage negotiation, parties involved in a dispute could choose the adjudication process if they preferred it. The passage notes that there was little debate in the legislative body (the House) over the optional adjudication method. This suggests that the focus of the discussion and consensus was on the importance of voluntary negotiation as the preferred mode of dispute resolution. However, Jagjivan Ram thought that the House might not agree on forced adjudication as a conflict resolution strategy. He advised the government to become involved in labour issues. Since the parties to such disputes were no longer only the injured employees and the injured employer, and sincere grounds of conflicts, were, no longer just breaches of contracts, Ram refused to view these industrial disputes as things exclusively under the private law of contracts.[37] In truth, the trade dispute, according to Jagjivan Ram, was a re-enactment of the economic conflict between capital and labour, in which the general public suffered just as much as the employer and workers involved in the business. The common mass was an essential party to trade disputes, even though these disputes were 'ostensibly bipartite engagements between capital and labour'. This was especially true when they involved goods and services that were vital to the community's well-being. In more concrete terms, a strike in public utility service would result in a 'loss of services and supplies to the community in addition to production and profit losses for the employer, employment losses, and wage losses for the workers'. Thus, as the government was to ensure services and supplies relating to the safety, health and welfare of the population, it had no other choice but to intervene in industrial disputes. Thus, Ram thought that the government should intervene in industrial disputes using a veto to promote interest.[38]

Jagjivan Ram believed that resolving industrial disputes required a swift readjustment of employer-employee relations through mutual agreement or compulsory adjudication. Prohibiting strikes and lockouts did not provide a long-term solution. He argued that government intervention was necessary to regulate workplace relations when employers and workers could not resolve disputes on their own. The Rule 81A within the Defence of India Rules during wartime and how these principles were incorporated into a new bill. It also emphasizes the importance of balancing the rights of employers and workers with the need to safeguard public interests in resolving industrial disputes. Rule 81A, a provision within the Defence of India Rules, granted the government the authority to enforce awards made by adjudicators and effectively handle industrial disputes during the wartime period. This rule was used to settle disputes between employers and workers, and the outcomes were reportedly satisfactory to both parties. This suggests that the government sought to adapt and refine the wartime rules for peacetime use, allowing for more flexibility in resolving industrial disputes. Jagjivan Ram emphasized that neither employers nor workers should have unrestricted rights to wage trade disputes that could potentially harm public interests. This reflects a recognition of the need to strike a balance between the rights of labour and management and the broader interests of society. In cases where public interests were at risk, the government had a role to play. It was the government's responsibility to intervene and secure relations between employers and workers. This intervention might involve private negotiation and conciliation, but if necessary, it could also include compulsory adjudication, where a formal decision would be made to resolve the dispute.[39]

The main aim of the Industrial Disputes Act was to minimize industrial disputes. Jagjivan Ram firmly believed that employers and employees can develop the habit of collective bargaining and can be free from harassment from courts, tribunals, boards, and committees. The Industrial Disputes Act of 1947 was practically the first effective venture in the field of labour-management relations, particularly, compulsory arbitration.[40]

The Industrial Disputes Act was intended to regulate the relations between workers and employers and recognized the importance of associating workers in the administration of industry, especially in matters affecting their health and comfort. The Act provided for the setting up of the joint committee, either by agreement or under direction from the Government. Works Committees promoted measures for securing and preserving amity or good relations between employers and workers. Any members of the committee could propose changes in definite matters of industrial relations and the decisions of the joint committee on such a proposal had the binding force of an agreement entered into by both labour and employer. During Jagjivan Ram's period, the Industrial Disputes (Appellate Tribunal) Act of 1950, was passed and a provision for a central Appellate Authority was made.

INDIAN TRADE UNIONS (AMENDMENT)

Jagjivan Ram's policy was always the recognition of labour as a partner in the industry. He placed more emphasiz on promoting trade unions because he believed that trade unions could solve the labour problem. We have seen for the first time in history that plantation and agricultural labour had been brought under a union. Jagjivan Ram recognized that the exploitation of the worker by interested parties could only be checked by a genuine trade union.[41] I have already mentioned that the All-India Trade Union Congress was established in 1920 as a central organization of labour. Though it was organized with the object of securing representation at the ILO Conference in Geneva, there was no doubt, a historical necessity for it. The All-India Trade Union Congress indeed received numerous supports from all corners. So, the trade union movement received a great impetus. Jagjivan Ram understood the necessity of trade unions in favour of the worker.

The Indian Trade Union Act of 1926, according to Jagjivan Ram, had been utterly unsuccessful. On 29 October 1946, he presented the Indian Trade Union (Amendment) Bill to Parliament under these conditions. Jagjivan Ram argued,

> ... the Bill provides for such a statutory recognition by the appropriate Government which in the case of Unions in the central sphere will be the Central Government and the Provincial Governments concerned regarding trade unions in the provincial spheres. The principal object of the Bill is that a trade union fulfilling the conditions provided in Clause 28(d) will be entitled to recognition by the employer and one of the important conditions is that the Union should be a representative trade union. Another important condition is that the Unions seeking recognition must have been registered under the Trade Unions Act for at least twelve months before they applied for recognition. This salutary provision will prevent too many trade unions from being formed hastily and applying for recognition straightaway. Opinions have been expressed that a trade union seeking recognition must contain not less than a prescribed percentage of workers in the undertaking or industry. In a Central Act which should meet the requirements both of the Central and the Provincial Governments, when conditions may be different in different areas, some elasticity is most desirable.[42]

He also stated,

> … provision has been made in Clause 28(g) of the Bill by which among others, the industrial court set up for the purpose will have the power to withdraw recognition of a trade union if satisfied that it has ceased to be a representative trade union. This provision along with that of Clause 38(d) will give power to the appropriate Government to impose suitable conditions to ensure that a large number of rival trade unions do not spring up thereby damaging the cause of workers instead of furthering it. The statutory provision is made for the recognition of trade unions and for giving such recognized unions certain rights and privileges, it is equally essential that such unions should also realise certain fundamental obligations. Therefore, certain practices by the trade unions have been defined as unfair practices and any recognized trade union guilty of unfair practice will be liable to have its recognition withdrawn. The unfair practices will be for a majority of the members of the Union to take part in an irregular strike or for the executive of the Union to advise or actively support or instigate irregular strikes. It is not of course the intention to forbid the declaration of strikes regularly in conformity with rules made by the Union laying down the procedure for declaring a strike. Also, it will be an unfair practice if the officer of a recognized union submits any return containing false statements. It is realized that while some responsibility and obligations are put on the members and executives of recognized trade unions, some essential conditions should be imposed on the employers also regarding their dealing with such Union.[43]

While it was against the law for employees to call strikes, it was also illegal for employers to declare a lockout. The Trade Union Act Amendment made it such that, while on the one hand, there were fewer instances of employers violating their workers' rights, on the other hand, the employers fully understood their responsibility to maintain amicable workplace relations in the industrial world. In India, this might be referred to as a revolutionary change.

FACTORIES ACT, 1948

The Factories Act of 1948 had a significant impact on legislation as a whole. The Bill's goal is to incorporate some significant new elements while also consolidating the existing law governing working conditions in industries. According to Jagjivan Ram, this 'current law' only applied to industrial companies where the manufacturing process was carried out using power, if 20 or more people were employed. There was a proposal that all industrial facilities that employed ten or more workers where power was used and twenty or more workers in all other circumstances should be subject to the law relating to factories. The number of businesses subject to control would probably triple as a result of this adjustment. There would be an instant rise from 25 to 35 lakhs in the number of workers, who were to gain protection under the Factories Act. The period of industrial expansion had begun in the nation. He agreed that to the greatest extent possible, this industrial expansion should not consist of a small number of huge plants, but rather of numerous modest industrial facilities dispersed throughout the nation. Therefore, it was vital to extend the application of our factory-related law to smaller establishments. The definition has been broadened in light of this viewpoint.[44]

This bill received special attention from Jagjivan Ram, who stated that the current Act distinguished 'seasonal and perennial factories'. The enforcement of regulations relating to safety and health was frequently lax because seasonal factories only operated for a portion of the year. The situation was unsatisfactory. A factory should be subject to the same safety, health, and welfare regulations whether it is operated all year long or just part of it. As a result, he refused to no longer distinguish between factories that were permanent and those that were temporary.[45] There were more pro-worker provisions in this amendment. He emphasized the importance of regulating workplace conditions such as cleanliness, ventilation, lighting, availability of drinking water and sanitary facilities, and proper fencing of machineries, regardless of the size of the workforce. It is also crucial to establish working hours, and weekly rest days, prohibit child labour, and reduce working hours for adolescents. However, the challenge lies in implementing these measures effectively. Section 86 of the clause grants provincial governments the authority to enforce these regulations in any facility that carries out manufacturing processes with or without power, but not those that rely solely on family labour.[46] This act brought within its domain the establishment of 10 workmen where power was used and 20 workmen where power was not used.

MINIMUM WAGES ACT, 1948

Jagjivan Ram introduced the Minimum Wages Bill soon after India gained independence, which was a significant step towards improving the lives of both agricultural and industrial workers. According to him, the bill was revolutionary not only because it aimed to benefit a large number of agricultural labourers, but also because it envisioned a scenario where India could achieve self-sufficiency in producing food grains.[47] During his presentation, he mentioned that Ambedkar, his predecessor, had originally introduced the measure in the previous Legislative Assembly in 1946. The Bill was referred to a Select Committee that same year, but due to changes in the Legislative Assembly, it needed to be referred again in November of that year. The Select Committee had since reviewed the Bill and issued a report based on Jagjivan Ram's presentation on 28 January 1948. This type of law was crucial in India, particularly for jobs where employees were unable to unite and demand that their valid grievances be addressed by their employers.

He remarked,

> In those industries where a large number of workers are employed or where there are facilities and conveniences for trade union workers to organize the labourers in those concerns, it is not so desirable as in the case of those workers who are scattered mostly in the rural areas where the trade union workers do not find it convenient to go and organize them and do something tangible for them. The inevitable result of all this has been that the workers in a very large number of industries, mostly situated in rural areas or small towns, get wages which are not at all consistent with the labour that is put in the operation of their work, and these industries are popularly known as sweated industries. The Bill provides that something might be done to improve the lot of the work in these sweated industries. The Schedule in which certain industries have been enumerated is not exhaustive. I would say the Schedule is simply illustrative. But while including the various industries in the Schedule, we had to take into consideration the factor that many of the provincial governments will not be in a position to take many industries at the same time, more so when we are limiting the period for the provisions of this Act to be put into execution only to two years in respect of Schedule I and to three years in respect of Schedule 4. But there is a provision that the Provincial Government concerned, if they so choose, may include in the

schedule any number of industries which they may find they are in a position to take into their hands as early as possible. The provisions of this Bill are not so complicated and there have been definite improvements made in the Select Committee over the original Bill. The Provincial Governments will set up Advisory Committees which, after making investigations, will make recommendations to Provincial Governments for the fixation of minimum wages in the industries given in the Schedule. The Provincial Governments may, on their initiative, also fix the minimum wages. This piece of legislation is very necessary. Sir, this should have been on the statute book long before. I hope that the House will unanimously adopt this legislation.[48]

The Minimum Wages Act, which was promulgated in March 1948, was a crucial law that protected workers. Jagjivan Ram stood out from other characters in this instance and will always be remembered for his sympathy for the cause of the oppressed people. The appropriate state government was given the authority to determine, review, and modify the minimum rates of wages that must be paid to workers in particular industries as a result of this act, which also moulded statutory provisions. This was a remarkable action to assist the disorganized industrial labour class. Agricultural labour was also included in this act.

EMPLOYEES STATE INSURANCE ACT, 1948

The Dominion Parliament approved the Employees State Insurance Bill. This Bill is designed to provide various benefits to workers, including those related to illness, pregnancy, or injury. These benefits are intended to offer a form of social security for workers. According to Jagjivan Ram, a prominent leader in the context of Indian labour rights and social justice, this bill is considered a milestone in the history of labour law in India. It signified the beginning of social security policies in the country, marking an important step towards ensuring the well-being of workers. While the Bill's initial scope may have been limited, Jagjivan Ram expressed the belief that the benefits provided could be expanded to cover a broader section of the working class in India. This suggests that the bill laid the foundation for future social security policies that could benefit a larger segment of the workforce. Jagjivan Ram also announced a commitment from various entities, including the corporation, Provincial Governments, and the Central Government, to seize the opportunity to expand the applicability of the bill as soon as possible. This indicates a willingness to work towards extending social security protections to more workers.[49]

During a Parliamentary session, Naziruddin Ahmed proposed an amendment to extend benefits to families and illegitimate children of employees. He emphasized that the House should focus on the benefits rather than mixing in questions of morality or ethics. Ahmed argued that if an employee was already providing for illegitimate children, then the Bill should extend help to those children as well. Thakurdas Bhargava, Ramnarain Singh, T.A. Ramalingam Chettiar, and Hoosam Imam supported the amendment. However, Jagjivan Ram opposed it, stating that workers often leave their legitimate families behind in their villages when they work in industrial areas. These workers may have illegitimate children from relationships they form in industrial areas, and accepting the amendment could lead to the disintegration of the workers' legitimate families. K. Santanam also opposed the amendment, and it was ultimately defeated. However, the House did agree to broaden the definition of 'family' for medical benefit purposes to include dependent parents of male workers. This amendment was moved by Ananthasayanam Ayyangar and accepted. During the third reading, members from all parts of the House congratulated the Labour Minister for his efforts in passing the beneficial bill for workers.[50]

During a discussion on social insurance schemes, Ananthasayanam Ayyangar, the first speaker, suggested that the Labour Minister should consider implementing compulsory State Insurance for all government employees, particularly those earning below Rs. 400 per month. The insured person could make full or partial contributions. Ayyangar also recommended that such a scheme should be extended to all other employees, not just those in government service. Meanwhile, Bishwanath Das congratulated Jagjivan Ram on the proposed measure, but pointed out that it would only benefit a small percentage of the population, specifically three million industrial labourers. Das reminded the House that over 150 million agricultural workers in the country's five lakh villages needed basic medical aid. B. Shiva Rao agreed with Mia Ray's suggestion that the Bill's passing would be meaningless if the provincial government did not take steps to implement its provisions. Rao cited how the Workmen's Compensation Act in Madras remained inactive for a long time until the trade union leaders translated the provisions into simple language and distributed them among workers, who then became aware of their rights. Prof. Ranga mentioned the issue regarding the implementation of these housing schemes. He seems to be challenging or addressing the positions held by individuals named Ray and Shiva Rao. He claimed that the provincial governments (referring to state governments within India) are not indifferent to the implementation of such housing schemes. Along with the change in the centre, the house forgot that the provincial governments had also changed. He remembered how provinces like Madras, Bengal, and Bombay had previously taken up the cause of labour upliftment zealously, even during the days of the former Congress Ministry. He believed that provincial governments were just as progressive as the Central Government. In fact, there were as many people interested in labour in the provincial legislatures as there were in the central legislature. He urged the house to trust provincial governments and legislatures to effectively and satisfactorily implement the provisions of the Bill. Renuka Ray acknowledged the changes in the provincial sphere but emphasized the lack of uniformity in implementing various schemes. She hoped that all provinces would implement the Bill uniformly without delay. K. Bhatt believed that labour was a rising force in the country and that the government needed to lay down careful labour policies. Many new parties were trying to exploit labour to gain power, and Congress governments needed to publicize measures like this Bill to benefit the people. Baba Ramnarain Singh stressed the importance of propaganda and approaching Indian villagers to support the National Government and its work for their benefit. Labour was the only wealth-producing section of the Indian population, and its needs and requirements should be given the highest priority. Kuladhan Chaltha believed that this bill would bring relief to nearly sixteen lakhs of workers in the country. R.K. Sidhwa disagreed with Harihar Nath Shastri, stating that special hospitals for labourers were essential because they would not receive proper treatment in general hospitals and not because they would sharpen class distinctions.[51]

Krishnamurti Rao stated that the Government holds a significant responsibility towards the States and must utilize its influence to implement similar social insurance benefits for labourers across different states. In response to the discussion, Jagjivan Ram explained that the constitutional position mandates dependence on Provincial Governments for the implementation of measures passed by the House. However, the Central Government ensures uniformity in the provinces and encourages honest efforts from Provincial Governments to implement measures according to their resources and capacity. The majority of Provincial Governments welcome these measures and promise to implement them as best as they can. Over the period of time, Provincial Governments have shown an increasing interest in labour welfare and legislation, and there is no reason to mistrust them.[52]

The Labour Minister expressed concerns about propaganda among India's mostly uneducated and unsophisticated workers. He believed that interested parties deliberately kept workers unaware of useful government measures so that they could exploit them for political purposes. The responsibility to educate workers fell on members of the House and other public workers. Jagjivan Ram had done the most for workers in the coalfields, but strikes were not caused by poor working conditions, but rather by political parties vying for control over the workers. The Minister opposed the establishment of exclusive hospitals for workers, but promised better facilities. The government was committed to providing suitable employment opportunities for all able-bodied individuals, but this would depend on the country's development. The Minister was confident that the States would not lag behind in implementing labour legislation.[53] It has been passed into a law.

EMPLOYEES PROVIDENT FUND ACT, 1952

In 1948, Jagjivan Ram proposed a Bill for Coal Mines workers' Provident Fund and Bonus, recognizing the need for social and economic security for the working-class. Despite ongoing debates, he was determined to ensure that passing the Bill would benefit workers. As labour minister, he continued to prioritize the social and economic security of working-class people and enacted the Employees Provident

Fund Act of 1952. This act established a compulsory and equal contribution scheme for both employers and employees, with funds invested in Central Government securities and earnings credited to the Fund. After retirement or in the event of premature death, the total amount was payable to the employee's heir or nominee, ensuring financial security for labourers in their old age.

Jagjivan Ram, a prominent Indian political leader, indeed played a significant role in initiating social security measures for the labour class in India. He was instrumental in the establishment of Welfare Funds for Coal Mines and Mica workers under the Coal Mines Labour Welfare Fund and Mica Mine Labour Welfare Fund Act of 1946. These funds aimed to provide various benefits, including medical, recreational, educational, and housing facilities, to workers in the coal mines and mica mines. In 1948, the Coal Mines Provident Fund Act and the Coal Mines Bonus Scheme Act were passed. These legislations were introduced to ensure the welfare and financial security of coal mine workers. The Coal Mine Provident Fund Act likely established a provident fund scheme for these workers, which helps them save for retirement. The Bonus Scheme Act may have provided additional financial incentives or bonuses to coal mine workers. Jagjivan Ram was also involved in the passage of the Dock Workers (Regulation of Employment) Act of 1948. This legislation focused on various aspects of labour welfare in the dockworker sector, including recruitment, training, health and safety measures, and provisions for paying a minimum wage during periods when labourers were unable to find employment or were only partly employed. It aimed to provide job security and improved working conditions for dock workers. His efforts contributed to the establishment of social security and welfare systems that aimed to provide essential benefits and protections to workers in these industries.

One of his greatest accomplishments was getting the plantation industry bill passed for the first time in India. Jagjivan Ram considered enforcing regulations on plantation labourers' working conditions. He stated,

> A fundamental change has taken place in our conception of the role of labour in industry. After the First World War, it was recognized that labour was not to be regarded as a commodity of commerce and that it was entitled to

humane conditions of employment. We have now advanced a little further. Labour is not only entitled to fair terms and conditions of employment but also becomes a partner in the industry in which he works. As partner labour is entitled to the benefits accruing from the partnership, but it must also learn to realize its responsibilities.[54]

This conception, the Labour Minister continued, was emphasized in the industrial truce resolution was adopted December last by the industries Conference which included representatives of Governments, Central, Provincial and States' employers and workers. He noted,

... the Tripartite Committee would have to assume new factories as a result of the industrial truce resolution. It will be the central machinery for the study and determination of fair wages and conditions of labour and fair remuneration for capital. In addition, it will have to devise ways and means for the association of labour in all matters concerning industrial production. I realize that plantation labour is less sophisticated than other industrial labour but it is neither possible nor permissible on that account to withhold the right to the partnership which is the keystone of future industrial policy. I hope that in this matter Government will have the fullest cooperation of the planters throughout India. For the proper implementation of the industrial truce resolution, we feel that it would be desirable to set up a smaller committee which will meet at more frequent intervals.[55]

About the wage issue, the Labour Minister stated,

... the committee set up to go into this matter would be able to arrive at an agreement which would do justice to the worker and credit to the industry. Jagjivan Ram also said that on the question of the medical care and treatment of plantation workers the industry agreed that Government might prescribe reasonable standards for plantations. Speaking on the proposals before the Committee in respect of legislation the Labour Minister maintained that although most employers might be ready to observe such standards as might be generally accepted as fair and reasonable, they had always to reckon with the few black sheep who gave a bad name to the industry. They must, therefore, be armed with legislative power to enable them to assume control where it was necessary.[56]

Jagjivan Ram expressed the expectation that the tripartite machinery for the plantations would become permanent and would assume its new and essential role by saying,

As time marches, we can see more clearly the almost revolutionary changes in the wake of the Second World War, which are silently but surely overtaking us. The old order is giving way to the new, requiring all round readjustment and reorientation. The changes may be liked or disliked but they are inevitable. It would be folly to resist all changes and to hope for the continuance of the old social and economic order. Wisdom demands that inevitable changes should be so directed as to bring about the greatest happiness for the greatest number. The common man is gradually coming into his own and it is our duty to help him in every possible way. He will need guidance and help.[57]

JAGJIVAN RAM AND INTERNATIONAL LABOUR ORGANIZATION (ILO)

The Indian delegation to the Conference of the International Labour Organization (ILO) was led by Jagjivan Ram. He had the honour and privilege of serving as the first Asian Chairman of the ILO conference, which was held in Geneva in 1950. Jagjivan Ram prioritized and pleaded for social justice and peace throughout the entire world.

In his Presidential address, Jagjivan Ram said,

... you know these well although it will not be out of place for me to say that certain decisions taken here, may perhaps not be of much significance in this part of the world but they are definitely important for the less-developed countries, for example, the issue of agricultural-labour, professional and technical training. However, you have also taken such decisions here which are of importance to the developed countries too from the industrial perspective as regards equal wages and unemployment, Today, the world is standing at crossroads. In future, human welfare will be determined on the basis whether we want to adopt the path of cooperation or conflict. If the team has the spirit of cooperation, then I have not the slightest doubt that man is capable of finding the solution to any problem. As my friend, Narwai observed, today, the issue is that we have to advance in a normal way, towards social peace. Ordinary peace, without social peace, cannot be termed as peace at all. ILO is trying to establish social peace and social justice in the world. However, to me, this appears to be quite strange and improbable because while making attempts to achieve social peace and realize the social dimensions of justice, we find ourselves in situations of conflict and resistance. The reason for this is that social justice and social peace, then it is essential that the privileges in the prevalent social order be reduced or done away with. In this, we may face opposition still, we shall have to create such circumstances in ILO and outside it, for social justice to become possible so that we can be successful in establishing social peace and the ultimate peace. Once more, I would like to repeat the belief that the feeling of cooperation and teamwork which have prevailed in this Assembly, not being restricted to the walls of this auditorium, may touch upon the international and national tasks, eliminate conflicts and promote peace.[58]

Jawaharlal Nehru led him to interest himself in the work of the International Labour Organization and said that 'the essential basis of world peace' should be social security, liberty and justice for all in every country. Through this address, Nehru gave an assurance to the world that India would religiously pursue the ideals propounded by the ILO 'for the emancipation of the worker'.[59] Jagjivan Ram also assured the world that there would be no change in the Government of India's labour policy following the ILO Conference. India had made 'substantial contributions to the ILO Conference'.[60]

Jagjivan Ram was a strong advocate for maintaining harmonious relations between employers and employees in accordance with international standards. He recognized that both production and labour welfare were crucial for the advancement of the country. He believed that in order to improve the overall quality of life for labourers, employers should strive to enhance the quality of production and expand industrial units. In 1966, International Labour Organization held in India at Mysore city. He addressed the session and said,

I am happy to learn that now ILO is focusing its attention seriously on Asia and its problems. Regional activities are quite necessary but the local needs should not be overlooked. However, regional activities should be covered under international jurisdiction because all should cooperate in the eradication of poverty and not just those who are badly affected. ILO shall have to show the world that it is desirous and capable of making the necessary contributions to solving problems. More than half of the world's population lives in Asia—most are poor. I have read, with interest, the plans and proposals prepared by ILO and its special agencies for economic reforms in less-developed countries. These plans should not remain only on paper. Work should begin on these and effectively so, Asia is looking and waiting. At the Asian Regional Conference in New Delhi, our Prime Minister expressed dissatisfaction, observing that Asia was not represented in it as was its due. In particular, we had discovered then that Indonesia was not represented. It is a matter of satisfaction for us that now Indonesia is a free country. Therefore, it is in a position to become a member of this organization and can play its role in promoting social justice. We will look forward to the presence of Indonesia's representative in the future meeting of the ILO. India's geographical location brings us in close contact with other Asian countries. We cannot live in isolation. Therefore, we have to keep in constant touch with our neighbouring countries. In particular, we are keen to maintain close ties with the people of China since they have been our friends and well-wisher, for centuries. I am sorry that in this session, no representative of such a large nation as China, is present. I am also disturbed by the absence of the Labour Ministers of Pakistan and Sri Lanka, who were unable to come, due to some important tasks in their own countries. I greet my friend, the Labour Minister of Burma (Myanmar), on my own and the people of India's behalf. I hope that this session of ILO shall bring the people of Asia closer and that Asia would also get close to the ILO so that peace and goodwill prevail all over the world.[61]

SPEECH OF JAGJIVAN RAM ON THE SUBJECT OF LABOUR

Jagjivan Ram attended the conference of the Assam Chamber of Commerce at Shillong, Assam on 16 October 1948 and said, that if prices and profits were to be stabilized, wages must also be stabilized. Jagjivan Ram added that under such a stabilization, wages for different industries would vary and the Labour Advisory Board would examine individual industries and fix the minimum wages. Due to the rise in the cost of living a corresponding increase in the dearness allowances had been granted to all salaried persons. To bring down the prices of articles the government were now introducing control measures, and the Minister felt that a condition might soon be created in which salaried persons might not feel the necessity of demanding an increase in dearness allowances.[62] He addressed the students at Lucknow University on 20 November 1948 and appealed to them, about the difficulties of the Congress Government and asked them to rationalize their thoughts and not to be led away by sentiments or slogans while criticizing the Administration. The Minister said that after the attainment of Independence, the responsibilities of the people had increased. Now the entire responsibility of improving the present conditions should not be placed on the government. The people should also share responsibility for it and should help the Government to tide over the present crisis. He thought that university education in India had not brought about a realistic approach to contemporary problems. He termed the labour issue as 'the most intricate problem not only in India but all over the world'. Thus, he offered the remedy by saying,

> The solution to the problem cannot be brought about by dealing with it on the surface. We have to go deeper and bring about principles and determine the same and fundamental change in our thinking. The Government cannot be progressive unless the people are progressive and for this, the intelligentsia should strive to bring about a progressive outlook among the people on the basis of detailed knowledge of our present conditions.[63]

Jagjivan Ram attended the Central Labour Advisory Council meeting on 22 November 1948 in Lucknow. Mr Khan, Dubhal K. Desai of the INTUC suggested that to meet the situation arising from the rise in food grain prices, the cereals were to be rationed and might be subsidized so that all could get cereals at cheaper prices. While he was unable to make any commitments on the topic, the Labour Minister said that he was interested in hearing how the employers' and workers' representatives felt about the idea. The report of the Committee on profit-sharing, which was submitted, was now being discussed again. However, there was no chance of a quick resolution of the differences between the companies' and workers' representatives' points of view. The chairman, Jagjivan Ram, advised that each group meet first separately, and then jointly for a consultation in order for the council to quickly come to a consensus on the fundamentals. The group overwhelmingly endorsed his proposal. Despite not being able to reach a firm decision about this complex issue of profit sharing, Jagjivan Ram declared, as the meeting come to a close, that they had made progress via their open and honest discussions.[64]

Jagjivan Ram in his speech delivered at the annual convocation of the Shastra Vidyalaya of the Kashi Vidyapith, Banaras on 10 February 1950, said,

> The working class in India has been chafing under the enormities of an unjust

social and economic order; exploitation of the poor and the weak have gone on unhindered for centuries. Fortunately, the old order is changing, yielding place to new. Today, we find a new awakening among the hitherto exploited, neglected and oppressed classes of India, who have so long suffered in silence. Mild tremors of discontent have begun to be felt. If not treated betimes, this volcano may erupt any moment and cause widespread dislocation and misery. An upsurge appears inevitable, being the result of the interplay of socio-economic factors. While the inevitable must happen, the undesirable features of this process of reorientation may yet be avoided by foresight and timely adjustment on the part of the privileged classes, who, unfortunately, instead of trying to reconcile themselves to the changes, seem to be preparing to fight with the windmill. There is going to be a radical transformation in India and a revolutionary change in the outlook towards the common man. He finds his Charter of Rights enshrined in the new Constitution of India.[65]

With the influence of industrialism and the rise of the working class with collective bargaining power, the subject of equating individual liberty with equality had come to the fore, argued Jagjivan Ram, in his speech at the Doaba College Convocation in Jullundur City on 25 March 1951. In order to maximize social welfare, the state must function as an institution. Since the idea of the police state, which operated until recently, could not plainly be converted to a welfare state all at once, this could only be done gradually. Evolution must be brought about with the least amount of resistance possible.[66]

In his speech at the political conference in Calcutta, Jagjivan Ram stated that the establishment of sound trade unionism on non-partisan lines was the screaming need of the hour. The beginning of the actual labour movement's demise occurred when various political ideologies intruded on trade unionism. Unfortunately, in India, unimportant issues seemed to take precedence over economic and social ones, which led to inter-union rivalry and weakened labour's ability to bargain collectively. Workers should prevent themselves from following the advice of persons who implemented 'exotic ideas' that were inappropriate for our economy and inflicted severe harm to the interests of the country.[67] He further added that there was a regrettable propensity for employers to hair-split the legislative requirements in an effort to circumvent them. One of the goals of labour law could only be achieved if employees exercised considerable restraint in expressing fair requests and refrained from initiating sudden strikes during all seasons, and if employers treated their employees with respect and adhered strictly to all legislative requirements. It was the national economy that suffered as a result of such tense labour relations. At a moment of such a contemporary crisis, it would be disloyal to take any action that might undermine economic stability rather than promote it. Employers and employees owe it to themselves and to the nation to take all feasible steps to encourage productivity. Both employers and employees were the essential components for the greater production of products and services in the contemporary economic system. They both required rewards. They should split the rewards of their labour and business venture equally. Additionally, both parties should bear the burden of making a sacrifice for the good of the country. Congress could also have a significant impact here. Congressmen should take a greater interest in the organization of labour and help them down the proper path in order to establish societal conditions that would put an end to all forms of exploitation.[68]

Jagjivan Ram consistently sided with labour, and he frequently asserted that no industry had a right to exist if it couldn't afford to give its employees a living wage. The government might finance that enterprise if it was necessary for the good of the community, but it had no right to exist by exploiting the working classes. He gave a thorough explanation of the five-year plan put forth by the Indian government to enhance working conditions for all worker categories.[69]

In addition to being aware of courts, tribunals, boards, and committees, Jagjivan Ram attempted to instill the practice of collective bargaining among employers and employees. He attended the 24th Session of the Tripartite Indian Labour Conference held in New Delhi on 29-30 July 1966. He presided over the Conference and said that the Indian economy had been put under severe restraints, prices had shown an upward trend and to solve this economic malice, one of the steps taken by the Government was the devaluation of the rupee. It was to be followed by the strictest discipline around, not only in the Indian economy but also in her national life, so that the full benefit of the devaluation could be utilized.[70]

On 18 January 1967, Babuji opened the Conference on National Movement on labour session in Bombay by stating,

> To me, this is a day of personal gratification. I have the privilege as free India's first Labour Minister and had a hand in formulating a Five-Year Plan for labour even before the Planning Commission came into existence. It is that Plan which laid the foundation and basic structure of the Government's labour policy. As I see in retrospect the passage of series of legislation in implementation of the Plan, has undeniably helped labour in bettering its lot and in wresting many concessions but has not, as was apprehended in certain influential quarters then, brought about a collapse of industry.[71]

In the 73rd Plenary Session of the Indian National Congress in Bombay in 1969, Jagjivan Ram said in his Presidential address,

> The industrial relations policy not only of the public sector enterprises, but also by private enterprises will need to be reviewed. In a society building socialism, there should be little scope for labour-capital clashes, for strides and slow-downs or lock-outs. The class feeling of employers and employees will have to be eliminated so that all those engaged in any undertaking regard themselves as workers in a common effort to enrich and serve the country. Workers' participation in the management is one way of imbibing this feeling and should be introduced in all undertakings.[72]

He said that India had to contend against many odds, both internally and externally. He cautioned the Indians that their very existence was endangered and their freedom was at stake. For sheer self-preservation, the countrymen had to wage a relentless war on the home front on which each farm and factory constituted a vital sector. Thus, each worker, irrespective of his field of operation, assumed huge importance for his sweat and toll, depending on the outcome of the national endeavour, the struggle for the country's economic freedom. Thus, each worker assumed the role of a soldier who held the key to the country's destiny. Hard and honest work and even more work became the call of India. He who thought or grumbled or otherwise obstructed the programme of essential economic development is a capitalist, labourer, or public servant was by common consent a traitor to the country whether he realized it or not.[73]

Jagjivan Ram's legacy as a champion for labour welfare and social justice is well-recognized. His tenure as the Labour Minister of India was marked by a strong commitment to improving the lives and working conditions of labourers. He consistently prioritized the welfare of the working-class during his tenure as Labour Minister. He was dedicated to addressing the difficult and often harsher conditions that labourers faced in various industries. Recognizing the need for comprehensive reforms, Jagjivan Ram appointed a National Commission on Labour. This commission's purpose was to review the existing labour laws and conditions and suggest improvements to enhance labour welfare. This initiative demonstrated his commitment to fairness and justice in labour relations. Jagjivan Ram firmly believed that a motivated and fairly treated labour force was essential for increasing industrial production. He understood that unless labourers received their fair share and were motivated to give their best, efforts to boost industrial output would be futile. His approach was not only about social justice, but also about economic productivity. His pioneering work in the field of labour welfare laid a strong foundation for subsequent labour legislation in India. Many of the reforms and principles he advocated for have had a lasting impact on labour rights and welfare in the country. Jagjivan Ram's efforts not only resulted in legislative changes but also created awareness among labourers about their rights and the importance of collective action to improve their conditions. He empowered the labour class to stand up for their rights and demand better treatment. The passage underscores the gratitude of the labour class for his bold and courageous stand on their behalf. He is remembered as a leader who fought tirelessly for their cause and made significant strides in advancing labour welfare and rights in India. His contributions as the Labour Minister and his dedication to the welfare of the working-class left a lasting legacy in India's labour history. His work paved the way for improved labour conditions and social justice for workers in the country.

NOTES

1. S.B. Upadhyay, *Historiography in the Modern World: Western and Indian Perspectives*, Oxford University Press, New Delhi, 2004, p. 149.
2. Bipan Chandra et al., *India's Struggle for Independence 1857-1947*, Penguin Books, New Delhi, 2016, p. 211.
3. John R. McLane, *Indian Nationalism and the Early Congress*, Princeton University Press, New Jersey, 1977.

4. Rajnarayan Chandavarkar, *The Origins of Industrial Capitalism in India: Business Strategies and the Working Classes in Bombay, 1900-1940*, Cambridge University Press, Cambridge, 1994.
5. Dipesh Chakrabarty, *Rethinking Working-Class History: Bengal 1890 to 1940,* Princeton University Press, Princeton, 1989.
6. Shapurji Saklatvala, 'Who is this Gandhi?', *Labour Monthly*, vol. 12, no. 7, July 1930.
7. R. Palme Dutt, *India Today*, Victor Gollancz Ltd., London, 1940.
8. Suniti Kumar Ghosh, *The Indian Big Bourgeoisie: Its Genesis, Growth and Character*, Subarnarekha, Calcutta, 1985.
9. Rakhahari Chatterji, 'Class Conflict and Nation Building: Gandhi and the Indian Labour Movement', *The Indian Journal of Political Science*, vol. 37, no. 4, 1976, pp. 42-57.
10. Dr. Sanjay Paswan and Dr. Pramanshi Jaideva, *Encyclopaedia of Dalits in India*, vol. 11, Kalpaz Publications: Delhi 2002, p. 81.
11. Ibid., p. 83.
12. A *halwaha* is a term used to refer to agricultural labourers or farmworkers, particularly those who engage in physically demanding work in the fields.
13. Ibid.
14. Ibid.
15. Ibid.
16. Indrani Jagjivan Ram, *Milestones: A Memoir*, Penguin Books India Pvt. Ltd., New Delhi, 2010, p. 66.
17. M.C. Saksena, *Struggle and Achievements*, Alka Publication, New Delhi, 1973, p. 305.
18. Ibid.
19. B.M.Turadagi, *Dr. Jagjivan Ram's life and Achievements: A Critical Analysis,* unpublished Ph.D. Thesis, Karnataka University, 2018, p. 87.
20. Ibid.
21. Ibid.
22. A.C. Sinha, K.L. Chanchreek, B.K. Tiwari and R.C. Shukla (eds.), *Struggle and Achivements: Babu Jagjivan Ram Commemoration Volume*, Alka Prakashan, New Delhi, 1973, p. 142.
23. S.R. Bakshi, *Jagjivan Ram: The Harijan Leader*, Anmol Publications, New Delhi, 1992, p. 171.
24. Ibid.
25. Jain, 'Babu Jagjivan Ram and Indian Labour', op. cit., p. 560.
26. Ibid.
27. Ibid., pp. 560-1.

28. *The Bombay Chronicle*, 10 January 1949.
29. Shachi Rani Gurtu, *Jagjivan Ram on Labour Problems*, Atma Ram & Sons, Delhi, 1951, p. 11.
30. Ibid., p. 12.
31. *The Bombay Chronicle*, 13 April 1947.
32. Ibid., p. 4.
33. Ibid.
34. Ibid.
35. Ibid.
36. Om Prakash Maurya, *Babu Jagjivan Ram*, Publication Division, Government of India, New Delhi, 2010, p. 110.
37. Ibid.
38. *Babu Jagjivan Ram in Parliament: A Commemorative Volume*, Lok Sabha Secretariat, New Delhi, 2010, p. 95.
39. Ibid.
40. Nau Nihal Singh, *Jagjivan Ram: Symbol of Social Change*, Sandeep Prakashan, New Delhi, 1977, p. 61.
41. Gurtu, op. cit., p. 9.
42. *Babu Jagjivan Ram in Parliament: A Commemorative Volume*, Lok Sabha Secretariate, New Delhi, 2010, p. 86.
43. Ibid., pp. 86-7.
44. The Constituent Assembly of India (Legislative) Debates, Official Report, vol. I, 1948, pp. 74-5.
45. Ibid.
46. Ibid, p. 75.
47. *Babu Jagjivan Ram in Parliament*, op. cit., p. 115.
48. The Constituent Assembly of India (Legislative) Debates, Official Report, vol. I, 1948, p. 339.
49. *The Bombay Chronicle*, 2 April 1948.
50. Ibid.
51. Ibid.
52. Ibid.
53. Ibid.
54. *Amrita Bazar Patrika*, Friday, 2 April 1948.
55. Ibid.
56. Ibid.
57. Ibid.
58. Gurtu, op. cit., pp. 98-100.
59. Ibid., p. 128.
60. *The Bombay Chronicle*, 17 July 1948.

61. Gurtu, op. cit., pp. 96-7.
62. Speech given by Babu Jagjivan Ram in the Conference of Assam Chamber of Commerce in Shillong, Assam on 16 October 1948, published in *The Bombay Chronicle.*
63. Lecture delivered by Babu Jagjivan Ram at Lucknow University on 20 November 1948, published in *The Bombay Chronicle.*
64. Babu Jagjivan Ram's statements at the Central Labour Advisory Council meeting on 22nd November 1948 in Lucknow, published in *The Bombay Chronicle.*
65. Gurtu, op. cit., p. 122.
66. Gurtu, op. cit., p. 141.
67. Gurtu, op. cit., pp. 145-6.
68. Gurtu, op. cit., p. 146.
69. *The Bombay Chronicle,* 12 March 1947.
70. Nau Nihal Singh, op. cit., p. 61.
71. S.R. Bakshi, op. cit., p. 81.
72. Devindra Prasad Sharan, *Jagajivan Ram – The Man and the Times*, Indian Book Company, New Delhi, 1994, p. 120.
73. *Amrita Bazar Patrika*, 22 March 1948.

6

The Lonely Harijan

Jagjivan Ram's Politics for the Depressed Classes

Ambedkar firmly rejected the Congress-led Nationalist Movement and Mahatma Gandhi's striving to elevate the *Harijans* by tearing down Gandhi's reputation as a champion of the cause of the Dalits. The majority of the 78 seats won by Congress in the 1937 elections, according to Dr Ambedkar, were secured with the help of Hindu votes, and as a result, those seats in no way represented the Scheduled Caste. Untouchables fought against the Congress by running candidates in nearly every constituency, he claimed. Ambedkar demonstrated the extreme hypocrisy of the Congress, which claimed to include Scheduled Castes in its plan to improve the lives of Dalits.[1] In the late twentieth century, another radical Dalit leader Kanshi Ram also scorned the Congress and pitted Dalit leaders as sycophants, who had been depriving the Dalits by ushering 'the *Chamcha* Age'.[2] Dalit activists, writers and historians generally join hands with such 'Ambedkarite' position regarding the attempt of the Congress leaders to uplift the Dalits. Scholars and activists like Gail Omvedt,[3] Arundhati Roy,[4] Kancha Ilaiah Shepherd have considered the 'suited and booted' Babasaheb, rather than the 'semi-naked Gandhi', to be the messiah of the downtrodden masses.[5] Journalist and politician Sagarika Ghose, following the same track, argues that without Ambedkar, the Dalit would have faced tremendous exploitation and marginalization under the Congress-led structure.[6]

There were quite a number more all-India *Harijan* political figures besides Ambedkar, but there hasn't been a significant study that focuses on how they helped the Dalits get a voice. Though detailed studies offers a dense understanding regarding the movements of Phule and his *Satyashodhak Samaj*,[7] Narayan Guru,[8] and that of various caste associations[9] and temple entry movements,[10] activities of other Dalit leaders have not been dealt with properly. The biography of Kanshi Ram by Abhay Dubey in Hindi[11] and the Adi-Dharma movement under Mangoo Ram by Mark Juergensmeyer[12] are two outliers. Till date, research seems to have focused on either the extreme Dalit leaders, or those leaders from lower castes, who started any religious movements, such as the Adi-Dharma movement and so forth.

However, this predominant focus on such radical Dalit leaders, which they genuinely deserved, does not imply the absence of a second front, which was, though much criticized, in a similar way tried to raise the voice of the lower caste people. Ghanshyam Shah categorizes these movements into reformative and alternative groups. Leaders of alternative movements such as those led by Ambedkar made efforts to build an alternative socio-cultural framework by promoting conversion to another religion or by emphasizing education, economic status, and political power, the former advocated caste reform to address the issue of untouchability.[13] Thus, new scholarship does not always portray the reformist stance of Gandhi in such a negative manner. Rather, scholars like Nishikant Kolge,[14] and Rajmohan Gandhi[15] have refuted the arguments of Roy by pointing out how Gandhi had fought against the caste system from a different approach. Refuting the predominant Gandhi *vs.* Ambedkar views, Aishwarya Kumar's important research delves into the complex, but complementary relationship they shared in establishing the contours of justice, equality, and democracy not only in India, but throughout South Asia.[16] However, even these scholars do not pay attention to the significant roles played by the other Congress leaders on the Dalit question. Thus, Kolge even mentions the contribution of Kanshi Ram,[17] but does not write a single line on leaders of the order of Jagjivan Ram, who belonged to the Dalit group himself, rose to prominence, received important portfolios in the postcolonial era, and utilized his political power to help the lower caste people.

In this prevalent historiography, leaders like Jagjivan Ram have always been criticized as 'Congress Agent'[18] to form an alternative front against Ambedkar. Thus, the intention of such '*Harijan* Elites'[19] has always been suspected in Dalit historiography. Thus, Jagjivan Ram, unlike other Dalit leaders like Bhola Paswan Sastri, has been condemned for doing so little for the Untouchable population and merely focusing on getting political power and economic affluence for their selfish reasons.[20] It should be kept in mind that Jagjivan Ram and Ambedkar reflected polar opposite Dalit sensibilities. D.R. Nagaraj, points out that while Ambedkar symbolizes 'pure fire' and 'defiance', Jagjivan Ram was more 'soft' and 'shrewd'.[21] Hence, in order to get a clear glimpse of the Dalit upliftment, along with the Ambedkarite versions, we need an alternative and complimentary, not contradictory, understanding of the activities of the leaders like Jagjivan Ram, who under the umbrella of Congress attempted to utilize his power and influence in the development of the lower caste people.

Jagjivan Ram's philosophy was a brand-new social order built on an uncommonly inclusive mentality. He had made every effort to promote his vision of a new social order built on the pillars of liberty, equality, and justice for all. His fight was driven by a desire to free Dalits from the shackles of untouchability. In 1969, Jagjivan Ram spoke in Anantapur City on democracy, secularism, and socialism. He said that it won't be a heavy price to pay when many people are ready to give their lives and, therefore, get ready to break free from the bonds of slavery. The goal of this movement, according to him, was to instil greater human ideals in the Indian society. And, in that, he favoured both socialism and democracy. Despite his reverence for socialism, he criticized the communist prioritization of class over caste. He said that it would be faulty to overlook the fact that democracy and caste cannot coexist.[22] Democracy or caste will prevail, but neither can coexist; an idea emanating out of all liberal democratic predecessors of Jagjivan Ram, which he planned to uphold. He further said that all discussions of socialism would be meaningless as long as caste exists, as caste and socialism are incompatible, and it is very challenging to instil human values in the community, as, long as socialism and democracy are not established in the nation. This is how Jagjivan Ram, reconstituted the old political-ideological dilemma of newly independent India, to remind its leadership cohorts which part he himself was, that traditional liability could not be dragged on when the nation had been planning for politico-structural modernization.

Jagjivan Ram was aware that democratic, socialist, and secular conceptions cannot be taken into account without the development of the oppressed classes' people on the social, economic, political, and educational fronts. It was disheartening to think that there were leaders with comparable stature, commitment, and skill to the best the world has ever produced. An organization larger than any political party on earth, the nation has not come close to achieving the objective it set for itself. Many questions arise whether it is headed in the right direction. Is this mess the result of conflicting beliefs and ideals? Is it just attributable to the Congress's multifaceted and multidirectional mass nature? Does Congress have a philosophical foundation that allows its members to make decisions about issues that they face? It is true that a precise description of the goal of political independence was not required during the pre-Independence era due to the form and functions of the Congress organization. Thus, Jagjivan Ram pointed out the changed scenario and the Congress' need to recapitulate its new-found position to meet the issue of an oppressed section of the society in hand. Many believed that the subject was only of academic importance, but, Jagjivan Ram's urge was to create a proper and adequate dialogue. Even then, the resolutions adopted by the Congress in successive sessions suggested that the Congress was uniting in the favour of a more precise definition of independence, the fusion of western industrialization with traditional cottage industries, and a compromise between Gandhian thought and the scientific method.[23] The result of a thoughtful study was the transformation of the social reformer into a nationalist politician. He envisioned a democratic, caste-free Hindu society. He consistently sought to implement democratic measures that would be advantageous to all. Jagjivan Ram ensured that social justice was written into the Indian Constitution as a member of the Constituent Assembly.[24]

The Indian Constituent Assembly, was responsible for drafting the Constitution of India. These discussions were indeed crucial in shaping the future of India as an independent nation. The Constituent Assembly did discuss the need for changes in the economic and the social structure of India. This included debates on issues such as land reforms, wealth redistribution, and social justice. The assembly debated and eventually enshrined a set of fundamental rights in the Indian Constitution. These rights included the freedom of speech and expression, right to equality, right to life, personal liberty, and more. Land reforms were indeed a significant part of the discussions. The assembly debated the need to abolish *zamindari* systems and bring about land reforms to benefit the landless and marginalized. The issue of estate taxes or death duties was discussed, but, it did not find a place in the final Constitution.

The assembly did discuss the role of the state in owning or controlling key industries and services. This led to the mixed economy model adopted by India, where both public and private sectors coexisted. Addressing poverty and unemployment was a pressing issue, and the assembly likely discussed policy measures and principles to promote economic and social welfare. Congress passed numerous resolutions during the course of the years before Independence, reflecting a developing consciousness, but it was unable to be held accountable because it had no influence over the legislative process. In the following comments, Jagjivan Ram urged the populace and the government to address the unemployment issue: 'The unemployment crisis has taken an alarming scale in the country.' Long periods of unemployment plant the seed of unhappiness, as he said, especially among young people. In addition to the enormous number of unemployed people, of whom the majority has been from the depressed sections, the nation also has millions of people who are underemployed or just partially employed. Numerous young men, including educated and trained young men, who are unemployed not only breed resentment, but, also waste the country's resources. This is how Jagjivan Ram perceived the upcoming Dalit rage among the youths which he thought might be problematic for the Congress Party. To combat the threat of unemployment, he proposed that the leadership must prepare the Indian economy to brace for this upcoming threat from below. If it isn't done, he argued, unpleasant behaviours like violence will permeate the political and social life of the nation.[25] To quickly solve the issue, the Government must approach it from all directions. He emphasized the development of a socialistic social structure as well. He made the following case for putting these goals into action:

> We proclaimed that the goal of planning should be the development of a socialistic pattern of society and we foresaw obtaining full employment within a period of ten years. We made the noble declaration that caste and class had no place in the social order within a few years, even before we were even close to achieving these goals, and we called for a revolution to be brought about through radical changes in the attitudes, outlook, and ways of thinking and living of the people through fundamental changes in the social and economic structure.[26]

Since his early years, Jagjivan Ram desired total unity within the lower classes. He had dedicated his life to eradicating casteism, which had long since been entrenched in Indian society. Due to casteism, which was at odds with modern society's notion of fundamental human dignity, members of upper-caste Hindu communities were denied equal opportunity in the social, political, and economic realms. Jagjivan Ram believed that it is the main obstacle to the full realization of human potential since he had personally experienced its negative repercussions, such as untouchability and marginalization. In response to the widespread caste-based prejudice that prevailed at the time and the ensuing marginalization of a sizeable portion of society, Jagjivan Ram dedicated his life to the advancement of the oppressed classes. He was actively involved in organizing young people from the lower socio-economic classes and worked to educate his neighbours about the importance of standing up for their rights and attracting the attention of political leaders. Such events strengthened his desire to stand up for justice, and he made it his life's work to work towards eradicating the societal ill that debilitated a sizeable portion of the population.

In 1933, he was chosen to serve as the Harijan Sevak Sangh's secretary of Bihar state. Jagjivan Ram organized the All-India Ravidas Sammelan in Calcutta in 1934 with great success. He interacted with various social workers during the Conference, with whom he discussed his ideas and proposed that all *Harijan* leaders should speak from a single platform. Kanpur hosted the Depressed Classes' Unity Conference in 1935. The All-India Depressed Classes League picked

Jagjivan Ram to preside over its Lucknow Session in 1936. Numerous such gatherings would follow in West Bengal, Uttar Pradesh, Bombay, and Punjab. He organized the underclasses and made efforts to express and broadcast their real complaints. Jagjivan Ram said that the country must 'fight for a socially interdependent society that would be so modified and revolutionized that they might participate in it in terms of equality of rights and obligations', urged the downtrodden classes in his appeal. Leaders like him were instrumental in the passage of the Scheduled Castes and Scheduled Tribes Act, which provides for state involvement to uplift socially disadvantaged sections through reservations in public jobs and legislative seats. He had a significant role in the development of the 1955 Protection of Civil Rights Act.[27] He held a strong belief in the worth of every person and their right to personal freedom.

The issue of how Jagjivan Ram adapted to the well-being of the oppressed people, comes to the fore as a poignant question. Has his life been affected in any way? According to Peter Friedlander, Jagjivan Ram's career was greatly influenced by his trust in a medieval Hindi lower caste poet-saint, Ravidas.[28] According to Jeffrey Haynes, these discussions now frequently centre on whether religion contributes to or facilitates peaceful conflict settlement. Jagjivan Ram preferred a non-confrontational approach to conflict resolution to advance Dalit rights as a result of his political career and his devotion to Ravidas, as, a religious tradition.[29] He was able to protest against Dalit prejudice in India and strive for their emancipation in a calm and non-confrontational manner within the Hindu fold.

Since Jagjivan Ram was born into a Chamar family, the name was later anglicized. In Hindi, this Chamar community was referred to as *achut*, Untouchable, or *asprisya*. Jagjivan Ram used the British government's term for the downtrodden class in 1928. It is mentioned that his father, Sobhi Ram, was a devout man and a priest of the Shiv Narayani Sant movement. The Shiv Narayani Sant movement is a religious and social movement that emerged in India, particularly in the northern regions. It is associated with the worship of Shiv (Lord Shiva) and Narayani (an incarnation of the Goddess). The movement emphasizes spiritual devotion, religious rituals, and the promotion of social and moral values.[30] Indeed, the life and deeds of Jagjivan Ram, whose father was a devout priest in the Shiv Narayani Sant movement, can be seen as a model that combines spiritual belief with a commitment to social reconstruction. His political career and advocacy for social justice were deeply rooted in his values and upbringing. Growing up in a family associated with a religious movement, Jagjivan Ram likely imbibed strong spiritual values. These values often emphasize principles like compassion, service to others, and moral conduct. Such beliefs can shape a person's character and guide their actions.

The Shiv Narayanis were distinguished by their inclusion of Hindus, Muslims, Christians, and members of the mixed population's lowest castes, as observed by H.H. Wilson. The Shiv Narayani Sant movement appears to be a syncretic religious and social movement that emerged in India during the eighteenth century. This movement seems to have drawn elements from both Hindu and Muslim traditions while emphasizing certain moral and social principles. Individuals could join the Shiv Narayanis assembly, and become part of the community by making offerings to a sacred text of the tradition, and by listening to its teachings. Unlike some other religious movements, it did not require the guidance of a guru for admission. Followers of the Shiv Narayani Sant movement continued to dress according to the conventions of both Hindu and Muslim communities, indicating a syncretic or inclusive approach to religious practices.

The teachings of this movement placed a strong emphasiz on moral characteriztics, such as truth, temperance, and mercy. This suggests a focus on ethical conduct and personal virtues. The movement's teachings included a prohibition on polygamy, indicating a stance on family and social values. The movement was founded by Shiv Narayanis, a Rajput of the Nerivan lineage from the village of Chandravan, near Ghazipur. He lived during the reign of Mughal emperor Muhammad Shah (1702-48). The Shiv Narayanis were primarily Rajputs, a prominent warrior caste in India. Some of them served as warriors (*sipahi*), while others worked as porters. They were mainly concentrated in the areas around Ghazipur and Calcutta.[31] According to Babu Bajirangi Lal, the Shiv Narayanis community had four primary centres in the Ghazipur region. However, by 1918, they had expanded their presence to other regions, including Cawnpore

(Kanpur) and Bombay. Shiv Narayanis could also be found in several locations, including Calcutta, Karachi, and Rangoon. This indicates that the community had spread to different parts of India and even beyond, possibly due to migration or the attraction of their teachings. There were Shahabad residents who had converted to Christianity, which is now a part of present-day Haryana. This highlights the religious diversity within the Shiv Narayanis community, with some members choosing to follow different faiths. It is noted that while many members of the society had once been Rajputs, most of the community's members by this time were Chamars, Dusadhs (another Untouchable group of landless agricultural labourers), and members of other Untouchable groups. This demographic shift suggests changes in the composition of the community over time, possibly due to a plethora of social and economic factors.[32]

Despite growing up in a world marred by deprivation, prejudice, and persecution, Meira Kumar, Jagjivan Ram's daughter, reminiscences about her father Jagjivan Ram's youth that 'her father Jagjivan Ram constantly strove to overcome the adversities in his life'. Jagjivan Ram, was a prominent Indian political leader who was a staunch advocate for the rights of marginalized communities. Jagjivan Ram's father played a role in the Shiv Narayanis movement by printing handbills of the movement's holy scripture, the *Anyas*. Jagjivan Ram had the opportunity to attend school from a young age, as earliest as six. However, his educational journey was not without challenges, as he encountered caste prejudice during his middle and high school years. Discriminatory practices, such as the provision of a separate water supply for Dalit pupils, were prevalent at the time. Jagjivan Ram's determination to challenge caste-based discrimination is highlighted in the description. He reportedly smashed every pitcher of water set up exclusively for Dalits, which ultimately led to the school administration ending this discriminatory practice. This act of protest demonstrated his early commitment to fighting societal and all pervasive injustice. The account also mentions an incident during a family trip to Khopira, where they had property. The family was instructed to put away their umbrellas and walk through the neighbourhood because the Brahmins in the village had a long-standing ban on Dalits using umbrellas or driving. This episode reflects the deeply entrenched caste-based discrimination prevalent in certain areas of India at the time. His early experiences with caste discrimination and his willingness to challenge such injustices played a significant role in shaping his later activism and political career.[33]

According to Eleanor Zelliot and Rohini Mokashi-Punekar, the untouchable saints included or accepted all castes and women into the fold of saints' tradition,.[34] The growth of anti-caste intellectual movements in India between 1500 and 1750, according to Omvedt, 'stressed a strong kind of devotional movement with a vision of equality, an emphasiz on empirical reasoning, and access to ecstasy for all'. Then, during colonialism, from roughly 1920 onward, anti-caste intellectuals had to construct their own perspective in opposition to the growing 'Hindu nationalism' of the elite.[35] Shiv Narayan's followers, according to Parshuram Chaturvedi, were known for putting a strong emphasiz on organizing, educating, and advocating for their community's overall well-being in addition to its spiritual well-being. If there were enough devotees, they would form an association (*sangathan*) known as a *santsipahi* (soldier *Sants*), and elect an organizing committee made up of a priest (the *mahant*), a minister (the *vazir*), and other office-holders. They would then raise money, submit a percentage to a higher-level movement centre to request registration, and spend the remaining cash for neighbourhood and local community projects.

Jagjivan Ram's promotion of Ravidas assemblies and the development of Ravidasi sect temples as focal points for the development of Dalit communities indeed appears to have been influenced by his early experiences and the values instilled in him, possibly by his family's association with the Shiv Narayanis movement. It reflects a commitment to creating spaces and institutions that could empower and uplift marginalized Dalit communities. The establishment of Ravidas assemblies and temples suggests a focus on community empowerment and solidarity among Dalits. Just as the Shiv Narayanis movement emphasized a sense of belonging and shared values among its followers, Jagjivan Ram may have sought to create similar bonds within Dalit communities. The development of Ravidas temples likely aimed at providing not only a place of worship but also a hub for social and community activities. These temples could have served as centres for education, cultural preservation, and social interaction, mirroring the role of religious centres in the Shiv Narayanis movement. Jagjivan Ram's experiences of caste-based discrimination during his upbringing may have inspired him to take actions that mirror the efforts of movements like the Shiv Narayanis. Just as he challenged discriminatory practices during his school years, he may have seen the need to create spaces and institutions that challenged caste-based inequalities.[36]

From 1928 onwards, Jagjivan Ram organized numerous Ravidasi Sabhas in Calcutta. The Ramdas General Assembly (also known as the Ramdas Mahasabha) was established in 1928, claims Beltz, by Jagjivan Ram. In 1929, the latter established the Akhil Bhartiya Ravidas Sabha, commonly known as the All-India Ravidas Assembly.[37] In her memoirs, Indrani Devi mentioned that while Jagjivan Ram was a student in Calcutta from 1928 to 1932, he was actively establishing Ravidas Sabha, and trying to bring together various Dalit communities around the persona of Ravidas. Along with it, he supported the Ravidas Jayanti processions.[38] According to Nau Nihal Singh, his organization of Ravidas Sabhas in various Calcutta neighbourhoods in 1928 suggests his commitment to creating spaces for the Dalit community to come together, discuss issues, and build a sense of solidarity. The significant gathering at Wellington Park in Calcutta, attended by about 15,000 Dalits, reflected the strong support and enthusiasm for Ram's efforts. His role as a young leader and reformer likely resonated with the audience. Jagjivan Ram's advocacy against the meat consumption and alcohol aligns with efforts to promote social and moral reform within the Dalit community. Such reforms were often seen as prerequisites for challenging traditional caste-based hierarchies and discrimination. The mention of the Shiv Narayan's legacy suggests that Jagjivan Ram's early efforts may have been influenced by the values and principles he learned from his family's association with the Shiv Narayanis movement. This legacy likely emphasized moral and social values, as well as community building. The information hinted at the possibility that initiatives were motivated by earlier caste meetings held by Dalit groups in northern India. These meetings could have served as examples of collective action and empowerment.[39] Hitendra K. Patel has stated that Dalit Sabha assemblies, which started in 1913–14 in Bihar, were modelled after higher caste assemblies from the late nineteenth century. In these gatherings, caste elders urged people to abstain from alcohol, embrace monogamy, refrain from poisoning animals to death, and claim the Brahmin rank for Chamars.[40]

The primary goal of the Ravidasi Sabha and the Ravidas Jayanti celebrations was to mobilize large numbers of Dalits, and Jagjivan Ram consistently supported this. Jagjivan Ram's understanding of what he was doing, was influenced by his own opinions on Ravidas and the examples provided by his Shiv Narayani ancestry. It is important to recognize that various movements and ideologies within India's social and political landscape have advocated for similar moral and social values as a means to uplift marginalized communities, including Dalits. Jagjivan Ram, his Shiv Narayani heritage already incorporated these virtues as essential for the upliftment of Dalits, which aligned with the principles of morality and social reform. This underscores the diversity of influences and sources of inspiration that shaped the beliefs and actions of leaders like him.

The INC played a pivotal role in the Indian independence movement, and it continues to be one of India's major political parties to this day. Jagjivan Ram himself was a prominent member of the INC and made significant contributions to Indian politics as a leader within the party. Its convention was place in the conference room of the Gokuldas Tejpal Sanskrit College in Bombay, under the direction of W.C. Bonnerjee. Participants in this session came from all over India and represented various communities. Participants at this conference included lawyers, educators, lecturers, principals of schools, owners of newspapers, doctors, barristers, business people, financiers, landlords, social reformers, and religious academics, among others. Sobhi Ram, the father of Jagjivan Ram, was a prominent social reformer and a watchful member of the Shiv Narayani community who attended this conference. After recognizing the fundamental notion of organizing national freedom, he pledged to spread it.[41]

The historical context and Jagjivan Ram's speech at the 1931 conference on untouchability in Patna highlighted his strong stance on the need for concrete actions to address the social and economic issues faced by Dalits. Jagjivan Ram emphasized that Dalits were no longer content with mere words and sermons from caste Hindus.

Instead, they demanded genuine treatment and tangible actions to improve their social and economic conditions. This reflects his commitment to advocating for substantive change rather than symbolic gestures. Jagjivan Ram made it clear that he did not support any form of religious conversion. This suggests his belief in the need for social reform and upliftment within the existing religious and social framework, rather than advocating for conversion as a solution.

Jagjivan Ram mentioned Jinnah, who was advocating for a separate Muslim-only nation (which eventually led to the creation of Pakistan), and Ambedkar, who was pushing for separate electoral districts for marginalized communities. Here, his position suggests that he had his own vision for addressing the issues faced by Dalits within the broader Indian context, distinct from these other prominent leaders. Untouchability must be eliminated. Every religion and *jati* must band together in large numbers to fight for freedom. He further said that Dalits are Hindu *achuts*, or outcasts. He said vehemently against any communal cessation likewise, 'We were all born Hindus, and we will all die as Hindus. The nation was not founded by us; rather, we made the nation. The country is ours. Society must be warned against conversion to another religion.'[42]

Following this talk, Jagjivan Ram travelled to Bombay with Rajendra Prasad in 1931, where he met Gandhi and joined the Congress's fight for independence. In Bihar, he became the leader of Gandhi's Harijan Sevak Sangh (Union for the Upliftment of the Untouchables).[43] Greatly influenced by Gandhi's ideals, he knelt before his mother Basanti Devi and made the following promise: 'With your blessings, I will work for the rights of the thousands of Untouchables in this country, for social equality, for helping the poor, for labour rights, and for India's self-rule. I shall make efforts to create a climate of peace, brotherhood, unity, benevolence, and amity throughout the nation.'[44]

After spending a few months with Gandhi, Jagjivan Ram left an enduring impression on him that can be seen in the private letters the latter wrote to him. As the Harijan Sevak Sangh's Secretary, he undertook a thorough tour across the province and gained first-hand knowledge of the social, political, and economic issues of the Depressed Classes. This knowledge served him well in his future plan of action as a leader of the neighbourhood. There was no all-India organization of the Depressed Classes up until this point that could stand up and air the complaints of the Depressed Classes on a national level. As a result, he established the All-India Depressed Classes League after consulting with other community leaders. The League was founded in 1934-5, and provided significant contributions to the cause of the downtrodden classes. He established the provincial branch of the League in the month of July 1935, and was unanimously elected its President; he held that position up to this point with a little hiatus because there was no political awakening and agitation for social reforms in his province. The fact that the downtrodden sections in Bihar have been politically and socially organized and made aware is entirely to his credit.[45]

An extraordinary earthquake that struck Bihar in 1934 resulted in unimaginable anguish and devastation. Jagjivan Ram immersed himself in his humanitarian work. A hurry sent Gandhi to Bihar. In order to help with the relief effort, he joined Gandhi's group of volunteers for the first time. Jagjivan Ram testified in front of the British-based Hammond Commission in 1935 and fervently argued for Dalits to cast ballots in the 1936-7 elections. In one of her addresses Meira Kumar mentions his efforts: 'In this connection (to guarantee Dalits acquire the priceless right to vote), he met Mansfield, the then Reforms Minister in Bihar.' In the same year, he also spoke before the Hammond Commission, which had travelled from England to look at numerous problems relating to Dalit voters' rights. He was well aware that a significant portion of our society would continue to view our democracy as irrelevant without the social and political uplift of the underprivileged sections.[46] Without a doubt, Jagjivan Ram's work was the greatest contribution made by *Harijans*. He was aware of the needs of the masses, which are the cause of their subjugation. As a result, he invariably decides in *Harijans'* favour.

Jagjivan Ram acted in accordance with Gandhi's instructions. Gandhiji's article in 23 March 1934, in the weekly magazine *Harijan*, which he quoted, stated that: 'Untouchability is, in my judgement, an entirely fabricated construct. For the simple reason that in Hindu society, the men who sinned, were described as Untouchables, who, are in every way equal for the moral and intellectual development to the highest among the caste Hindus, but, who are treated as Untouchables, it has no relation to the moral or intellectual development of the people'.[47] Fighting for freedom also meant fighting against our frailties. Casteism was a cancer that was eating away at the foundation of our civilization. This context is necessary to comprehend Gandhi's different uplift programmes for *Harijans*. Therefore, Jagjivan Ram was inspired by Gandhi's actions. A great mind is one that shapes others' thoughts, in fact.

RE-EXAMINING JAGJIVAN RAM AND DR B.R. AMBEDKAR

Indeed, both Jagjivan Ram and Ambedkar were influential figures in the twentieth-century Indian politics who came from Dalit backgrounds and fought for the rights and upliftment of Dalits. However, as it is mentioned, they held divergent perspectives on the role of religion in the Dalit struggle for rights. This divergence had significant implications for their respective approaches. Ambedkar had a complex relationship with Hinduism. He believed that the caste system, deeply rooted in Hindu society, perpetuated discrimination and social injustice against Dalits. As a result, he concluded that meaningful emancipation for Dalits was not possible within Hinduism. He famously declared in 1935 at the Yeola Conference that he would not die a Hindu, despite having been born one. On the other hand, Jagjivan Ram, while also hailing from a Dalit background, did not advocate for religious conversion as a solution to the problems faced by Dalits. Instead, he remained within the fold of Hinduism and worked within the framework of the Indian National Congress, and the Indian political system to champion the cause of Dalits. He believed in bringing about social change and improving the conditions of Dalits while remaining within the existing religious and social structure. These differing approaches reflected the diversity of strategies and perspectives within the Dalit movement in India during the twentieth century. While Ambedkar pursued religious conversion as a means to address social inequalities, Jagjivan Ram focused on political and social reform within the existing system. Both leaders made significant contributions to the upliftment of Dalits, and the broader struggle for social justice in India.[48]

Trilok Nath claims that Jagjivan Ram disagreed with Ambedkar's viewpoint and asserted in speeches before the public that Dalits, who, converted to other religions would still bear the stigma of Untouchability, and run the risk of alienating other Hindus.[49] He argued with him that, despite their conversion to other religions like Sikhism, etc., Dalits continued to face discrimination within that faith and that, rather than resolving the issue through conversion, the only viable option was a transformation that had an impact on all of the Indian society.[50]

Jagjivan Ram said that, 'To be preached at by caste Hindus to give up eating meat, stop drinking alcohol, and live pure lifestyles, now won't work any longer', during the convention of Untouchability Society in Patna in 1931, when Rajendra Prasad was the principal guest. Now, Dalits demand genuine treatment rather than simply words; there must be a tangible action. They no longer wanted to hear sermons. Jinnah is pushing for an Islamic nation, and Ambedkar is pushing for arrangements for separate electoral districts. He said,

> I don't support any kind of religious conversion. We are Hindu *achuts,* or outcasts. We were all born Hindus, and we will all die Hindus. The nation was not founded by us; rather, we made the nation. The nation is ours. Society must be warned against conversion to another religion. Untouchability must be eliminated. Every religion and *Jati* must band together in large numbers to fight for freedom.[51]

Ambedkar said at the Bombay Presidency Depressed Classes Conference in October 1935 that the Dalits should completely leave the Hindu religion after the Poona Pact failed to satisfy their electoral demands. Ambedkar maintained that inequity was the entire foundation and ethics of the Hindu faith and that it was useless to delude one into thinking that the depressed classes would ever attain their full manhood while remaining in the Hindu fold. Mahatma Gandhi opposed the divisive action. Openly criticizing Ambedkar's failing attempts was Jagjivan Ram. Ambedkar was surrounded by media attention. He received constant support from people of all faiths, including Sanatanists, Arya Samajists, Buddhists, Sikhs, and Christians. The oldest community was in the danger of being upended by Ambedkar's departure from Hinduism. Many Dalits were converted to Christian and Sikh religions.[52]

'We are Hindus, and those of us who want to leave the Hindu religion are cowards', Jagjivan Ram once remarked at the Depressed Classes League meeting held at the Gandhi Grounds. There were a sizeable number of Scheduled Caste members in the Constituent Assembly. The League's Vice President, Radhanath Das, was seated in the chair. A portion of the audience sang 'Dr Ambedkar Zindabad' and 'Jai Bhim', as Jagjivan Ram entered to address the conference. The conference was in disarray for roughly five minutes before the police intervened to assist restore order. 'I tell you that if you want to accept Christianity or Islam you are at liberty to do so,' Jagjivan Ram stated that 'going away would be better since it would purge the sad class. He questioned what he had been doing since 1936 and what he had been thinking for the last ten years. Why didn't you convert to Islam? It is better for you to experience it first-hand and identify your areas of strength.' He stated that 'religion is a question of faith rather than a tool for negotiating political rights. Don't compromise your religion for political objectives.' At this point, roughly 50 conference attendees chanting slogans exited the event. There has long been a difference of opinion between Ambedkar and him, according to Jagjivan Ram. Who is on the correct path will only become clear with time. 'We do not belong to the group that denigrates and disparages others,' he continued. He then issued a warning to Hindus, urging them to treat the lower classes equally with other Hindus and grant them all Hindu rights; otherwise, if things continued as they were, it was feared that there would be no Scheduled Castes left in the Hindu religion in a hundred years. He urged Hindus to act right away to improve the lot of the underprivileged classes.[53]

The All-India Depressed Classes League vice-president and a member of the Constituent Assembly, Dharm Prakash, stated, 'In 1941, when the Viceroy's Executive Council was expanded for the first time, no Scheduled Caste representative was taken in it.' At this point, Ambedkar made a statement criticizing the Council's exclusion of any *Harijan*. At the time, Ambedkar and the late M.C. Raja served on the War Advisory Board. Both of them were requested to resign from it by the Depressed Classes League in protest. However, Ambedkar was unwilling to step down since he simply could not afford to anger his British overlords.[54] When Ambedkar was appointed to the Executive Council in 1942, he was asked not to accept the councillorship since the Scheduled Castes' representation was insufficient. He did not, however, care for how the community he is currently crying so much over was represented. Moreover, he remained in his position despite the resignations of Aney, Sarkar, and Sir Homi Mody from the Council in opposition to the oppressive policies of the British government. When the British Cabinet Delegation convinced him of his unrepresentative character and invited Jagjivan Ram as the true representative of the Scheduled Castes,[55] Ambedkar did not hesitate to appeal to Churchill and Amery to save him. By listing his 'Loyal faithful services to the British Government and thereby appealing to the mercy to sustain his lost leadership,' Prakash accused him of writing to the Viceroy and the Cabinet Delegation.[56]

Ambedkar founded the Republican Party of India (RPI), which was an independent party, and was fighting for the Dalit rights. On the other hand, within the Congress, a mainstream party, Jagjivan Ram campaigned for Dalit liberation and rights. The latter was portrayed by Christophe Jaffrelot as a 'social reformer'. As opposed to Ambedkar's strong rejection of caste-based Hinduism, the latter placed more emphasiz on Sanksritization, and the imitation of high-caste Hinduism.[57] According to Jaffrelot, he used the Gandhian idea to fight casteism in India. The Congress Party attempted to use him as a counterweight to Ambedkar's more extreme strategy for opposing caste in India, which was rising in favour.[58] According to my claim, Jagjivan Ram spent his entire life working within the Congress Party to advance Gandhi's Dalit upliftment doctrine. But his battles for Dalit rights lacked any artificiality. Both Mendelsohn and Vicziany reached the conclusion that Jagjivan Ram's contribution to the Dalit community was somewhat constrained by his position within the Congress Party and that his career's longevity was a result of both 'his competence and also his carefulness not to engage in dissent and controversy and that it was hard to estimate how much power he wielded within the Congress Party over the years.'[59]

Sanjay Paswan and Pramanshi Jaideva described that in the post-Ambedkar era, Ambedkar was mentioned as a champion of the Dalits.[60] Jagjivan Ram made significant contributions to the upliftment and welfare of Dalits in India, earning him recognition as a champion of the Dalit community. Jagjivan Ram played a pivotal role in advocating for the rights of agricultural labourers, including Dalits. His efforts led to the establishment of minimum wage policies for agricultural labourers, which was a significant step toward ensuring fair wages and economic security for this vulnerable group.

As the Railway Minister, Jagjivan Ram made a ground-breaking move by integrating Dalits into Indian Railways food services. This meant that Dalits could eat with higher-caste people all over India, breaking down age-old social barriers and promoting social equality. Jagjivan Ram founded the Dalit Varga Sangh (Depressed Classes Union) with the aim of economically uplifting the Dalit community. This organization worked to address the economic disparities faced by Dalits and empower them through various initiatives. His skilful handling of parliamentary work and his unwavering commitment to advocating for the rights of Dalits within the political system earned him respect and recognition as a champion for their cause.[61] With regard to his devotion to work among Dalits, I think, no doubt, there is no artificialness in his work. He always thought towards the upliftment of Dalits because he came from an Untouchable family and he knew the reality. Jagjivan Ram was very much influenced and followed Sant Kabir's ideology by stressing upon universal upliftment and equality. Badri Narayan has written in his one chapter about the *Chamcha* (stooges, agents or tools) age, he argues that the Scheduled Caste politician had sold out their community's interests in favour of personal advancement. I think it is his personal opinion though it is not true in all cases. The concept of a *Chamcha* always existed in all categories or parties, and not in only in the Scheduled Caste community. In a party-based democratic system, interest groups existed in this system. We have seen sometimes that elected members of their party joined another party for their interest. According to Kanshi Ram, these were the *Chamchas* created by mainstream political parties to oppose and compete with the genuine champions of the Dalit cause.

All Dalit leaders, including old-timers of the order of Jagjivan Ram and Kanshi Ram's contemporary, Ram Vilas Paswan, were encompassed within this definition of *Chamcha Raj*. K.C. Das in his book, *Indian Dalits: Voices, Visions and Politics*, Kanshi Ram criticized Jagjivan Ram and other 'stooges'. Kanshi Ram said that Jagjivan Ram, who had been in the Congress Party before moving to the Janata Dal, was not a leader, but a stooge.[62] It was the opinion of Kanshi Ram about Jagjivan Ram, but, my argument is that he was the able leader of the Congress Party, and he was not dependent on the Congress leadership. His work on Dalits is a witness to what he was. He followed the ideology of Gandhi and he always openly opined this way. Jagjivan Ram held to a desire to maintain beliefs inherited from his Sant heritage in his long political life.

Comparing the philosophical ideologies and activities of Ambedkar and Jagjivan Ram, it would be quite unfair as they had different personalities and approaches. The former was a revolutionary who rebelled against the system, while Jagjivan Ram was a freedom fighter who believed in evolutionary reforms. He believed that sustainable social justice for minorities could only be achieved by converting the minds of the majority and securing their support. Both dedicated their lives to uplift the downtrodden and fought for Dalit rights using different approaches. Ambedkar founded the Republican Party, while Jagjivan Ram founded the All-India Depressed Classes League.

MESSIAH OF DALITS

Jagjivan Ram founded the Akhil Bhartiya Ravidas Mahasabha, Khetihar Mazdoor Sabha, and All-India Depressed Classes League. Through these groups, he included the Depressed Classes in the freedom struggle movements and made an appeal for all Dalit leaders to band together not only to demand social reform but also equal political representation. Jagjivan Ram appeared before the Hammond Commission in Ranchi on 19 October 1935, a significant day in the history of modern India, and he urged that Dalits be given the right to vote.[63] Nau Nihal Singh claims that Jagjivan Ram founded Ravidas Sabhas in a number of Calcutta neighbourhoods to promote awareness of the underprivileged. A big conference was conducted at Wellington Park in Calcutta when Jagjivan was 20 years old, and 15,000 *achuts* had assembled as an audience to hear him speak.[64] According to Singh, Jagjivan Ram advocated avoiding eating meat and consuming wine because he thought that doing so would help the Untouchables' uplifment in advance.[65] As a result, Ram took his responsibility seriously and was always thinking of ways to better the situation of the poor.

Jagjivan Ram emphasized upon Dalit-related concerns. The main focus of his fight was the advancement of Dalits. He was a pioneer in implementing social programmes aimed at improving Dalit conditions. It would take a while to bring about a dramatic reconstruction of the socio-economic order. However, even the size and styles of welfare project implementations are woefully inadequate. It was expected that as these communities' conditions improved, people there would strive to live honourable lives. Equally predictable was that they would reject traditional treatment as their knowledge and their attendant grasp of their rights grew. But tyranny and harassment have returned everywhere this movement has appeared, especially in the rural areas. It is a sign that upper-caste psychology has not changed significantly; rather, there has simply been a grudging adjustment. Even supposedly liberal people have the same mindset; their expression is just different. How else could one account for the frequently praised expressions of pity and the widely publicized desire to help the downtrodden and oppressed communities? A positive development has been the addition of an extra ten years to the Constitutional reservation of seats for these classes. But, there will be a lot more work to do. There should be an end to all activities that separate Hindus from other castes and reinforce discrimination. Scheduled Caste separate settlements shouldn't be built. In both urban and rural settings, there should be a mix of them. Liberal stipends should be offered to all students from Scheduled Castes and Tribes, technical education should be encouraged and facilitated, and fair representation in public offices should be ensured.[66]

The Bihar Provincial Depressed Classes Conference's second session was held at Gopal Ganj in 1937. 'Let's organize the agricultural labourers', Jagjivan Ram remarked during his presidential address at this conference. Heavy obstacles will need to be overcome. Additionally,

Jagjivan Ram stated that in rural areas, there were limitations on Scheduled Castes purchasing agricultural land in specific portions of the country.[67] The most astounding aspect of this restriction was that castes that were absolutely necessary to agricultural operations were classed as non-agriculturalists. After the Constitution went into effect, these prohibitions were lifted; however, it has since come to light that even arable wasteland is no longer accessible to them. As a result, people are forced to labour in agriculture to survive.[68] He understood the issue they had. He was a true leader with a strong foundation among the oppressed people.

Jagjivan Ram, in his letter to N.R. Malkani, President of Harijan Sevak Sangh, Sindh, expressed his concern for the *Harijans* of Sindh. He argued that some special safeguards and protections should be given to the Scheduled Castes of Sindh. Although, there was some confusion regarding the Scheduled Caste status of the Jatias, he confirmed that the Bhangis, Chamars, Musahars, or Meghwals should be provided with special safeguards.[69]

As I have already mentioned, Jagjivan Ram was keenly aware of rural development and was aware that more people lived in rural areas. He, therefore, placed a value on property ownership. In light of the National Policy on Tenancy, he desired the implementation of land reforms. In July 1967, a conference of chief ministers was held to hasten the efficient implementation of land reforms. In conformity with the general structure of national regulations, ceiling legislations had been updated. In March 1976, during his second term, a conference of Chief Ministers was held when the issues with the implementation of the 20-point programme were, especially, reviewed in relation to the measures for land reform.[70] Due to this, by the end of June 1975, more than 11.8 lakh acres of land had been declared excess, of which 8.11 lakh acres had been given to the original landowners. He had a particular interest in how surplus land was distributed to landless agricultural labourers, especially those who were members of the Scheduled Castes and Scheduled Tribes. A total of 13 lakh people are now the proprietors of the land, for they had spent their entire lives cultivating and producing.[71]

Jagjivan Ram began to strongly express the cause of constructing a society based on social justice, inclusion, and political and economic equality without which democracy will be inadequate, said Meira Kumar, in a statement about her experience with her father. For this reason, he concentrated on the voting rights of the underprivileged classes back in 1935. He met Mansfield, the then Reforms Minister in Bihar, in this context.[72] In the same year, he also spoke before the Hammond Commission, which had travelled from England to look at numerous problems relating to Dalit voter's rights. He was well-aware that a significant portion of our society would continue to view our democracy as useless, without the socio-political improvement of the underprivileged classes. He made efforts to attain the objectives of social and political empowerment of disadvantaged groups while preventing social unrest or discord among the populace. Democracy cannot coexist with exclusivity and isolation, which creates a gap between the rich and the underprivileged. He firmly believed that those who are on the receiving end of the social order are rendered meaningless without economic freedom and distributive justice. If we minimize his significance to just that of a Scheduled Castes leader, history will be distorted.

Throughout his brilliant public career, Jagjivan Ram campaigned for the eradication of casteism's horrors and for easing the suffering and privations of the once Untouchables. He was unwavering in his promotion of their cause. However, the scope of his concerns was considerably broader. Following the Poona Pact, the All-India Hindu Mahasabha convened a meeting on 29 December 1935, at Poona, Maharashtra, with Malaviya serving as its President. 'Let the Harijans not forsake it and we put the dust under their feet to our foreheads.' Malaviya pleaded with the Harijans to maintain the Hindu religion. He promised to take away the thorns that had been placed in the *Harijan's* path. Except for intermarriage and interfaith marriage, which extended to the rest of the Hindus as well, they planned to abolish all of their handicaps.[73] He attended the All-India Hindu Mahasabha meeting because it was open to everyone at the time, and the resolution was approved as Jagjivan Ram had requested. The Mahasabha reiterated its previous resolution to grant all Hindus equal access to all public facilities and institutions, including schools, wells, Ghats, water supply points, hotels, roads, parks, *dharmashalas*, temples and other public places of worship, cremation grounds, etc., regardless of their caste or creed. When Jagjivan Ram pressed his resolution, there was a fight between him and the Shankaracharya of Puri, there were over 15,000 people present in the open session. It advocated the removal of all caste and birth-based differences in Hindu society. If his resolution was not adopted, Jagjivan Ram threatened to leave the convention. The resolution was supported by Malaviya, and the Shankaracharya was overthrown. Not only his group but even many of Ambedkar's supporters congratulated him on his bold stand and henceforward, he became known as a reckonable leader among leaders in the country.[74]

Since he was aware that empowerment is the key to the depressed class's achievement or upliftment, Jagjivan Ram placed more focus on the Depressed Classes' rights to equality and empowerment. He urged the downtrodden classes to fight for a socially interdependent society that would be so altered and revolutionized that they might take part in it in terms of equality of rights and obligations.[75] As Jagjivan Ram was constantly optimistic, he was motivated to struggle against the constraints of our societal structure or system again and again. A nation or society, according to him, could never become strong or withstand the onslaughts of other countries, if, any elements in that society were suppressed or lacked progress.[76] The daring and lucid statement made by Jagjivan Ram that the chain was only as strong as its weakest link, which brings us back to the construct of John Rawls. The community and country as a whole could not be strong if any segment of the population continued to be weak.[77]

As an advocate for the protection of the oppressed classes in the Constituent Assembly, Jagjivan Ram has made significant contributions. He placed more emphasize on making sure the new Republic of India's Constitution contained enough clauses to outlaw untouchability and caste-based discrimination. He played a key role in getting the Protection of Civil Rights Act of 1955, passed and included in the country's Constitution. He also had a significant impact on the creation of the state's intervention policies, which included reserving jobs in the public sector and seats in the legislature for members of the Scheduled Castes and Scheduled Tribes.[78] His accomplishments in this sphere were viewed as a significant step forward for the underprivileged. Indrani Devi claims that he served as the patron of practically all organizations dedicated to resolving issues affecting underprivileged people in general and Scheduled Castes in particular.[79] Jagjivan Ram informed the then Prime Minister, Indira Gandhi in 1969, following the nationalization of banks, about the inadequate participation of the Scheduled Caste and Scheduled Tribes at different levels of posts in banks and the government's financial organizations. He took the initiative to make it mandatory and constitutional to only hire people from these classes for the positions designated for reservation at all levels in banks and government financial institutions.[80] Jagjivan Ram is aware of how crucial reservation was in enhancing the socioeconomic standing of Dalits.

The National Commissioner for Scheduled Castes and Scheduled Tribes was first appointed by Jagjivan Ram. According to Article 378 of the Constitution, the President of India has appointed this unique and national-level officer to carry out the following tasks: (a) review any issue involving the protections for the Scheduled Castes and Scheduled Tribes specified by the Constitution, and (b) reports to the President on how well these protections have operated since 1950. Currently, it resembles a National Commission for SCs and STs. He issued orders mandating the presence of Scheduled Castes in hotels, mess halls, restaurants, tea shops, coaches, dining cars, and *Pani Pandey* (who served drinking water to the passengers) in all major stations when he was the railway minister. Although it might seem insignificant, it was a brilliant idea that allowed lower-caste Dalits to mingle with upper-castes while travelling across the nation. He came to understand that the Scheduled Castes were still experiencing an economic crisis. As a Minister of Communication, he made significant contributions to the advancement and benefit of the Scheduled Castes. He issued orders stating that only members of Scheduled Castes should be hired for the fourth grade.[81]

Thousands of underprivileged individuals had the chance to find employment as a result of this attempt. It is because of his serious outstanding political ideas that he could awaken a great mass of Depressed Classes from their age-long slumber and, thus, he became a cynosure of life to the ignorant masses, Ramesh Chandra and Sangh Mitra wrote.[82] He urged Indian society to create the conditions necessary for the creation of the Depressed Classes in the nation before displaying lofty ideals. Despite obstacles, he managed to instil in the Depressed Classes an eternal attitude of sacrifice and duty without upsetting the high-caste Hindus. It was merely an example of his political savvy. Special facilities and advantages should not be viewed as incentives for picking sides, but rather be understood as lawful dues to be provided for years of hardship, he argued.[83] Thus, he became the legitimate leader and representative of the *Harijans* in India.

FIGHT FOR ERADICATION OF CASTES AND CLASS SYSTEM

The social division in society is a result of the caste system. 'The bastion of caste is tottering and it is going to fall,' declared Jagjivan Ram.[84] According to him, the caste system's presence in human society is a disgrace. He continued,

> It is a challenging task. I don't believe in passim. I feel this scourge can be readily eradicated if intercaste marriages are made mandatory. Additionally, it would be better if Hindus of lower castes dropped their caste names and adopted their birth names. The legal system must be vigilant and powerful. In some of my talks, I've advocated for a separate judiciary for this reason. But one thing is certain: as democracy and socialist forces gain power and science and technology advance, the caste system will eventually come to an end on its own. Even in a primitive culture, untouchability would be unacceptable. Our efforts will be fruitful because society is undergoing a quiet, peaceful revolution.[85]

Anything done by caste Hindus to improve the lives of *Harijans* on a governmental or public level, in Jagjivan Ram's opinion, is not in their best interests. But given that they have been compelled to live in subhuman conditions for generations and still, considered to be a repentance of their misdeeds.

The caste system prevented social mobility, stratified occupational talents, and impeded the growth of national integration, according to Chanchreek. India cannot develop as a result unless the caste system is effectively eradicated. A reform is necessary for the entire social system. The only way a caste-free society can be established is in this manner. Talking about democracy, socialism, and contemporary society, in my opinion, is worthless if the caste-based social structure is not altered. Many of the old moral and ethical standards will become frightening as society becomes more and more materialistic and technological. Modern society, on the other hand, is one that is devoid of superstition, rigidity, and social preconceptions, and is more liberal and scientific in outlook. The caste system has been maintained by forbidding marriages between members of other caste groups, shunning those who broke this rule, and denying the children of such marriages the right to inherit, membership in the caste, and a respectable standing in the society. The pillars that support the caste system must be removed to end it.[86] Jagjivan Ram believes that the caste system can be abolished if same-caste marriage is outlawed and intercaste marriage is encouraged, but, it may take some time.

ABOLITION OF UNTOUCHABILITY

Untouchability is viewed as the lowest form of human life in Indian culture. Jagjivan Ram to a crusade to end the practise of being untouchable. When he attended BHU and Arrah High School, he himself experienced untouchability. Hemlata Swaroop wrote that he underwent the humiliation first-handedly, and that an entire class of people had been subjected to as a result of the offensive caste system. As a young student, who endured the caste-based slurs and discriminatory behaviour of other boys both in the school and at BHU. Even though he was a science student, personal struggles led him to become a serious student of the humanities as well. His numerous writings, speeches, and utterances are full of fire that burned in his young heart and made him resolve to devote himself fully to improving the conditions of his people. He could comprehend the odd social and economic interplay that resulted in 20 per cent of India's people living in dehumanizing conditions, such as discrimination, denial, starvation, hunger, and public humiliation. Shudras and other members of the Depressed Classes, constituted the majority of landless farmers and craftsmen.[87]

The cause of their backwardness, according to Jagjivan Ram, were the social disabilities that prevented them from advancing economically and educationally. They did not lacked brains or a desire to learn because of God or nature, but they were not given the chance to pursue their education in public institutions. These primitive people were unable to set up their own plans for the education of their dependents and offspring. They were forced to live in segregation and lead wretched lives as domestic servants, landless farmworkers, or renters with no rights. It is important to realize that the issue is not solely social or economic due to decades of subjugation on both the fronts. The social issue is inextricably linked to the economic one, and social backwardness prevents even attempts at economic liberation from succeeding.[88]

According to Jagjivan Ram, the deep-rooted caste structure of the Hindu social order has a huge number of minor and great groups with varied degrees of status, respect, and control over socio-economic interactivity, primarily determined by birth. Millions of modest men from lower-castes have been oppressed and dehumanized, as a result of superiority based on birth or caste. They were regarded as semi-slaves or servile animals for generations and denied opportunities for social equality, natural justice, moral development, and economic prosperity.[89] Jagjivan Ram went on to argue that the Kshatriyas and the Vaishyas enjoyed respectability, and social and economic inclinations, whilst the Brahmins at the top of the caste hierarchy felt themselves as very respectable and highly positioned.

These three *varnas* quickly established themselves as a close-knit and a powerful clique in society since they had all of the land, riches, and social status from the very beginning. On the other hand, castes and groups that worked in physical labour or the arts were regarded as beneath society and considered untouchable. There were only the *Aryas* (Aryans) and the *Anaryas* in the early Vedic era. The *Aryas* were outsiders with a penchant for violence. They were exceedingly intelligent and skilled in the ways of combat. The Indus Valley Civilization's *Anaryas* were extremely sophisticated and peaceful people. They had mastered the technique of fostering societal harmony for a while and no longer needed brutish force or other tools of oppression and subjection of people. They had forgotten about fighting techniques and weapons, due to the extended period of peaceful life. These helpless Indians were attacked by the warlike *Aryas*. The *Aryas* came here after violently slaughtering or enslaving these people and capturing the entire Indus Valley. These extremely unfortunate slaves from the first invasion of India evolved into the untouchables of the Vedic era throughout time.[90]

The conflict between the Aryan conquerors and India's native population, he continued, accentuated not just cultural, but, also occupational and functional distinctions. The creation of the Shudras, a fourth caste, occurred and the *chaturvarna* society developed. The sages have sung about it being immortal. Gradually, men began to think that the order had been set by God. The conquered natives, also known as, *the Broken Men,* lost all rights to a place in the divinely ordained social structure and on the common lands. They were made to live outside the hamlet and were given jobs that were deplorable and lowly. They were known as the *Asparshyas* and they were the forbearers of the Untouchables. Despite being a part of the Hindu society, they did not belong to it because, they, were not given a place in the *chaturvarna* social caste ladder.[91] 'Ever since my undergraduate days, I was naturally worried about a lot of my fellow comrades', he wrote. 'I had been promoting the idea that Hindu society's socio-economic fabric was woven with untouchability's denial of opportunity and element of serfdom. As a result, I believed that it could only be destroyed by a thorough redesign of the socio-economic order.' It meant a revolution grander than any the world has seen thus far on the social, economic, and political fronts.[92] He asserted that some quick steps to stop the practise of untouchability included inter-caste marriages, mixed-race communities, dropping the inclusion of caste in last names, and psychological changes in thinking and mores. A significant contribution to this approach will also come from the radical reorganization of social and economic relations. He pointed out that the issue of untouchability was an economic one and should be addressed from that specific perspective. It is not because it offers a solution to their financial problems that Scheduled Castes and Scheduled Tribes are eager to obtain adequate representation in the government service, but, rather because it enhanced their prestige and provides them with a position in society.[93] The impoverished and underprivileged found in him a strong champion of their cause, according to K.C. Pant, as his stature in national affairs continued to increase. He yelled out against exploitation and injustice. He did it with conviction, without making any concessions, and without inciting animosity. His remarks affected many facets of society because of this tenor of voice.[94]

JAGJIVAN RAM'S SPEECH ON DALITS

In his letter, Jagjivan Ram extended his warmest congratulations on the *Harijan*'s liberation, which he claimed was long overdue, to the people of Hyderabad in general, and the community in particular. He maintained that the criminals of Hyderabad and their minions had been spurred to their wistful eyes to the exploitation of the *Harijans* for their own selfish and evil goals. The *Harijans* bravely resisted being used as pawns in these gangsters' schemes. Fortunately, the forces of liberation have destroyed their ambitious edifice and their vicious hold. These *Harijan* masses will now be able to partake with the rest of the population as the start of his new age in Hyderabad will enable them to break the bonds, which had so long held them in servitude, and saddened their souls.[95] New opportunities are knocking on Hyderabad and India's doors. They should place their fears aside and get ready to work with all the progressive forces to create a new system free from social, economic, and political exploitation.

Jagjivan Ram participated in the All-India Harijan Workers Convention's second session in New Delhi and demanded 'new sacrifices' for the nation's Scheduled Caste's economic liberation. Over 400 *Harijan* workers attended the Convention, and he asked them to educate the public about the Indian Constitution by outlining its ramifications. The Constitution would have been created in vain if the people, are not encouraged to realize the potential made possible by the grant of an equal right to vote. On 15 April 1950, the Convention got underway here to develop a common strategy and plan for the advancement of the *Harijan* masses.[96] Additionally, Jagjivan Ram stated that every member of the community must work to make all of the Constitution's provisions that were intended to improve their lot's effectiveness. Success comes to those who are committed to their goal and would rather die than live a life of shame. Anyone fighting for a just cause may overcome any force on earth. referring to the group of *Harijans* known as *Bhangis*. Only after the sweepers among them attained a respectable level of economic prosperity were the *Harijans* expected to have made significant advancements. He suggested the formation of a special committee and urged *Harijan* employees to pay more attention to the spread of education among the Scheduled Castes.[97]

The convention provided the Indian government with unwavering backing as it implemented the Indo-Pakistan agreement on minorities. The convention adopted a resolution that expressed concern over the racial unrest in East and West Bengal and cited the Indo-Pakistan Agreement as the sole and ideal solution to the issue. The convention guaranteed the government that it would have the 'support and confidence' of every Scheduled Caste member in whatever measures it took to combat communalism or to protect minorities. The convention stated in another resolution that improving the economic standing of the Scheduled Castes was the only way to free caste Hindus of what it called the 'untouchability complex'. Untouchability is a stain on Hindu society that cannot be removed by legislation that forbids it or permits temple entry. The resolution said that the change wouldn't occur until the government took actions to better the lives of *Harijans* by giving them more possibilities and special privileges in the commercial and industrial spheres.[98] The convention established a subcommittee to develop a ten-year strategy to bring Hindus and Scheduled Castes closer together and bridge the gap that now exists between them. The Convention required that a separate department be established at the Centre to coordinate and monitor the actions of various State Governments towards the uplift of the Harijan people. A resolution on the subject stated that the question of the Scheduled Castes and the Scheduled Tribes is an all-India question and no State can be allowed to go slow in this matter.[99]

In a statement to the convention, Sardar Patel stated that it was crucial that nothing be done that would further create division in Hindu society. Instead, we should work to put things in order so that the term 'Scheduled Castes' is no longer included in our Constitution or laws.[100] 'My *Harijan* friends know how precious their cause is to me and how zealously and devotionally I have been working in that cause,' he added. 'It has been my sincere goal to eradicate untouchability as quickly as possible, and in doing so, I am merely trying to emulate the great master who was the first to demonstrate a workable solution to this significant issue plaguing Hindu society.'[101] The idea that they belonged to a low or inferior society or caste should be eradicated, according to Mr Gadgil, from the minds of the *Harijans*.[102] The constitutional guarantees of equality of opportunity and status for all would become 'infructuous' in their eyes if they didn't comply. The session was presided over by N.S. Kajrolkar, president of the Bombay Provincial Depressed Classes League.

In an article titled, 'Friend of Labour and Harijan unique achievements of Jagjivan Ram, President, All-India Depressed Classes League,' which appeared in *The Bombay Chronicle* on 3 April 1953, it was stated that Jagjivan Ram had long been recognized throughout India as the person who had lit a fire in the hearts of millions of people. His exemplary character, courage, unwavering resolve, and unwavering sense of responsibility will forever serve as a beacon light for India. He has demonstrated how one can be wealthy in squalor, high in ugliness, and self-respecting while experiencing public humiliation. His great judgement and common sense have frequently rescued the nation, and he has unquestionably dedicated his life to serving the country. The irresistible drive to serve the nation and the underprivileged community overrode the temptations of higher education. Ram founded the Ravidas Sabha while still a student to promote the social progress of his community.[103]

As the first assessment of the political and social achievements of the *Harijans* in the post-Independence era, the convention of *Harijan* lawmakers and workers held in Nagpur has a unique significance. It is only inevitable that early successes fell short of the pledges and goals because the nation was dealing with Partition, refugee rehabilitation, and scarcity on all fronts. Despite this, the government has long-term plans like abolishing *zamindari* and other programmes specifically for the *Harijans*. Given that they make up the majority of the agrarian, industrial, and artisan classes, the *Harijans* stand to gain from the Five-Year Plan and community projects. In his presidential address, Jagjivan Ram lamented that despite the Constitution's abolition of untouchability and the prohibition of discrimination based on race, religion, or caste, social conventions, prejudices, and caste superstitions continued to control society and hampered the *Harijans'* progress. When Jawaharlal Nehru urged the *Harijans* to analyse their issues in relation to the bigger issue of eradicating poverty and unemployment in the nation and establishing a classless society based on equality of opportunity, the issue was elevated from a local to a national stage. Even though they are a disadvantaged group that needs specific assistance, India's overall affluence affects how the *Harijans* are treated and how far they can advance. They must fully fulfil their responsibility as the main producers, if they want to benefit from the freedom and all that it entails. In all spheres of life, Mahatma Gandhi waged a fierce fight against the evils of untouchability. He understood with clarity that political independence would be hollow until all classes and masses, including the *Harijans*, rose to the status of equals and shared in its rewards. By opening up temples to the *Harijans*, untouchability was eradicated at the highest level thanks to his inspiration. However, he saw even this significant accomplishment as the first in a succession of actions that would be taken to help the *Harijans* come into their own. His constructive programme was a war on poverty, disparity of wealth and status, and elevating the common man to the top. He connected the *Harijan* issue with the *Daridra Narayan* issue.[104] Even his suggestion that Congress meetings take place in small towns rather than major cities was intended to strengthen the national organization's support among the populace and ensure that the villagers benefited from the high costs associated with a Congress meeting. This was an example of mass contact.

When speaking to a crowd in Bezwada on his way to Madras on 26 December 1946, Jagjivan Bam, a Labour Member in the interim government, said: 'We have now achieved the threshold of our aim of *Purna Swaraj* by the message of "*ahimsa*", provided by Gandhi. He continued, 'We may have to step up the last fight to accomplish our dearly held aim. Nothing is more expensive than freedom, so we must always be prepared to battle and should not care how many of us die in the process of obtaining our nation's freedom.'[105] He continued by saying that no force on earth could prevent Indians from obtaining total independence. Turning to the *Harijans*, they were the oppressed and the exploited, and only freedom could bring them redemption.

They, therefore, represented a higher need for freedom than other groups. He urged them to keep up with the others in the impending battle.

Jagjivan Ram, while a Labour Member in the interim government, advised a delegation from the Madras Depressed Classes League that the *Harijans* in south India should strengthen the cause of All-India Depressed Classes League. The Labour Member further assured them that the *Harijans* would have adequate protections in the future Indian Constitution to guarantee their political, social, and economic rights. The delegation, which was led by League President, Dakshayani Velayudhan gave a thorough explanation of the League's past accomplishments to the Labour Members. They also asked Jagjivan to alert the Constituent Assembly and the Interim Government to the urgent necessity for statutory legislation on an All-India basis to remove the disabilities of *Harijans*.[106]

In his speech to the Harijan Legislature Convention in Nagpur on 30 October 1952, Jagjivan Ram noted the gap between the profession, law, and reality, despite the Constitution's Article 17 ban on Untouchability, and its guarantees.[107] Hence, he said that the Scheduled Castes' chronic and ongoing problems with poverty and plague persisted. The misery and suffering of the underprivileged classes will be the reason, communism, if it ever does, spreads throughout the nation. No other source or nation will be used to deliver it. The goal is to establish a society without classes that offer everyone the same possibilities. What else could the vision be than communism, and the downtrodden classes shouldn't worry about it since all they stand to lose is their chains? No class that fights to free itself from the bonds of servitude has ever been able to do so without experiencing excruciating pain and agony brought on by the oppressive party. It has consistently paid a high price for its freedom.[108]

Jagjivan Ram addressing the Scheduled Castes and Scheduled Tribes Social Welfare Association at Madras on 16 August 1972 urged an end to the caste system. He called for a frontal attack on the caste system to demolish it completely from Indian society.[109] According to him, even after 25 years of independence, the light of Independence has not reached millions upon millions of our compatriots. When the Scheduled Castes and Scheduled Tribes Social Welfare Association of

Madras congratulated him, he responded, 'The sadness of the whole situation is that 80 per cent of the population needs to beg from the other 20 per cent. Is there a tragedy more tragic than this? Despite vast sums being spent on numerous projects, money set aside for scholarships for the poor has remained the same.'[110] The *Socialist India* published an article on 18 September 1971, describing the plight of the *Harijans*. The editorial emphasizes the plight of the *Harijans* nationwide. The editorial also includes a passage from a speech given by the leader on 13 September 1971, in Gujarat, during which he called on members of the Backward Classes and *Harijans* to fight for their legitimate needs and place in society. He emphasized that entrenched interests were responsible for the creation of caste divisions and are currently responsible for maintaining them.

Jagjivan Ram went on to say that it is past the time for us to pay attention to this seriously unhealthy component of our culture. The government should not only pass laws but also tighten them up and vary the penalties accordingly. But the general public must also work to establish an environment in which every member of *Harijan* can talk and live freely without fear. He must not be reliant on the Hindu castes who have long denied him access to any independent source of income.[111]

This is one of the oldest schools of social work created in the country for postgraduate study in social work, according to Jagjivan Ram, who spoke at the annual day function of the Delhi School of Social Work, University of Delhi, on 8 March 1968. The injustice of our social order first attracted organized public attention during the fight for freedom. The elimination of social injustices and irrational practises, such as the segregation of women and prejudice against significant segments of the population on the basis of caste, language, and other factors, caught the attention of our leaders during the social reform movement led by Gandhi. Gandhi emphasizes the importance of addressing issues like rural reconstruction, tribal welfare, the eradication of caste discrimination, and Hindu-Muslim unity. In order to awaken the nation's conscience to the plight of a society built on disparities and depriving a very significant section of a life of self-respect, he assembled a group of committed workers of varying origins, education, and socio-economic backgrounds.[112]

Jagjivan Ram spoke at the Mahatma Gandhi Centenary Celebrations in New Delhi about the civil rights leadership and social change. While Gandhiji expanded and emphasized his understanding of caste and *varna* in the hope that the Hindu conscience would catch up with the new thinking, he believed that the eradication of Untouchability was an urgent problem. He researched the social history of India and the evolution of social consciousness.[113] 'Gandhi did not succeed in bringing about a dramatic transformation in the Hindu social order, which was impacted and corrupted by Islamic and Christian order as well,' he stated while summarizing his speech. But, Jagjivan Ram also argued that Gandhi did not strive for it. However, he, at the same time, 'did not put untouchables on the road to emancipation.'[114]

TEMPLE ENTRY MOVEMENT BY JAGJIVAN RAM

It was reported that *Harijans*, Jagjivan Ram would lead the first group of pilgrims to Tiruvarur Temple once the citadels of Gods were opened to him. The lower castes in Tamil Nadu broke open Hindu temples for worship. K. Koti Reddi, Minister for Hindu Religious Endowments, Madras, who arrived here led the *Harijan* men, women, and children for worship into the historic Sri Subramania Temple at Thiruparankundram, about four miles south of Madurai, whose doors had previously been closed to the *Harijan* community. The *Harijans* shouted *Mahatma Gandhi Ki Jai*. As the Minister and the *Harijan* party entered the temple to the sound of pipe music, the residents gathered in front and cheered loudly. The minister drove to Tallakulam in the north of the city, where he performed worship alongside a group of *Harijans* at Sri Prasanna Venkatesa's Vaishnava Temple. The Minister raised the Congress flag in front of the temple as he led the *Harijan* inside. It was recorded when *Harijans* entered the two temples. The Minister next went to the Sri Meenakshi Amman Temple, which was the first in Tamil Nadu to be accessible to *Harijans* seven years ago. *Harijan* was granted access to the well-known Sankarakoil Temple Wednesday morning under the direction of Reddi.[115] 'The excitement of the people to admit *Harijans* into the temples is adequately evident in the opening of a number of temples recently', Reddi told the press.[116] The Provincial Government is currently debating whether or not to capitalize on the public's enormous enthusiasm by ensuring that all legal barriers preventing *Harijan* friends from participating in temple worship are removed. According to the reports, Jagjivan Ram began his visit to south India by travelling in Grant Trunk Express. He will go to technical centres and employment exchanges. In addition to them, he will visit a lot of temples that recently opened their doors to *Harijans*. He will also speak at a number of public gatherings organized by the province's Congress Committee and *Harijans* in various locations. On 1 January, Jagjivan Ram, a Labour Member of the Government of India, will declare open to *Harijans* the old and historic temple of Sri Thiagarajaswami at Tiruvarur in Tanjore District. The Mahatma gives his blessings by stating, 'My blessings to temple admission movement should be presumed. In this situation, I am working alone against the odds.'[117] Gandhi gave this message to the United Press of Media, who then relayed it to B.S. Murthy, Parliamentary Secretary and President.

I have previously mentioned that Jagjivan Ram was the main author of the resolutions adopted by the Hindu Mahasabha. These resolutions aimed to provide equal access to all public facilities and institutions to all Hindus, regardless of caste or creed. This gave *Harijans* more opportunities to worship nearby temple gates, allowing them to breathe easier. Brindaban Das, however, describes him as a man of the people who always prioritized the needs of the working class, farmers, and underprivileged, regardless of his position. His extensive knowledge and experience enabled him to excel in every role he held, and he was deserving of every honour. His supporters hope he will continue to lead the nation and serve it for years to come.

NOTES

1. B.R. Ambedkar, *What Congress and Gandhi Have Done to The Untouchables*, Thacker & Co, Bombay, 1945.
2. Kanshi Ram, *The Chamcha Age: An Era of the Stooges*, Vedic Mudranalaya, New Delhi, 1982, pp. 89-116.
3. In these works, Omvedt argues that Gandhi idealized the fourfold *varna* system as the core of the Hindu society, and thus, his conservative and reformist stance failed to help the lower caste people. Gail Omvedt, *Dalits and the Democratic Revolution: Dr. Ambedkar and the Dalit Movement in Colonial India*, SAGE, New Delhi, 2014. See also, Gail

Omvedt, 'Gandhi and the Pacification of the Indian National Revolution', *Bulletin of Concerned Asian Scholars*, vol. 5, no. 1, 1973, pp. 2-9.

4. Roy dismissed Gandhi's efforts to tackle the caste issue by referring to him as the latest in a long line of privileged caste Hindu reformers. Roy slammed Gandhi's deception, believing that Gandhi was effectively reducing the subject of caste exploitation to the question of removing stigmas associated with the acts of bhangis. See Arundhati Roy, *The Doctor and the Saint: Caste, Race and the Annihilation of Caste, The Debate between B.R. Ambedkar and M.K. Gandhi*, Haymarket Books, Chicago.
5. Kancha Ilaiah Shepherd, 'Gandhi was not a Caste Abolitionist', *The Week*, 22 June 2019.
6. Sagarika Ghose, 'The Dalit in India', *Social Research*, vol. 70, no. 1, 2003, p. 97.
7. Anupama Rao, *The Caste Question: Dalits and the Politics of Modern India*, Permanent Black, Ranikhet, 2010. In her first chapter, Rao extensively focuses on the contributions of Jyotiba Phule, Gopal Baba Walangkar, and Shivram Janba Kamble. See also, Rosalind O'Hanlon, *Caste, Conflict and Ideology: Mahatma Jotirao Phule and Low Caste Protest in Nineteenth Century Western India*, Cambridge University Press, Cambridge, 1985.
8. K.V. Cybil, 'Narayan Guru and Formation of Political Society in Kerala', in Simhadri Somanaboina and Akhileshwari Ramagoud (eds.), *The Routledge Handbook of the Other Backward Classes in India*, Routledge, London, 2022.
9. Eleanor Zelliot, 'Learning the Use of Political Means: The Mahars of Maharashtra', in Rajni Kothari (ed.), *Caste in Indian Politics*, Orient Longman, New Delhi, 1970, pp. 29-69.
10. Dilip M. Menon, 'Intimations of Equality: Shrines and Politics in Malabar, 1900-1924', in Sumit Sarkar and Tanika Sarkar (eds.), *Caste in Modern India: A Reader*, vol. I, Permanent Black, Ranikhet, pp. 474-510. See also, Robin Jeffrey, 'Temple-Entry Movement in Travancore, 1860-1940', *Social Scientist*, vol. 4, no. 8, 1976, pp. 3-27.
11. Abhay Kumar Dubey, *Kanshi Ram: Ek Alochanatmak Adhyayan*, Rajkamal Prakashan, New Delhi, 1997.
12. Mark Juergensmeyer, *Religious Rebels in the Punjab: The Social Vision of the Untouchables*, Navayana, New Delhi, 2009.
13. Ghanshyam Shah, 'Anti-Untouchability Movements', in Vimal Shah (ed.), *Removal of Untouchability: Proceedings of a Seminar*, Department of Sociology, Gujarat University, 1980.

14. Nishikant Kolge, *Gandhi Against Caste*, Oxford University Press, New Delhi, 2018.
15. Rajmohan Gandhi, 'Response to Arundhati Roy', *EPW,* vol. 50, no. 30, 2015.
16. Aishwary Kumar, *Radical Equality: Ambedkar, Gandhi and the Risk of Democracy*, Stanford University Press, Stanford, 2015.
17. Kolge, op. cit., p. 166.
18. Ramnarayan S. Rawat, 'Making Claims for Power: A New Agenda in Dalit Politics of Uttar Pradesh: 1946-48', *Modern Asian Studies,* vol. 37, no. 3, 2003, p. 596.
19. Oliver Mendelsohn, ' "A Harijan Elite?": The Lives of Some Untouchable Politician', *EPW,* vol. 21, no. 12, 1986.
20. Ibid.
21. D.R. Nagaraj, 'The Flaming Feet and Other Essays: The Dalit Movement in India', Permanent Black, Ranikhet, 2010, p. 219.
22. S.R. Bakshi, *Jagjivan Ram: The Harijan Leader*, Anmol Publications, New Delhi, 1992, p. 179.
23. Ibid., p. 17.
24. S.K. Malik and Ankit Tomar, *Revisiting Modern Indian Thought: Themes and Perspectives*, Routledge, New York, 2022, p. 128.
25. Ibid., pp. 40-1.
26. Ibid., p. 18.
27. Jagjivan Ram, *Caste Challenge in India*, Vision Books, New Delhi, 1980, p. 22.
28. Peter Friedlander, 'Reassessing Religion and Politics in the Life of Jagjivan Ram', *MDPI Journals*, vol. 11, no. 5, 2020, p. 1.
29. Ibid.
30. Jagjivan Ram, 'His Select Speeches in Parliament', in *Babu Jagjivan Ram in Parliament: A Commemorative Volume*, Lok Sabha Secretariat, New Delhi, 2005, p. 2.
31. H.H. Wilson, *Siva Narayanis: In Sketch of the Religious Sects of the Hindus*, Trubner & Company, London, 1861, pp. 358-9.
32. Grierson George Abraham, 'The Siva Narayanis', *The Journal of the Royal Asiatic Society of Great Britain and Ireland,* 1918, pp. 114-17.
33. Meira Kumar, 'My Father's Childhood', in *Babu Jagjivan Ram in Parliament: A Commemorative Volume*, Lok Sabha Secretariat, New Delhi 2005, pp. 34-8.
34. Eleanor Zelliot and Rohini Mokashi-Punekar (eds.), *Untouchable Saints: An Indian Phenomenon*, Manohar, New Delhi, 2005, p. 14.

35. Gail Omvedt, *Seeking Begumpura: The Social Vision of Anticaste Intellectuals,* Navayana Publishing, New Delhi, 2008, p. 23.
36. Parshuram Chaturvedi, *Uttar Bharat Ki Sant Parampara,* Bharati Bhandar, Allahabad, 1972, pp. 633-50.
37. Johannes Beltz, *Mahar, Buddhist and Dalit: Religious Conversion and Socio-Political Emancipation*, Manohar, New Delhi, 2005, p. 100.
38. Indrani Ram, *Milestones: A Memoir*, Penguin, New Delhi, 2010, p. 49.
39. Nau Nihal Singh, *Jagjivan Ram: Symbol of Social Change*, Sundeep Prakashan, Delhi, 1977, p. 37.
40. Hitendra K. Patel, 'Aspects of Mobilizations of Dalits in Bihar (1913-1952)', *Contemporary Voice of Dalit*, vol. 9, no. 1, 2017, pp. 63-72.
41. Om Prakash Maurya, *Babu Jagjivan Ram*, translated by Rupali Kishore, Publications Division, Ministry of Information and Broadcasting, New Delhi, 2010, p. 3.
42. Sant Saran, *Babu Jagjivan Ram Aur Dalit Andolan,* Vani Prakashan, New Delhi, 2017, p. 137.
43. Maurya, op. cit., pp. 30-1.
44. Ibid.
45. *The Bombay Chronicle*, 22 September 1946.
46. Address by former Lok Sabha Speaker, Meira Kumar as the part of fourth Babu Jagjivan Ram Memorial Lecture held on 6 April, 2011, please also see Sudarshan Ramabadran and Guru Prakash Paswan, *Makers of Modern Dalit History*, Penguin Books, New Delhi, 2021, p. 11.
47. Bakshi, op. cit., pp. 179-80.
48. Beltz, op. cit., pp. 50-8.
49. Trilok Nath, *Politics of the Depressed Classes,* Deputy Publications, Delhi, 1987, p. 194.
50. Indrani Ram, op. cit., pp. 52-3.
51. Saran, op. cit., p. 137.
52. Sanjay Paswan and Pramanshi Jaideva (eds.), 'Jagjivan Ram: Champion of Dalits', in *Encyclopaedia of Dalits in India: Leaders,* vol. 4, Kalpaz Publications, Delhi, 2004, pp. 111-12.
53. *The Bombay Chronicle*, 16 December 1946, vol. XXXIV, no. 287, p. 7.
54. Ibid., 31 August 1946, vol. XXXIV, no. 208, p. 7.
55. Ibid.
56. Ibid.
57. Christophe Jaffrelot, *India's Silent Revolution: The Rise of the Lower Castes in Northern India*, C. Hurst & Co., London, 2003, p. 98.
58. Ibid., p. 102.

59. Oliver Mendelsohn and Marika Vicziany, *The Untouchables*, Cambridge University Press, Cambridge, 1998, pp. 207-8.
60. Sanjay Paswan and Pramanshi Jaideva (eds.), op. cit., p. 15.
61. Ibid., pp. 82-91.
62. Badri Narayan, *Kanshiram: Leader of the Dalits,* Penguin Books, New Delhi, 2014, p. 68.
63. Meena Charanda, 'Jagjivan Ram', in Suratha K. Malik and Ankit Tomar (eds.), *Revisiting Modern Indian Thought: Themes and Perspectives,* Routledge, London, 2022, p. 129.
64. Nau Nihal Singh, op. cit., p. 37.
65. Ibid.
66. Bakshi, op. cit., pp. 33-34.
67. Paswan and Jaideva (eds.), op. cit., p. 83.
68. Ibid.
69. NMML, K.R. Malkani Papers, Correspondence with Jagjivan Ram on 12 March 1947.
70. B.M. Turadagi, 'Dr. Jagjivan Ram's Life and Achievements: A Critical Analysis', unpublished Ph.D. thesis, Department of Political Science, Karnataka University, 2018, p. 194.
71. K.L. Chanchreek, *Babu Jagjivan Ram: A Nation Builder*, vol. 1, Shree Publications, New Delhi, 2006, p. 250.
72. *Journal of Parliamentary Information*, vol. LVII, no. 3, September 2011, New Delhi, Lok Sabha Secretariat, Government of India, pp. 261-2.
73. Prabhakar Machave, *Sri Jagjivan Ram: The Man and Thoughts*, Saumya Publications, Bombay, 1977, p. 84.
74. Devendra Prasad Sharma, *Jagjivan Ram: The Man and the Times,* Indian Book Company, New Delhi, 1994, pp. 38-9.
75. *Babu Jagjivan Ram in Parliament: A Commemorative Volume*, New Delhi: Lok Sabha Secretariat, 2005, p. 10.
76. *Babu Jagjivan Ram: A Builder of Strong India*, Social Welfare Department, Karnataka Government, 2007, p. 54.
77. Ibid., p. 63.
78. Turagadi, op. cit., p. 181.
79. Indira Ram, op. cit., p. 110.
80. Jagjivan Ram, op. cit., p. 56.
81. Turagadi, op. cit., p. 182.
82. Ramesh Chandra and Sangh Mitra, *Dalit Identity in the New Millenium: Caste System in India,* Commonwealth Publication, New Delhi, 2003, p. 78.

83. Jagjivan Ram, op. cit., p. 56.
84. *Babu Jagjivan Ram: A Builder of Strong India*, op. cit., p. 62.
85. Chanchreek, op. cit., p. 111.
86. Ibid., p. 112.
87. Ibid., p. 83.
88. Ibid., p. 84.
89. Jagjivan Ram, op. cit., p. 104.
90. Ibid., pp. 104-5.
91. Ibid., p. 10.
92. Ibid., p. 45.
93. *Babu Jagjivan Ram: A Builder of Strong India*, op. cit., p. 64.
94. K.C. Pant, *Babu Jagjivan Ram in Parliament: A Commemorative Volume*, Lok Sabha Secretariat, New Delhi, 2005, p. 74.
95. *The Bombay Chronicle*, 20 September, 1948.
96. Ibid. 16 April 1950.
97. Ibid.
98. Ibid.
99. Ibid
100. Ibid.
101. Ibid.
102. Ibid.
103. Ibid., 3 April 1953.
104. Ibid., 9 November 1952.
105. Ibid., 28 December 1946, vol. XXXIV, no. 298, p. 4.
106. Ibid., 4 January 1947, vol. XXXV, no. 3, p. 4.
107. Bakshi, op. cit., p. 177.
108. Ibid., pp. 177-8.
109. A.C. Sinha, *Struggles and Achievements: Babu Jagjivan Ram Commemoration Volume*, Alka Prakashan, Delhi, 1973, p. 181; See also *Motherland* (New Delhi), 16 August 1972, p. 4.
110. Ibid., see also *Indian Express* (New Delhi), 16 August 1972, p. 4.
111. Ibid., see also *Socialist India* (New Delhi), 18 September 1971, p. 1.
112. Ibid., pp. 182-3.
113. Ibid., p. 183.
114. Ibid.
115. *The Bombay Chronicle,* 25 December 1946, vol. XXXIV, no. 295, p. 1
116. Ibid.
117. Ibid., 27 December 1946, vol. XXXIV, no. 297.

7

The Repentant Politician
Jagjivan Ram, Caste Politics, and His Departure

Jagjivan Ram, originated from the rural regions of Bihar, a state in India characterized by a pervasive caste system that restricted opportunities and fostered prejudice. Despite these challenging circumstances, Jagjivan Ram exhibited unwavering determination and embarked on a relentless pursuit of his goals, ultimately achieving unparalleled achievement as a leader in contemporary Indian history. He was a figure of inspiration in the fight for freedom, displaying adeptness in parliamentary affairs, exhibiting innovative leadership as a Union Minister and Deputy Prime Minister, and serving as a steadfast advocate for the rights of many underprivileged individuals in India. It is widely acknowledged that in 1928, Jagjivan Ram relocated to Calcutta with the intention of pursuing higher education. However, it was during this period that he became actively involved in the realm of politics. He gainfully exhibited a heightened level of engagement in matters pertaining to social changes and politics.

During his time as a student at Vidyasagar College, Jagjivan Ram orchestrated a gathering, known as a *sammelan*, which brought together labourers and individuals from lower castes in Wellington Square.[1] Indrani Devi reported that the demonstration witnessed a substantial turnout of approximately 30,000 to 35,000 individuals, indicating a notable level of success as a public gathering. In his address, he emphasized the interdependence of all individuals in determining the progress of the nation. 'It is imperative for us to remain vigilant regarding potential adversaries and maintain a high level of organization.'[2] In August 1929, the All-India Ravidas Sabha was established by the individual in question with the aim of disseminating the notion that Dalits ought to engage in self-organization, pursue education, and abstain from alcohol consumption.

The Congress leaders closely monitored his actions and were duly impressed by his activities. Following the completion of his Bachelor of Science degree, he wholeheartedly dedicated himself to engaging in activities aimed at promoting the advancement of Dalits. He established his objective by contemplating the path he intended to pursue, which encompassed two distinct goals: advocating for the liberation of the nation and promoting social reform and equality. Jagjivan Ram founded the Akhil Bharatiya Ravidas Mahasabha in Calcutta in 1934, and subsequently launched the All-India Depressed Classes League in 1935. The primary aim of forming this association was to involve the marginalized classes in the struggles for liberation, while also advocating for Dalit leaders to unite not only for social reform but also to demand equitable political representation. In the year 1937, he founded the Khetihar Mazdoor Sabha, an organization aimed at promoting the advancement and empowerment of impoverished labour. On 19 October 1935, a significant event unfolded in India as Jagjivan Ram presented himself before the Hammond Committee in Ranchi, advocating for the enfranchisement of Dalits.[3] This moment holds historical significance in the country's narrative.

In December 1928, Jagjivan Ram had the opportunity to witness and attentively observe Mahatma Gandhi deliver a speech during the Indian National Congress gathering held in Calcutta. Gandhi's teachings and actions had a profound impact on the enlightenment of several individuals. Jagjivan Ram was duly impressed and significantly affected by the beliefs and ideology espoused by Gandhi.

Subsequently, in 1935, Jagjivan Ram assumed membership in the Congress Party. He had his initial encounter with Gandhi during the latter's visit to Bihar, where he aimed to engage with the individuals affected by the significant earthquake of 1934. He was engaged in humanitarian efforts to provide relief to the populace. Gandhi travelled the calamity-stricken region in the company of him, and a multitude of individuals hailing from diverse regions across the nation. Jagjivan

Ram was assigned the responsibility of overseeing the fulfilment of various dietary requirements within a diverse group. Additionally, a newsletter was disseminated to provide updates on relief operations to funders, sympathizers, and workers. The strong association with Gandhi served as a catalyst for his early involvement in the war for independence and the upliftment of marginalized individuals who were subjected to a lower social status due to the caste system. In the year 1936, Jagjivan Ram received a nomination to serve as a member of the Bihar Legislative Council. Subsequently, in 1937, he participated as a candidate representing the All-India Depressed Classes League and successfully secured a seat in the Bihar Legislative Assembly. Furthermore, he played a pivotal role in securing victories for all the 14 reserved constituencies, which were contested by candidates from the All-India Depressed Classes League.[4]

The present analysis pertains to the primary objective of Jagjivan Ram as a Dalit politician and the reasons for his affiliation with the Indian National Congress. The individual exhibited a high level of clarity and objectivity in expressing his desires. He had been affiliated with the Congress Party for an extended period of time. However, an inquiry emerged on the reasons for Jagjivan Ram's departure from the Congress Party. Initially, his intention was to depart from Congress or he was compelled to depart from Congress. Were the circumstances a determining factor in the decision to leave Congress, or was time the primary factor?

Jagjivan Ram emerged as a prominent figure in the Dalit community, attaining national leadership status. Despite garnering significant respect from various religious, social, and political entities, he had a strong affinity towards the Dalit people. One aspect of his focus was to explore strategies for establishing a connection between the Dalit community and the Congress Party. He had observed that the policies of the Congress Party also aimed at the upliftment of the Dalit community. He expressed a lack of support for the success of the independent Dalit movement among the Hindu community. Gandhi had prior knowledge of his thoughts, as Dr Rajendra Prasad had apprised him of his notable contributions in the field of humanitarianism. Mahatma Gandhi delegated to him the task of overseeing the Harijan Sevak Sangh.[5] Babu Jagjivan Ram willingly embraced this responsibility, and established a direct association with Mahatma Gandhi, the freedom movement, and the initiative aimed at uplifting the marginalized class.

Following the tenure of Jawaharlal Nehru, the subsequent Prime Minister and the potential retention of political dominance by the Nehru family inside the Congress Party are subjects of inquiry. The inquiry at hand was of considerable magnitude, and it is crucial to ascertain the stance adopted by Jagjivan Ram. Upon analysing the prevailing political climate within the Congress Party, it becomes apparent why Jagjivan Ram made the decision to tender his resignation from the aforementioned political organization. In 1959, the Congress Working Committee had initially chosen S. Nijalingappa as the future President of the Congress Party. However, this choice was overridden, and Indira Gandhi was appointed as the president instead. This appointment was accompanied by the implementation of the Kamaraj Plan, which involved the resignation of top Congress ministers to aid Indira Gandhi's ascent through the party hierarchy.

In adherence to the Kamaraj Plan, a prominent member of the cabinet voluntarily relinquished their ministerial position, while Jagjivan Ram similarly resigned and assumed the role of a party worker. Lal Bahadur Shastri assumed the position of Prime Minister due to the support garnered from the majority of the Congress Working Committee. Shastri made a public declaration of his government, consisting solely of three individuals: Neelam Sanjiva Reddy, S.K. Patil, and Indira Gandhi. The move faced opposition from Jagjivan Ram's supporters, who protested against it. However, he skilfully navigated the situation, recognizing the presence of a potential conspiracy within Congress. The Kamaraj Plan was perceived as a superficial measure.[6] According to the analysis provided by Indrani Devi, individuals have shifted their focus from party concerns to self-oriented considerations. Within the States, a notable lack of unity, accompanied by negative emotions such as ill feelings, jealousy, and even hate, was observed among members of Congress. Limited efforts have been made to rejuvenate the political party. The presence of internal divisions, rivalries, and hostilities inside the Congress Party ultimately benefited the opposition parties.[7]

The demise of Lal Bahadur Shastri in 1966 came as a sudden and unforeseen event, leading to the appointment of Gulzarilal Nanda, who held the position of Home Minister, as the interim Prime Minister. The Congress Party consisted of three Prime Ministerial contenders, namely Nanda, Indira Gandhi, and Morarji Desai. Subsequently, Nanda departed from the scene, while Desai maintained his conviction that it was imperative to engage in the struggle. The support rendered by Jagjivan Ram proved to be crucial, ultimately culminating in his endorsement of Indira Gandhi. Mrs. Gandhi garnered a total of 355 votes, while Desai secured 169 votes. Subsequently, she assumed the position of Prime Minister. She summoned Jagjivan to her apartment. Indrani Devi provided a detailed account of Jagjivan Ram's return home, noting that he arrived within a short span of time, visibly distressed and exhibiting a countenance marked by intense rage. The latter expressed that he was assigned the labour ministry, and while he did not object to this allocation, he noted that he was being presented with a subordinate role inside the cabinet, which was considerably lower in rank compared to his previous post. He had subsequently declined. He found himself rendered speechless.[8] However, subsequent to this occurrence, individuals expressing good intentions urged him to consider accepting the cabinet position, suggesting that any objections may be voiced at a later time. Both Indrani Devi and Meira Kumar expressed opposition, but he himself acquiesced albeit with a sense of discontent.

An internal conflict arose between Morarji Desai and Jagjivan Ram when the latter expressed his support for Indira Gandhi's bid for the position of the Prime Minister. Jagjivan Ram expressed dissatisfaction upon receiving notification from Finance Minister, Morarji Desai, on his failure to submit income tax returns for a period of ten years. It should be noted that Jagjivan Ram did not get any warning from the income tax department. According to his wife, it may be inferred that Morarji Desai harboured feelings of envy towards her husband since the inception of their relationship, perhaps stemming from their political rivalry.[9] Given these conditions, Jagjivan Ram had a sense of indignation and contemplated submitting his resignation. Indira Gandhi urged him to refrain from resigning due to the fact that certain cabinet ministers had not fulfilled their obligation to file income tax returns. During that period, the syndicate exhibited significant influence and was characterized by its division into two distinct factions. The syndicate exhibited opposition towards the progressive programmes implemented by the Government and the Congress. Desai emerged as a major leader inside the syndicate. If Jagjivan Ram were to retire, it is likely that the syndicate would derive advantages from the ensuing power dynamics. Gandhi possessed an understanding of the significant stature held by Jagjivan Ram as a prominent leader of the Dalit community, recognizing his crucial contribution to her successful election as the prime minister. Two distinct factions arose, each characterized by divergent beliefs, perspectives, and frequent disagreements on various matters. One segment, referred to as the syndicate, comprised Patil, Nijalingappa, Desai, Chadrabhan Gupta, Reddy, Kamaraj, and others. The progressive faction, comprising notable figures such as Indira Gandhi, Jagjivan Ram, Fakhruddin Ali Ahmed, and various other personalities, formed the opposition side.[10]

Following the untimely demise of President Dr. Zakir Hussain on 3 May 1969, the imperative arose to initiate the process of electing a successor to assume the presidential office. The All-India Congress Committee convened in Bangalore on 9 July 1969. The plan for the nationalization of banks was presented by Indira Gandhi, but, it faced opposition from the syndicate. The parliamentary board put out Neelam Sanjiva Reddy as a candidate for the position of president; however, Indira Gandhi expressed her opposition to this nomination. She nominated Jagjivan Ram as a potential candidate for the position of president. Morarji Desai expressed opposition to the nomination of Jagjivan Ram for the position of president. Indira Gandhi was cognizant of the syndicate's inclination to reject any name she put forth. Ultimately, the selection of a new president yielded no outcome. The members of the Congress Party included Indira Gandhi as the chairman, along with Y.R Chavan, Jagjivan Ram, Fakhruddin Ali Ahmed, S.K. Patil, and Morarji Desai. The astuteness of Indira Gandhi's diplomatic manoeuvre was evident. Instead of V.V. Giri, she recommended the name of Jagjivan Ram.[11] This occurrence resulted in a rift between him and the syndicate. Mrs. Gandhi's primary objective was to strategically leverage Jagjivan Ram's influence in order to secure electoral victories in the future. Nageshwar Dwivedi congratulated him for becoming the President, but at the same time mentioned in a letter to him that he was going to wear *kanton ka taaj* (A Crown of Thorns).[12]

V.V. Giri both served as the acting President and the Vice-President of India. On 12 July 1969, the Congress parliamentary board officially announced Reddy as their nominated candidate for the position of President. Furthermore, Giri had officially announced his campaign for the Presidency. Mrs. Gandhi provided reassurance to Giri by providing complete and unwavering support. Mrs. Gandhi and Jagjivan Ram expressed their opposition to the syndicate's discretionary judgement. Giri tendered his resignation from the position of acting president, while Reddy similarly resigned from the post of Speaker of Lok Sabha. Chief Justice of the Supreme Court Mohammad Hidayatullah assumed the responsibility of acting as the President. Both Reddy and Giri submitted their nomination papers on 29 July 1969. Jagjivan Ram held a neutral stance. Indrani Devi asserts that a significant statement made by Giri was, 'I have assumed the role of a candidate due to the dictates of my conscience, guided by my personal inner voice'.[13] Jagjivan Ram played a pivotal role in this context by urging all legislators from each province to exercise their voting rights based on their individual conscience. However, the legislators interpreted his appeal as an imperative to exercise their individual conscience when casting their votes.

During the electoral proceedings, Neelam Sanjiva Reddy comprehended the unattainability of triumph. During this period, the President of the Congress, Nijalingappa, sought the assistance of the Swatantra Party and the Jana Sangha in favour of Neelam Sanjiva Reddy. Jagjivan Ram expressed his disapproval of the individual's actions as being contrary to the party's interests, and subsequently dispatched a letter on 11 August, requesting the Congress President to provide clarification regarding the individual's anti-party conduct. Nijalingappa's response to the concerns highlighted by Jagjivan Ram was not deemed satisfactory. In the present matter, a syndicate meeting was convened whereby it was determined that the Congress President made a decision based on personal interests rather than the interests of the party. Mrs. Gandhi presented a letter to the president of the Congress Party, which made a reference to Jagjivan Ram's letter. She expressed that participating in this election served as a method to safeguard our principles. The act of voting serves as an expression of solidarity with these core principles.

> It is inconceivable for me to envision a scenario in which I would emerge victorious in an electoral contest by disregarding our core principles and beliefs. Given the prevailing circumstances and in light of constitutional considerations, I am of the opinion that it would be inappropriate to issue a direction sometimes referred to as a 'whip'.[14]

It is evident that Mrs. Gandhi did not endorse the actions of Nijalingappa, who held the position of Congress President. The declaration of the election date occurred on 16 August 1969, at which point two factions within the Congress Party cast their votes in support of their preferred candidate. Subsequently, the counting date was announced to take place on 20 August 1969. After tabulating the votes, Giri garnered a total of 420,077 votes, while Reddy secured 405,427 votes.[15] The former became victorious in the election, assuming the position of President of India. Jagjivan Ram played a pivotal role in shaping the outcome of this election.

On 21 August, individuals who were in favour of the syndicate's Presidential candidate convened with the Congress President, urging him to initiate measures against Mrs. Gandhi, Ahmed, and Jagjivan Ram. Additionally, they expressed the call for the removal of individuals from the membership of the Congress Party. The Congress Working Committee convened a meeting wherein, prominent members such as Kamaraj, Patil, Nijalingappa, Desai, and others expressed their endorsement for taking action against Jagjivan Ram, Ahmed, and Mrs. Gandhi. However, the majority of the Congress Working Committee members did not lend their support to this course of action. Jagjivan Ram expressed his dissent with the policies of Nijalingappa and his adherents in a public manner, which subsequently became a topic of discussion in the debates held in the Lok Sabha.

The crisis developed when the Congress President, Nijalingappa, dispatched a letter to Jagjivan Ram, outlining the reasons for his potential expulsion from the party due to his contravention of the Congress' regulations. This identical letter was also sent to Indira

Gandhi and Fakhruddin Ali Ahmed. Ultimately, the president of the Congress Party decided to dismiss three members from its ranks. The Congress Party had a division, resulting in the emergence of two factions. The original Congress faction became often referred to as Congress (O) or organization, attracting the participation of esteemed senior officials. The formation of the new Congress Party, officially named the All-India Nationalist Congress (I), was characterized by the inclusion of only three prominent leaders: Jagjivan Ram, Ahmed, and Mrs. Gandhi. The syndicate perceived itself as possessing significant authority; however, the complete control over the administration rested with the newly established Congress. Chidambaram Subramaniam assumed the role of interim president within the newly-formed Congress Party. In the final week of December 1969, a significant Congress central committee conference took place in Bombay. Jagjivan Ram assumed the presidency of the Congress (I) through a democratic election process.[16] The new Congress Party steadily emerged as the dominant political force in India, while concurrently necessitating the neutralization or dissolution of the old Congress Party.

The declaration of a general Lok Sabha elections occurred in 1971. Indrani Devi considers that Jagjivan Ram acquired knowledge of a highly influential campaign that was initiated against Mrs. Gandhi. A faction of the Brahmin community expressed the viewpoint that Jagjivan Ram was a political adversary of Mrs. Gandhi, and hence advocated against casting ballots in his favour. Numerous rumours were disseminated, although he chose to disregard them. Following the publication of the outcome, the Congress (I) secured a majority. The Lok Sabha consisted of a total of 520 seats, with the Congress (I) party securing 352 seats and the Congress (O) party obtaining a mere 16 seats. Subsequently, Jagjivan Ram resolved the ambiguity surrounding his relationship with Mrs. Gandhi, thereby putting out the nomination of Mrs. Gandhi for the position of leader. She assumed the position of Prime Minister of India, while Jagjivan Ram was appointed as the Defence Minister.[17] Nageshwar Dwivedi compared the latter with the Hindu deity Hanuman for his shrewd tactics, bravery, and humble attitude.[18]

Following the attainment of a majority during the tenure of

Jagjivan Ram as the president of the new Congress Party, he made the decision to relinquish his presidency of the Congress (I) Party. One perspective is that Jagjivan Ram made a deliberate choice to prioritize matters pertaining to national defence. Was there any external or internal pressure exerted on the incumbent party president to vacate their position? The current state of knowledge on this matter remains uncertain. Despite effectively managing both the positions of party president and Minister of Defence, he encountered no significant challenges. The presence of escalating cross-border threats may potentially contribute to the situation at hand.

The commencement of the civil war in Pakistan occurred in March 1971. The region of East Pakistan expressed a desire for autonomy and independence from West Pakistan. The conflict gradually escalated, with India providing indirect support to the East Pakistani population in their resistance against the Pakistani army, which had resorted to terrible violence against civilians. A significant proportion of individuals departed from their respective countries and migrated to India. A significant influx of refugees seeking safety has been observed in the Indian border states, namely West Bengal, Assam, Tripura, and Meghalaya. In an abrupt turn of events, Pakistan initiated an attack on India, instigating the India-Pakistan conflict. Despite its relatively short duration of fourteen days, the war concluded with Pakistan being pushed to surrender. During that period, P.N. Haksar, an adviser to Indira Gandhi, advocated for a quick cessation of hostilities on the Western front. Jagjivan Ram argued that given India's current possession of both moral and military superiority, it would be unwise to pursue a course of action that would embarrass and inflict additional harm upon West Pakistan.[19]

The much decorated, Gen. Sam Manekshaw expressed agreement with the notion that a unilateral ceasefire was the appropriate course of action. Following the dissatisfaction of Defence Minister, who had been largely disregarded by Mrs. Gandhi throughout the crisis and had his voice suppressed, the Cabinet supported the concept of exercising restraint. Consequently, she publicly declared an immediate ceasefire on the Western front. In response to speculations regarding the influence of superpowers and the perceived threat posed by Nixon's Seventh Fleet on India's decision to declare a ceasefire, Indira Gandhi confidently asserted during an interview with the *Time* magazine that the decision was autonomously made within India. She further emphasized her personal resilience against external pressures, affirming her steadfastness in not succumbing to any form of coercion, be it from individuals or states.[20]

The Internal War or Internal Emergency of 1975 marked a significant event that brought about a pivotal shift in the political trajectory of Jagjivan Ram. This turning point led him to make the decision to disassociate himself from the Congress Party, an organization in which he had ascended to considerable prominence, in order to advocate for the restoration of democratic principles. The commencement of the second phase of his political trajectory occurred in 1977. Following the demise of Ahmed, he tendered his resignation from the Cabinet as a Minister of Irrigation and Agriculture and defected from the Congress Party. Subsequently, he established a new political party known as the Congress for Democracy, which promptly aligned itself with the Janata Party. Despite his extensive affiliation with the Union Cabinet and the Congress Party spanning fifty years, Jagjivan Ram made the decision to relinquish his positions within both entities. On 2 February 1977, a significant event occurred in the nation's history when Jagjivan Ram submitted resignation letters to Prime Minister and the Congress President D.K. Barooah.[21] In these letters, Jagjivan Ram elucidated the underlying reasons rooted in their lifelong commitment to ideas and beliefs that had shaped their struggles.

Dear Madam Prime Minister,

When I called on you last evening at 4.45 p.m., I pleaded with you for lifting 'the Emergency' as the prevailing conditions in the country do not justify its continuance any longer. I further explained that any situation arising after the lifting of the Emergency can be dealt with by the normal laws of the land and no extraordinary measures were necessary. You expressed your reluctance to end the Emergency as the Home Ministry had already examined it and did not find it possible to lift the Emergency. After this it was unnecessary to further pursue the matter and I left. The country today is under double Emergency. Besides, there are some extraordinary laws in operation. Citizens of the country have been deprived of all their freedoms—freedom of expression, freedom of association, freedom of assembly, freedom of movement, etc. Life and liberty of the citizens are not safe. Any citizen can be deprived of his life, his liberty and his property by the government without any remedy—legal or administrative—being available to him. Executive today is vested with extraordinary powers with no check on their action.

There are instances where innocent citizens have been detained only because some politician in the power of his henchman or an executive was displeased with them. Houses of many citizens in many parts of the country have been demolished. A fear psychosis has overtaken the whole nation. People are living in a state of constant fear and are silently suffering. This is bad for any country, more so for a Democracy. Therefore, it is necessary that the Emergencies are ended, all extraordinary laws are made inoperative and freedom of the people are restored so that the entire nation can be rescued from the state of importance to which it has been reduced at present. It is, however, obvious that you are not prepared to do this. Therefore, one will be justified in drawing the conclusion that the government wants to sustain it—perpetuate itself—by measures like the Emergencies and the extraordinary laws. It is difficult for me to associate myself with such a dispensation any longer. I am, therefore, sending my resignation herewith from your cabinet and request you for its immediate acceptance. I would like to take this opportunity to express my thanks to you for all the respect, courtesy and consideration you have shown to me during all the eleven years that I have been a member of your Cabinet. Wishing you speedy recovery and sound health,

I remain,
Sincerely yours,
JAGJIVAN RAM[22]

LETTER TO CONGRESS PRESIDENT MR D.K. BAROOAH

Dear Mr. President,[23]

Following their departure from the Congress (I), Jagjivan Ram and his supporters, including H.N. Bahuguna, the former Chief Minister of Uttar Pradesh and former General Secretary of the All-India Congress Committee (AICC), Nandini Satpathy, former Chief Minister of Orissa, N.D.Tiwari, former MP, K.R. Ganesh, former Minister in the Government of India, and Raj Mangal Pandey, former Minister of Uttar Pradesh, have announced their intention to establish a new political party known as the Congress for

Democracy. The advent of Citizens for Democracy (CFD) had a significant role in facilitating political transformation inside the nation, as it provided a means for individuals who were deeply dissatisfied with the prevailing political circumstances to voice their concerns. This period of discontent arose during the tenure of Mrs. Gandhi, who had declared a state of Internal Emergency, exacerbating the urgency felt by the populace. During a news conference held on 4 February 1977, in New Delhi, he expressed that the primary goal of the newly formed political party was to establish a socio-economic framework based on socialist principles. The purpose of this component is to represent socialism, encompassing both theoretical and practical aspects. Moreover, he articulated that his political party had made a commitment to reinstate propriety and ethical conduct inside the realm of public affairs. He self-identified as a unifying entity within the opposition.[24] A multitude of individuals in positions of leadership, intellectual prowess, academic expertise, and social service have aligned themselves with the CFD organization. During a news conference held by the CFD, Sumitra Kulkarni, the granddaughter of Gandhi, expressed her apprehension regarding the gradual abandonment of the party's core values. The individual experienced a perception that a significant portion of the ideologies promoted by the Congress Party during its ninety-year tenure were progressively disregarded over the recent three to four years. Consequently, she arrived at the determination to align herself with the political party that espoused democratic principles.[25]

During the period of emergency rule in the 19th month, there was a notable transformation in the political landscape. Opposition parties such as Lok Dal, Jan Sangh, Congress (O), and Socialist Party, among others, collaborated to form a political entity known as the Janata Party. Led by Jayaprakash Narayan, this coalition played a pivotal role in consolidating democratic forces to combat the autocratic rule of Mrs. Gandhi. Jagjivan Ram collaborated with Jayaprakash Narayan by integrating his political organization, the CFD, into the Janata organization alliance. This alliance played a pivotal role in establishing the Janata Party government, marking the first instance of a non-Congress government assuming power at the Centre subsequent to India's attainment of Independence.[26] JP, Jagjivan Ram, and other major leaders conducted massive nationwide campaigns aimed at shaping popular sentiment against Mrs. Gandhi. These efforts included organizing several rallies. An endeavour has been undertaken to concentrate on the contributions of Jagjivan Ram. According to JP, the outcome of these elections would play a crucial role in shaping the future trajectory of India's history. It was incumbent upon the citizens of India to be cognizant of the matter. Individuals are faced with the decision of embracing either democracy, which encompasses the entitlement to a fair trial and freedom from arbitrary detention, or authoritarianism. Individuals possess the agency to determine their own future as well as shape the trajectory of future generations. The matter at hand was not solely confined to the act of voting, but rather pertained to the act of determining one's own future through personal agency. One must make a decision either the desire for personal freedom or the acceptance of servitude. It is advisable to exercise prudence and ensure that you exercise your voting right in favour of the Janata Party, supporting the principles of democracy and freedom.[27]

Atal Bihari Vajpayee, Lal Krishna Advani, George Fernandes, Desai, Chandrasekhar, and Chaudhary Charan Singh were prominent political figures in Indian political history. The individuals in question are Charan Singh and Jagjivan Ram. The latter and other prominent individuals played a vital part in the transition of power from the Congress dictatorship, introducing novel ideologies inside the political sphere of the nation. The Janata alliance, consisting of the Janata Party with 270 seats and the CFD with 28 seats, acquired a total of 298 seats. This coalition formed the government with Desai as its leader. In contrast, the Congress Party led by Mrs. Gandhi was defeated, earning only 153 seats, a significant decrease from their previous count of 353 seats.[28] The role played by Jagjivan Ram was of great significance as he effectively influenced the mindset of voters with his motivating rhetoric. He played a significant role in facilitating the establishment of the Janata Party government, which emerged as a consequence of the Emergency declared by Gandhi, disregarding democratic norms.

Jagjivan Ram had received assurances from Vajpayee and Nana Goray of the Socialist Party concerning their support for his candidature for the position of the Prime Minister. Consequently, he harboured optimism regarding his prospects of assuming the role.

During a conversation with Subramanian Swamy, he recounted an experience involving Jagjivan Ram and discussed the potential social transformation that could arise from the appointment of a Prime Minister belonging to a Scheduled Caste community. Jagjivan Ram, in addition to belonging to the reserved caste, was widely recognized as one of the most proficient Ministers in post-Independence India. Jagjivan Ram possessed exceptional qualities that would have made him an outstanding candidate for the position of Prime Minister. However, it is worth noting that inside the Janata Party, there existed a single factor that worked against his candidature. He was the individual responsible for proposing and advocating for the approved resolution of the Emergency situation.[29] Charan Singh expressed opposition to Jagjivan Ram assuming the position of Prime Minister. According to Charan Singh, the support he extended towards the Emergency resolution was deemed unforgivable. Charan Singh raised concerns regarding Jagjivan Ram's failure to file income tax returns for a period of ten years. In addition to the aforementioned point, it is worth noting that Charan Singh, being a member of the Jat community, expressed his disapproval towards the notion of appointing a Prime Minister from the Scheduled Caste. The leader of the Parliamentary Party, Vajpayee, discreetly approached JP and Acharya Kripalani, informing them of his decision to swap allegiances.

However, Jagjivan Ram was unaware of this fact. Jagjivan Ram displayed a high level of confidence in his anticipated majority, as seen by his prearrangement of celebratory items such as sweets and firecrackers to commemorate his ascension to the position of Prime Minister. However, he was unaware of the subsequent act of betrayal perpetrated by Vajpayee. Upon receiving the news of Morarji Desai's selection by JP, Jagjivan Ram became visibly agitated and expressed his discontent by forcefully displacing chairs and tables. The nation failed to seize a significant historical opportunity to witness the appointment of a leader from the Dalit community as the Prime Minister. Jagjivan Ram got over his sadness and joined the Desai's cabinet as Defence Minister. Subsequently, Morarji Desai appointed him to the position of Deputy Prime Minister. However, the government led by Desai was ousted in July 1979, leading to the ascension of Charan Singh as the Prime Minister. Singh garnered the backing of the Congress Party, which was under the leadership of Gandhi at the time.

The downfall of Charan Singh's government might be attributed to his refusal to comply with Gandhi's request to eliminate the Special Court responsible for adjudicating matters involving her and Sanjay. Jagjivan Ram declined to provide him with assistance in the parliamentary setting. Jagjivan Ram became the leader of the Janata Party in Parliament, succeeding Morarji Desai. However, the Janata Party fell short of a majority by 18 MPs, while the All-India Dravida Munnetra Kazhagam (AIDMK) had 19 MPs. M.G. Ramachandran presented Subramanian Swamy with a letter expressing support, accompanied by a request for the appointment of two ministers.[30] Upon receiving the communication, Jagjivan Ram experienced a sense of exhilaration. President Reddy dissolved the Lok Sabha without affording its members the opportunity to establish a government, potentially influenced by personal animosity. The nation missed out on another opportunity to benefit from the expertise of a highly skilled administrator from a Scheduled Caste background.

In the year 1980, the Seventh Lok Sabha Elections witnessed the re-election of Jagjivan Ram from the Sasaram constituency. However, on this occasion, he assumed a place with the opposition, marking the first instance in his extensive political trajectory. The Congress Party regained power while the Janata Party experienced a decline in popular support and subsequently disbanded.

In March 1980, Jagjivan Ram established a novel political party known as the Congress (J). Subsequently, in the general elections held in December 1984, he achieved another notable triumph by securing a successful re-election to the Lok Sabha. Jagjivan Ram's election history has remained remarkably untarnished since entering the political arena, having successfully secured a seat in all the eight Lok Sabha sessions held since the country's independence. His political career has made a lasting impact on the history of India. Throughout his tenure as a minister, he has reflected a particular focus on the well-being of individuals. During his tenure, he implemented several significant measures aimed at improving the conditions of marginalized communities. He established a strong basis for the development of contemporary India. With a notable track record in administration, he has had a lasting impact. The individual in question made significant contributions to India's parliamentary system of governance, serving as both a Member of Parliament and a Minister. The individual demonstrated a profound level of political acumen and comprehension when addressing the various difficulties faced by the nation, whether they pertained to matters of national defence or agricultural affairs. He possessed the knowledge and skills necessary to effectively navigate bureaucratic systems and optimise outcomes.

NOTES

1. Indrani Jagjivan Ram, *Milestones: A Memoir*, Penguin Viking, New Delhi, 2010, p. 38.
2. Om Prakash Maurya, *Builders of Modern India: Babu Jagjivan Ram*, Publications Division, Government of India, New Delhi, 2010, p. 14.
3. Meena Charanda, 'Jagjivan Ram', in Suratha Kumar Malik and Ankit Tomar (eds.), *Revisiting Modern Indian Thought: Themes and Perspectives*, Routledge India, 2022, p. 129.
4. Ibid., pp. 120-30.
5. Maurya, op. cit., p. 30.
6. Ram, op. cit., pp. 203-4.
7. Ibid., p. 205.
8. Ibid., p. 214.
9. Ibid., p. 231.
10. Ibid., pp. 231-2.
11. Ibid., pp. 232-3.
12. NMML, Nageshwar Dwivedi Papers, Correspondences with Jagjivan Ram on 3 December 1969.
13. Ibid., p. 234.
14. Ibid., p. 236.
15. Ibid., pp. 237-8.
16. Ibid., pp. 239-41.
17. Ibid., pp. 252-6.
18. NMML, Nageshwar Dwivedi Papers, Correspondence with Jagjivan Ram on 27 December 1971.
19. Katherine Frank, *Indira: The Life of Indira Nehru Gandhi,* HarperCollins Publishers, Great Britain, 2001, p. 306.
20. Ibid.

21. Ramesh Chandra and Sangh Mitra, *Jagjivan Ram and His Times*, Commonwealth Publishers, New Delhi, 2003, p. 218.
22. Ibid.
23. Ibid.
24. Ibid., p. 227.
25. B.M. Turadagi, 'Dr. Jagjivan Ram's Life and Achievements: A Critical Analysis', unpublished Ph.D. thesis, Department of Political Science, Karnataka University, p. 160.
26. Ibid.
27. K.L. Chanchreek, *Jagjivan Ram's Crusade for Democracy*, S. Chand & Company, New Delhi, 2008, p. 56.
28. www.General Election-1977.
29. Turadagi, op. cit., p. 163.
30. Ibid., pp. 163-7.

8

Conclusion

From an early age, Jagjivan Ram harboured a strong aspiration for complete solidarity with the lower socio-economic strata. Having been born into a *Harijan* household and having encountered the rigidity of the caste system imposed by the broader society, he possessed a profound understanding of the actual conditions faced by the *Harijans*. The individual in question had devoted his entire existence to the elimination of casteism, a deeply ingrained social phenomenon inside Indian society. The denial of equal opportunity in the social, political, and economic domains to members of upper-caste Hindu groups was a consequence of casteism, which contradicted modern society's concept of essential human dignity. He held the belief that discrimination poses a significant barrier to the complete actualization of human potential, as he had personally encountered its adverse consequences, including untouchability and marginalization. Jagjivan Ram committed his life to the progress of marginalized social groups in light of the prevalent caste-based discrimination and subsequent marginalization experienced by a significant segment of society in that era. He actively engaged in the organization of young individuals from lower socio-economic backgrounds and endeavoured to teach his community members about the significance of advocating for their rights and garnering the attention of political figures. These occurrences bolstered his determination to advocate emphatically for justice, and he dedicated his entire career to striving for the elimination of the prevalent social problem that severely affected a significant segment of the populace.

Jagjivan Ram gave a significant attention on the challenges pertaining to the Dalit community. The primary objective of his struggle centred on the progress of the Dalit community. He was a trailblazer in the implementation of social activities with the objective of enhancing the socio-economic conditions of the Dalit community. The individual expressed that achieving a significant reorganization of the socio-economic structure would require a considerable amount of time in order to capture the attention of the populace. Nevertheless, the scale and methodologies employed in welfare project implementations are significantly insufficient. It was anticipated that with the improvement of conditions inside these communities, individuals residing there would endeavour to lead lives characterized by integrity and virtue. It was also foreseeable that as their understanding and awareness of their rights increased, they would decline conventional therapy. However, the presence of this movement has led to a resurgence of authoritarianism and harassment, particularly in rural areas. This observation suggests that there has been limited transformation in the psyche of the upper-caste, with just a reluctant adaptation taking place. Even individuals who identify as liberal can possess similar cognitive frameworks, but their outward manifestations may vary. What other explanations exist for the commonly lauded demonstrations of compassion and the well-acknowledged inclination to assist marginalized and oppressed populations? An encouraging advancement has been the extension of an additional decade to the constitutional provision of reserved seats for these social groups. However, it is anticipated that a substantial increase in workload will be required. There is a need for the cessation of all practices that perpetuate the segregation of Hindus based on caste and discriminatory treatment. The construction of segregated villages for Scheduled Castes should be discouraged. In order to achieve a balanced and sustainable environment, it is imperative to incorporate a combination of urban and rural elements in both urban and rural settings. It is recommended that comprehensive financial support in the form of liberal stipends be extended to students belonging to the Scheduled Castes and Tribes. Additionally, there should be a concerted effort to promote and facilitate technical education. Furthermore, it is imperative to establish mechanisms that guarantee equitable representation of these marginalized communities in public posts.

Jagjivan Ram systematically laid the foundation to advocate for the rights of the *Harijans*, as well as the working class and other marginalized groups. Saksena accurately asserts that while he is widely recognized for his political leadership, he also played a significant role as a Trade Union Leader. Under his leadership, the working-class inhabitants of Bihar initiated their monumental endeavour. Upon his election as Vice-President of the Bihar Trade Union Congress in 1940, he garnered significant admiration and recognition as a prominent figure in the realm of labour activism. The efforts made by Jagjivan Ram towards the welfare and empowerment of many elements of Indian society, such as the working class, are undeniably noteworthy. Jagjivan Ram's proactive engagement in the establishment of organizations and alliances aimed at representing landless labourers, village craftsmen, and marginalized communities serves as evidence of his dedication to addressing the socio-economic difficulties encountered by these populations. It is frequently observed that leaders who have significantly advanced workers' rights and social justice are often referred to as 'saviours' and 'liberators' of the working class. However, it is crucial to acknowledge that the pursuit of workers' rights and social justice in India was a collaborative endeavour encompassing numerous individuals and movements. The work of Jagjivan Ram was in accordance with the overarching objectives of social and economic justice that were pivotal to the Indian independence struggle. The individual's active support for the rights of workers, particularly those belonging to marginalized and oppressed groups, had a substantial impact on the development of policies and legislation designed to enhance the well-being of labourers in India. He had shown a strong awareness and concern for the well-being of the working-class.

Throughout the twentieth century, three notable individuals in India placed considerable emphasiz, and stress on the importance of achieving equality within the caste system. The persons who accepted leadership roles were Ambedkar, a highly esteemed scholar, Jagjivan Ram, a significant political figure, and Kanshi Ram, a committed activist. All three individuals originated from families affiliated with the Untouchable caste and collectively pursued the goal of eliminating the caste system and promoting a social framework based on principles of human equality. Nonetheless, it is worth noting that within the realm of current scholarship, there exists a want of consistent recognition of Jagjivan Ram's status as a notable figure or advocate for the Dalit community. However, it is imperative to acknowledge his importance as a leader of the Dalit community, as he was the only person to hold a ministerial role and actively champion the rights of underprivileged groups until his passing. The examination of his leadership position within the Dalit community should not be subjected to questioning, given his endeavours in advancing the welfare of socio-economically disadvantaged people, and his unique approach to championing social justice within the realm of Dalit politics. The primary focus of his efforts centred on the critique of the caste system and the fight against untouchability, issues that were frequently disregarded or insufficiently addressed by established political factions. He exhibited a steadfast commitment to the principles of Gandhian ideology. The individual in question is commonly recognized as originating from a socially advantaged upbringing and devoting his endeavours to pushing for the progress of the Dalit community. He maintained a position that was contrary to the caste system.

Annexure

Caste Challenge in India

Jagjivan Ram

The author has discussed the origins of caste and gradual changes in its meaning. Here, he has described how the previous tribal concept of caste was changed after the coming of the Aryans, and how later, both tribal and Aryan concepts of caste were mixed in a phased manner. According to the author, before the Aryans, the tribal people used to obey the caste system on the basis of clans. Endogamy was not allowed between two different tribal groups, even if they belong to the same place, or the same language group. But, the Aryan society was based on the occupational caste system, beginning it was three tired, later, by adding the Sudra caste it became fourfold system, or *chaturvaranya*. The Aryans had created another caste that was Untouchable. They used to consider the conquered aboriginals or the broken men as Untouchables. They were not assigned to the social hierarchy of the *chaturvaranya* system. Gradually, this system became popular in the society, and both the Aryans and the tribes started to become a part of it. As learning and spiritual knowledge were considered esoteric virtues, the Brahmins were exempted from manual labour, along with the powerful class, i.e. Kshatriyas.

Until the fifth century BC, there was no strong territorial power in India, which could divert tribalism into the harmony of a nation. Even though there was no equality before and this inequality resulting from caste, and it was supposed to be ordained by God and thus, the lawmakers prescribed different kinds of punishments and taxes for different *varnas*. This concept not only eliminated all the possibilities of revolt by the exploited majority, but also there was a concept that, if they would perform those social duties willingly, then they would probably be born in a higher group in their next birth. But this concept of Hindu society was threatened when the Muslim invaders and Christian missionaries came to India with their proselytizing attitude and the concept of equality and brotherhood among their followers. This concept raised several revival movements to achieve social equality. But they ultimately failed because they were not organized.

The new religions sought to reform the people of the country and inculcate in them a new belief in the equality of all men before God. But, the people had been living for so long in psychological cages and had become so acquiescent to prevalent Hindu Brahmanical beliefs, that the efforts of the saint reformers failed. According to Jagjivan Ram, though many of these sects exist even today, they have lost their old dynamism. Their mentalities and ideas are not distinguishable from the prevailing Brahmanical beliefs. Ram further added that even the Untouchables were not successfully made free from the caste within other religions like Islam and Christianity. Even with the advent of the British and their industrial revolution, the caste system got a huge blow in urban areas, but the village remained the same.

Jagjivan Ram suggested that people should be judged by their merits, and not by the caste. Here, he referred to the change of mind in the cerebral notions of the upper caste. In this respect, he suggested recalling the renaissance, which provided a new socio-economic basis by changing the intellectual as well as the moral attitude of the European people. He believed that people should change their way of thinking and thereby complete the unfinished work of the reform movements or renaissance. He believed that the renaissance in Europe succeed because it did not imply a break with the past, but developed what was original in early ideas and shattered the narrow mental barriers and recovered the idea of freedom in real terms.

Jagjivan Ram further described that Buddha failed because he was a reformer who was too advanced for his time, and the reforms initiated by the other saints failed because their followers became segregated with time. Here, he also mentioned Gandhi who did not challenge the present Hindu Brahmanical concepts directly, he accepted it, but then gave it the highest virtues. In the last part of chapter, Ram concluded that the caste system is unsuitable for the overall development of the country. Thus, it should be abolished by its roots.

SOCIAL CONFLICT AND CULTURAL CRISIS

In the second chapter, Jagjivan Ram is found to stand forth with strong point that, unless the caste system is abolished, the talk of culture, high moral value, democracy, and civilization, all, are meaningless. Here he raised the significant question that what is the reason behind this crisis? According to him, if the ideal life of society is inconsistent with the realities of our society and is unattached to it, then that ideal is simply an illusion. According to him, ancient beliefs and traditions somehow bound the concept of social equality, and looking at the past should be the only purpose of finding the links that bind us as a nation. Here he referred to the President Rajendra Prasad's speeches, which reflect the same at the inauguration of Somnath Temple.

Jagjivan Ram shared his view that, without equal opportunity for development, cultural values are meaningless. Here in this chapter, he has mentioned the Vedas, *Upanishads*, and the Shankaracharya's discourses. He said, that the Hindu upper caste people used to decide rules according to their profit and link it with the traditional Hindu religious texts and the systems, which could not get the support of the Vedas, *Upanishads* or the *Srimad Bhagavada Gita*, was named divine. The person who broke the rules was outcasted from the four *varnas*. The man born into a low caste was a slave to everybody. There was a complete absence of any kind of likelihoods for the enhancement of the interpersonal relationship between the master and the slave.

Jagjivan Ram here pointed out an important fact, that though the caste system was maintained very strictly, it could not be denied that, under the caste system each *varna* became a loose set-up mixture. After many years with the advent of different religious groups in India, and their ultimate assimilation with the Hindu religion, the Indian society lost its concept of caste purity and thus, it was not merely an Indian, but an assimilation of thousands of integrated societies. Though he distinguished Islam and Christianity here by saying that, Islam in itself was such a complete and undivided entity that it could not be assimilated into the religious confederation. The same was the case with Christianity.

MAHATMA GANDHI AND SOCIAL CHANGE

In the third chapter, Jagjivan Ram started from the standpoint where he ended the second chapter. At the beginning of the third chapter, he wrote that it was in the very past that the process of intermixing and *Hybridization* was completed, and nothing like skin, colour, hair form, or skeletal traits marks out any single region as being peopled by a pure racial group. It is the sentiments that bind men together, sentiments of a common race, of common religion, traditions, customs, habits of thoughts, of language and literature, achievements and sufferings. He further contended that, caste does not indicate inborn superiority or inferiority, rather, it recognizes different outlooks and corresponding modes of life. It was impossible to create an integrated nation if people remain rigidly exclusive and socially alien to each other by claiming superiority over each other. The only way to national progress is through widening the circle of social activity. And unless the mentality of caste difference is ended, it may not be possible to explore a new way to a homogeneous society.

Herein, he mentioned a common fact that, from the beginning of elections, practically all politicians and all political parties have made full use of the caste structure for electoral purposes, which is wrong. Because, the actual democratization of politics, offers an opportunity for the suppressed communities to forge new alliances and break up the monopoly of political and economic power held by the upper caste. He contended that caste and democracy cannot co-exist. And casteism is harmful to a creative and cooperative society. He urged for the treatment of social matters equal to political and economic matters. He wrote that the racial elements are powerful enough to resist assimilation and organized enough to maintain their separate entity. And, with the acrid caste system when linked with *karma*, reincarnation raised the status of the caste system. These kinds of ideas emanating from the Brahmanical centres of teaching and learning, later infiltrated the masses with their varied traditions, customs, beliefs and therefore diversified. According to Ram, many of these assumptions have a social purpose. They make to eliminate competition and to confirm stability. They are not divinely ordinated and have no divine origin.

Jagjivan Ram said, that all the thinkers of the order of Buddha, Mahavira, and Vivekananda to Rammohan Roy, made the same mistake by considering caste as a religious institution because it's a social institution. Here, in this respect, he compared Gandhi with God and his idea of Hinduism as wide as the skies. But, he also claimed that Gandhi's ideas were inconsistent because, during the *swaraj* revolt, he had contended that *swaraj* could not be granted even by God, but had to be earned. But the same person said in Bihar, that the occurrence of an earthquake was a divine retribution by God for the sins of untouchability. Again the same man believed in the inner sense, when, he said that, his fasting was ordered from within. He showed some proof, that Gandhi ultimately supported the Marxist concept that, man's involvement with commerce influenced his political ethics and overall social life. But in the later period, Gandhi considered nationalism as the reality beyond all questions.

Jagjivan Ram said that Gandhi, later, he wanted to revive the *chaturvarnic* concept in all its pristine purity. According to Gandhi, *chaturvaranya* and heredity were accepted as the rule of nature and as the supreme regulatory principle of social life. The four *varnas* are therefore, fundamental, natural, and essential, while the castes and subcastes are excrescences. To Gandhi, if we do not efface untouchability, we shall be effaced from the face of the earth. Abolition of the caste system is the best possible adjustment to social stability and progress. He was in the favour to use *varna* and caste as interchangeable terms and believed that all types of men can be categorized under four broad occupations: teaching, defending, wealth-producing, and manual labour.

Jagivan Ram recalled his student life and wrote when he was a student, he used to propagate the harmful effects of untouchability on the socio-economic fabric of Indian society. To abolish the caste differences, he suggested a complete reorganization of the society. In this chapter, he also spoke about his drastic step when he strongly attacked the caste system at a conference of the Bihar's anti-Untouchability League (later known as Harijan Sevak Sangh) and how he sought the attention of Dr. Rajendra Prasad and ultimately, entered public life for the first time by becoming the secretary of the League. He mentioned how Gandhi's huge efforts against untouchability failed. He mentioned that a huge number of people used to join his campaign praised his thoughts but went home unchanged.

In this chapter, Jagjivan Ram shared his experiences with Gandhi when he accompanied him on his Bihar tour in March 1934. He mentioned how the worst situations like agitations, brickbats skirmishes and exchange of *lathi* blows and so on, could not limit the courage of Gandhi, and how he ultimately completed his target with patience and preached against untouchability. Herein, he also focused on the fact of how the Gandhian movement took women into the active political sphere of the society.

One notable thing that Jagjivan Ram concluded about Gandhi, was that the latter, in the initial stage, never directly attacked the caste system, but wanted to reform it and convert the sentiments of Hinduism into the shape of nationalism. But later he changed his mind and worked for the complete abolition of caste. Here, Gandhiji preached about the necessity of caste Hindu girls marrying Harijan husbands. However, he believed that there had to be a change in the moral and intellectual attitudes of the people and thus, the old orthodox concepts had to go. He shared that he was happy when Gandhi's viewpoint transformed.

According to him, caste differences or untouchability is more like an economic problem rather than a social quagmire. These social divisions could be tackled with economic revival. He believed that the spiritual and moral resources of the nation should be mobilized, and a crusade should be organized against the caste system before it harms the democracy of our nation. The concept of national unity must have to be extended beyond caste and region. And it is also a mental revolution. He said that, although Gandhi could not bring a radical change to the Hindu social order, but was successful in putting the Untouchables on the way to emancipation.

THE PROBLEM OF THE SCHEDULED CASTE

The fourth chapter is based on Jagjivan Ram's thoughts on the problems of the Scheduled Caste community. Though today, according to the Indian Constitution, none can be marked as an Untouchable. But Jagjivan Ram says, that the traditional division is still living in the minds of the people and thereby, is prevalent in the society. Even the intellectuals failed to eradicate this concept in the routinized rituals of their daily life. He believes that the gap between the percept and practice of individuals ultimately creates a gap between law and enforcement.

In this chapter, Jagjivan Ram had made a critical review of the mentality of the liberal leaders of the Scheduled Castes, who were concerned about upgrading the condition of the lower caste people but not about their amalgamation with the mainstream of society? They were concerned to upgrade them without changing their pre-decided occupation, living places, i.e. outside the mainstream of society, etc. By mentioning some examples here, he attempted to prove his words about the gap theory.

Here, Jagjivan Ram urged for the total abolition of distinct identities. This solution, mentioned about the reorganization of social and economic order along with the attendant ideological changes. He suggested that with the upgradation of their condition of them, they (the Untouchables) would treat themselves as equals and side by side insist others to simultaneously treat them as equals. He suggested that social reformers needed to find out the hidden roots of caste discrimination. Similarly, he also believed that it was economic exploitation, and the religious concepts were connected to give it a strong social and ideological base. He mentioned the other possibilities which could be a social matter, and by connecting it with the economic sector they tried to prove it lawful. He urged for the removal of all kinds of exploitation, rather than only the removal of caste exploitation to improve our Indian society. He also argued to provide necessary facilities to the Scheduled Castes, so that they could get over the barriers and at least avail a normal life. He was in favour of reservation in every public sector, such as services, education, housing facilities, and other things not only for the upliftment, but, as their rightful dues because, they were deprived of it for centuries. He denied terming the special assistance as a favour.

Jagjivan Ram also paid attention to the women's role in removing the caste discrimination. He said that the women, who control the household atmosphere, their thoughts and behaviour may affect a child's thinking. Thus, if one can encourage the woman to change her thoughts about caste, then they can easily blow up the existing concept of caste discrimination.

CASTELESS SOCIETY—A DREAM

In the fifth chapter, Jagjivan Ram wrote his views that caste and communal appeal is always a factor paralysing every aspect of our national life in terms of social, educational, administrative and political perspectives. It can be revived by holding a revolution in our daily lives, the way of our thoughts and thinking, work and the resultant deeds. He marked that, the caste system is not restricted to the Hindu society alone, as it infested the entire society of India. And, thus it seems like a dream, that the Indian society after becoming a casteless society will be utterly transformed into a prosperous society. He believed that science and technology, rapid urbanization and fast industrial growth are ultimately helping in changing society's outlook. And, when the process would complete only then it will reflect the humanistic strands of our thought and tradition. He said that the entire society will have become partners in creating a united nation. This will be the real strength of the nation.

Since the upper caste people are totally against the abolition of caste differences or reservations for the lower castes in educational and economic sectors, Jagivan Ram said that if the majority of the society is in favour of equality, such opposition will become ineffective and weak. Here again, he remembered Gandhi, who gave us the idea of *Sarvodaya*, where every man will be able to achieve his highest aims without any social obstacles. In this chapter, he showed his support for the fundamental belief of the democrats that, in a democratic society, the individual should be treated as a unit and not as a part of a caste, class or community. He said that this will be possible with the inculcation of a new sense of values through reorientation. He is found to share his thoughts in the favour of reservation by saying that, reservation for all, those who are socially, educationally and culturally backwards is not inconsistent with democratic principles in the peculiar context of our country.

Jagjivan Ram further contended that the excision of caste would mean an automatic abolition of untouchability. He added that the legislation can only show the way, but the attitude of the people should be change, otherwise, such legislations can never be effectively implemented. Here, he also mentioned scavenging as an unnecessary occupation that should be banned by law. Because, according to him, this profession is not vital for the society.

Lastly, he said that if a complete reorganization of our economy would be possible, along with full employment and social security assured to the poor and deprived people, and also with the total abolition of dehumanizing occupations, conditions could be created where the attitudes of the people towards manual labour would change and productive labour would come to be valued.

THE WRONGED FIFTH

In the sixth chapter, firstly, he mentioned some numerological figures to present an idea of the share of SCs and STs in the total population of the country along with their housing conditions, literacy rates, employment rates, etc.

In this chapter, he paid special attention to the agriculturists. In the matters of farmers, Jagjivan Ram mentioned that it is true that the Constitution of India has totally abolished feudalism, but, the feudal mentality is still alive and to abolish it from its roots, he was in favour of land distribution among the agriculturists. Here, he indicated some land types that are available and could be distributed.

He advocated for a cooperative economy, where the literate SC and ST people would participate and thereby take advantage. Here, he also pointed out some facts that, in rural areas, the SC and ST artisans would face difficulties in getting raw materials, newer techniques, better tools and most importantly, marketing products was an uphill challenge. So, here in this respect, he urged for governmental help. According to him, if the government becomes successful to turn the traditional artisans into modern artisans, then a large number of employment facilities would extend to all and sundry. He also contended that if the governmental policies and the government employment falls in the same line, then the SCs and STs would get a fairer chance.

In this chapter, he marked that how an economic crisis and poverty could bind a poor farmer and in this way revive the process of feudalism again and again. Later, he talked about two special occupational classes of people, i.e. sweeper and scavenger. He suggested special care for their child in matters of education, employment training, house allotment, etc. with the mainstream of the society, and not separately.

RESERVATION

The name of this chapter suggests that Jagjivan Ram shared his feelings about providing special assistance to the lower caste people. He believed that economic weakness does not offer any option to them, but to remain an unlettered and ignorant for life. This resultant backwardness reduced them to the status of virtual serfdom.

Jagjivan Ram discusses how the process of reservation started and gradually spread its wings. He said, in the early phase the policy of reservation was only confined to the matter of recruitment of the central government services. But later it also affected the policies of the state governments, but the private sectors were not ready to adopt it. He said, it was because of the general presumption, that the upper caste Hindus are born with competence and capability and it is only the SCs and STs who are supposed to be born incompetent and have to prove their competence and capability at every stage. Here he extended some instances of that, how in the economic sectors the upper caste people used to blame the lower caste people for any kind of disputes without having any proof. So, only the initiation of reservation was not sufficient, because it would not safeguard them from humiliation.

Here, he also presented some data, to show how caste discrimination used to work in this economic sector where five persons have been offered an appointment and out of whom only one person belongs to the SC category. He said that, when the orthodox traditional Hindus failed to secure the complete abolition of reservation in the services, they argued that reservation should not be based on the caste and birth of the individual, but, on his or her economic condition. According to him, it was nothing, but a tricky proposal because, in his view, appointments to the services are not only meant for the economic advancement of the person but his entire advancement. He further said that a Brahmin caste person will never salute a Yadav caste, however, superior the social status of the latter may be. On the other hand, if a Yadav personage is appointed as a sub-inspector of Police, the Brahmin police constable would compel to salute him. This insignificant matter would mark the beginning of a great social change. He believed that the real objective of such reservations is not economic development only, but, many more beyond it. As education today is depends on the economic condition of the family, he urged for a fair chance and fair competition for the children of backward people.

SOLUTION- CHANGE OF RELIGION?

This is the last chapter before the conclusion. In this chapter, Jagjivan Ram discussed a litany of reasons, which ultimately paved the way for religious conversion for the lower caste people. Here, he brought forth some examples of some tortures inflicted by the masters to his servant. But he believed that conversion can not be a proper answer to the problems of the Scheduled Castes because, it does not provide any solution to their problems. He gave some reason that the lower caste was attracted to other religious groups because, for example missionaries have opened schools and colleges for the tribal children and also arranged for their higher education in foreign countries in various disciplines, such as engineering, medicine, theology, etc. But, no such arrangements were done by Hindu philanthropic institutions or social reformers.

Jagjivan Ram was totally against the concept of conversion. Because he believed that, such conversions are insufficient to raise the socio-economic condition of those people. According to him, the Hindu religion was so flexible that it ultimately attracted the other religions within its shade and besides, it was not a matter of religion anymore, it was about the mentality, that remained unchanged with or without conversion. As the landlords, rich, and powerful communities still controlled the social, economic, and political life of the society for their gains. He is found to hold the thought of revolution. He said that the so-called lower caste people present in India in crores were scattered all over, and if they all united and gathered their strength, they can even forge a new nation. He compared the Indian society with the society of other countries, where knowledge and education decided superiority, but, unfortunately in India, caste does the same.

As in the previous chapters, where he also wrote that the village pattern still follows a deal pattern and the worst forms of exploitation are prevalent there. And, unless this discrimination is abolished, land redistributed and equal opportunities given to the deprived people, India cannot prosper adeqauately and fastly. Here he propounded an idiom to decrease the effects of caste by denying the use of surnames and titles identifying castes. He also preached for intercaste marriages, which could be encouraged by the members of the upper castes.

CONCLUSION

In this chapter, Ram mentioned how the early concept of caste superiority ultimately provided special facilities to the upper caste people in the matters of social-economic sectors and thereby, deprived the lower caste people for over a century. So, it is very difficult to uplift the conditions of the so-called lower caste.

It is still in India, that caste discrimination co-exists along with the advancements of science and technological developments. Though the Constitution has banned the word 'Untouchables', the concept still exists in the larger and ingrained mentality of the people. Even in the minds of so-called reformers, who urged for the social, political, economic and educational development of the people and the government initiated some welfare policies, the implementation of the welfare policies were slow and tedious. He said that, though legislative orders are in their favour, in reality, the higher authorities used to place myriad obstacles in their way. Because all the institutions are indeed made for the SCs and STs, but, are simultaneously dominated by the upper-class elites. Therefore, Jagjivan Ram urged to put some restrictions on the appointment of rich members in the co-operative sectors. Here, he also said that he is not against the rich but is in the favour of equal opportunities. To abolish the caste system, he also urged for a mixed-house colony, where all classes of people would live together.

Bibliography

A. PRIMARY SOURCES

Nehru Memorial Museum and Library (NMML)

Private Papers

Brahmananda Papers
K.R. Malkani Papers
Nageshwar Dwivedi Papers
Jayaprakash Narayan Papers

Official Government Documents

Dr. Babasaheb Ambedkar: Writing and Speeches (compiled by Vasant Moon), vol. 1, no. 21, Dr. Ambedkar Foundation, Government of India, 2014.

General Elections in India, 1951-72 (Lok Sabha), Report of the Election Commission, Government of India, New Delhi.

Annual Report for 1953-4 and 1955-6, Ministry of Communications, Government of India.

Annual Report for 1956-7, Ministry of Communications, Government of India.

Annual Report for 1962-3, Ministry of Communications, Government of India.

B. SECONDARY SOURCES

Agarwal, R.C., *Political Theory*, S. Chand & Company Ltd., New Delhi, 1993.

Ahir, D.C. (ed.), *Dr Ambedkar on British Raj*, Blumoon Books, New Delhi, 1997.

Ambedkar, B.R., *What Congress and Gandhi Have Done to The Untouchables*, Thacker & Co., Bombay, 1945.

Bakshi, S.R., *Jagjivan Ram: The Harijan Leader*, Anmol Publication, New Delhi, 1992.

Bandyopadhyay, Sekhar, *Namasudras of Bengal, 1872-1947*, Curzon Press, London, 1997.

Basu, D.D., *Introduction to the Constitution of India,* Wadhwa and Company, New Delhi, 2001.

Bayly, Susan, *Caste, Society, and Politics in India from the Eighteenth Century to the Modern Age*, Cambridge University Press, Cambridge, 1999.

Beltz, J. Mahar, *Buddhist and Dalit: Religious Conversion and Socio-Political Emancipation*, Manohar, New Delhi, 2005.

Beteille, Andre, *Backward Classes and the New Social Order*, Oxford University Press, New Delhi, 1981.

Bhambri, C.P., *The Janata Party: A Profile*, National Publishing House, New Delhi, 1980.

Bharadwaj, A.N., *Problems of Scheduled Caste and Scheduled Tribe in India*, Light & Life Publishers, New Delhi, 1979.

Bolton, G., *The Tragedy of Gandhi*, George Allen and Unwin Ltd., London, 1934, pp. 266-7 (accessioned 2019).

Brass, P.R., *The Politics of India since Independence*, Cambridge University Press, Cambridge, 2006.

G. Campbell, *Modern India: A sketch of the system of civil government, with some account of the natives and native institutions.* J. Murray, 1853.

Chahal, S.K., *Dalit Patronized: The Indian National Congress and Untouchables of India, 1921-1947*, Shubhi Publications, Delhi, 2002.

Chakrabarty, D., *Rethinking Working-Class History: Bengal 1890-1940,* Princeton University Press, Princeton, 1989.

Chandel, M.P.S., *A Social Force in Politics: Study of Scheduled Caste of U.P.*, Mittal Publications, New Delhi, 1990.

Chanchreek, K.L., *Babu Jagjivan Ram: A Nation Builder*, 2 vols., Shree Publishers, New Delhi, 2006.

———, *Jagjivan Ram: A Select Bibliography—1908-1975*, S. Chand & Company, New Delhi, 1975.

———, *Jagjivan Ram's Crusade for Democracy,* Sultan Chand Publications, New Delhi, 1978.

Chand, S., 'Four Decades of Jagjivan Ram's Parliamentary Career', *The Statesmen*, New Delhi, 1977.

Chandra, Bipin, *India's Struggle for Independence*, Penguin Books, New Delhi, 1989.

Chandra, Kanchan, *Why Ethnic Parties Succeed: Patronage and Ethnic Head Counts in India*, Cambridge University Press, New York, 2004.

Chandra, R. and Sangh Mitra, *Jagjivan Ram and His Times*, Commonwealth Publishers, New Delhi, 2003.

Chandavarkar, R., *The Origins of Industrial Capitalism in India: Business Strategies and the Working Classes in Bombay, 1900-1940*, Cambridge University Press, Cambridge, 1994.

Charanda, Meena, 'Jagjivan Ram', in Suratha Malik and Ankit Tomar (eds.), *Revisiting Modern Indian Thought: Themes and Perspectives*, Routledge, New York, 2022.

Chatterjee, Devi, *Ideas and Movements against Caste in India*, Abhijeet Publication, New Delhi, 2010.

Chaturvedi, P., *Uttar Bharat Ki Sant Parampara,* Bharati Bhandar, Allahabad, 1972.

Das, K.C., *Indian Dalits – Voice, Vision and Politics*, Global Vision Publishing House, Delhi, 2004.

Dasari, S., *Socio-Political Background of Babu Jagjivan Ram*, Ambedkar Fraternity Printing Publication, New Delhi, 1990.

Datt, K.K., *History of the Freedom Movement in Bihar*, 3 vols., Government of Bihar, 1957.

Dodd, L.C., *Coalitions in Parliamentary Government*, Princeton University Press, New Jersey, 1976.

Deshpande, G.P., *Selected Writings of Jyoti Rao Phule,* Leftword, New Delhi, 2002.

Devi, I., *Milestones—A Memoir*, Penguin Books India, New Delhi, 2010.

Dev, Acharya Narendra, *Kisan Movement in U.P. in Socialist and Nationalist Revolution*, Padama Publications, Bombay, 1946.

Dube, Ishita Banerjee (ed.), *Themes in Indian History: Caste in History*, Oxford University Press, New Delhi, 2010.

Dube, Saurabh, *Untouchable Pasts: Religion, Identity and Power among a Central Indian Community, 1780-1950*, State University of New York, New York, 1998.

Dubey, Abhay Kumar, *Kanshi Ram: Ek Alochonatmak Adhyayan*, Rajkamal Prakashan, New Delhi, 1997.

Dutt, R.P., *India To-Day*, Victor Gollancz Ltd., London, 1940.

Franco, Fernando and Archana Sinha, *Dalit Identity in Uttar Pradesh*, Indian Social Institute, New Delhi, 2002.

Frank, Katherine, *Indira: Life of Indira Nehru Gandhi*, HarperCollins Publishers, Great Britain, 2007.

Fadia, B.L., *Indian Government and Politics*, Sahitya Bhavan Publications, Agra, 2004.

Gandhi, M.K., *The Story of My Experiments with Truth: An Autobiography*, Navajivan Publishing House, Ahmedabad, 2001.

Ghosh, S.K., *The Indian Big Bourgeoisie: Its Genesis, Growth and Character*, Subarnarekha, Calcutta, 1985.

Gooptu, Nandini, *The Politics of the Urban Poor in Early Twentieth Century India*, Cambridge University Press: Cambridge, 2001.

________, *Swami Achhutanand and the Adi-Hindu Movement*, Critical Quest, New Delhi, 2006.

Gore, M.S., *The Social Context of an Ideology: Ambedkar's Political and Social Thought*, Sage Publications, New Delhi, 1993.

Gruthu, G.S., *Jagjivan Ram on Labour Problems*, Atmaram Publication, New Delhi, 1951.

Guha, Ranajit, *Dominance without Hegemony: History and Power in Colonial India,* Harvard University Press, Harvard, 1997.

Guha, S., 'Ethnic Parties, Material Politics and the Ethnic Poor:The Bahujan Samaj Party in North India', unpublished PhD thesis, Department of Political Science, McGill University, Montreal, 2008.

Gupta, R.C., *Great Political Thinkers (East & West)*, Laxmi Narayan Agarwal Publishers, Agra, 1980.

Gupta, S.K., *The Scheduled Castes in Modern Indian Politics*, Munshiram Manoharlal, Delhi, 1985.

Guru, Gopal, *Dalit Cultural Movement and Dialectics of Dalit Politics in Maharashtra*, Vikas Adhyayan Kendra, Bombay, 1997.

________, *Dr. Ambedkar's Concept of Political Power and the Question of Dalit Movement*, B.R. Ambedkar Trust, Hyderabad, 1993.

Guru, S., *Jagjivan Ram on Labour Problems*, Atma Ram & Sons, Delhi 1951.

Hardtmann, E.M., *The Dalit Movement in India: Local Practices, Global Connections*, Oxford University Press, New Delhi, 2009.

Ilaiah, Kancha, 'Productive Labour, Consciousness and History: The Dalit Bahujan Alternative', in Shahid Amin and Dipesh Chakraborty (eds.), *Subaltern Studies*, vol. 9, Oxford University Press, Delhi, 1996.

Jagjivan Ram in Parliament: A Commemorate Volume, Lok Sabha Secretariat, New Delhi, 2005.

Jaffrelot, Christophe, *India's Silent Revolution: The Rise of the Lower Castes in Northern India*, C. Hurst and Co. Publishers, London, 2003.

Jain, S.K., *Party Politics and Centre-State Relations in India*, Abhinav Publications, New Delhi, 1994.

Janda, K., Jeffery M. Berry and Jerry Goldman, *The Challenges of Democracy; Government in America*, Mifflin Company, Houghton, 1992.

Jangam, R.T., S.H. Patil and S.S. Patagundi, *Political Analysis*, Oxford & IBH Publishing Co., New Delhi, 1997.

Jurgensmeyer, Mark, *Religious Rebels in Punjab: The Ad Dharm Challenge to Caste*, Navayana, New Delhi, 2009.

Kadam, K.N., *Dr Baba Saheb Ambedkar and the Significance of His Movement: A Chronology*, Popular Prakashan, Bombay, 1991.

Kalhan, P., *Jagjivan Ram and Power Politics*, Allora Publications, New Delhi, 1980.

Kamble, J.R., *Awaking of Depressed Classes in India,* National Publishing House, New Delhi, 1979.

Kananaikil, J., *Scheduled Castes in the Constituent Assembly*, Indian Social Institute, New Delhi, 1982.

Kashyap, S.C., *The Framing of India's Constitution and Process of Institution Building*, Indian Institute of Public Administration, New Delhi, 1990.

Keer, Dhananjay, *Dr Ambedkar: Life and His Mission*, Popular Prakashan, Bombay, 1962.

———, *Mahatma Jyotirao Phule,* Popular Prakashan, Bombay, 1974.

Khare, R.S., *The Untouchable as Himself: Ideology, Identity, and Pragmatism among the Lucknow Chamara*, Cambridge University Press, Cambridge, 1984.

Kolge, Nishikant, *Gandhi Against Caste*, Oxford University Press, New Delhi, 2018.

Kshirsagar, R.K., *Dalit Movement in India and its Leader, 1857-1956,* M.D. Publishers, New Delhi, 1994.

———, *Political Thought of Dr. Babasaheb Ambedkar,* Intellectual Publishing House, New Delhi, 1992.

Kumar, Aishwary, *Radical Equality: Ambedkar, Gandhi and the Risk of Democracy*, Stanford University Press, Stanford, 2015.

Kumar, Vivek, *Dalit Leadership in India*, Kalpaz Publication, Delhi, 2002.

Kumar, Ravinder, *Western India in the Nineteenth Century: A Study in the Social History of Maharashtra*, Routledge and Kegan Paul, London, 1968.

Lynch, O.M., *The Politics of Untouchability: Social Mobility and Social Change in a City of India*, National Publishing House, New Delhi, 1974.

Machave, P., *Sri Jagjivan Ram: The Man and Thoughts*, Saumya Publications, Mumbai, 1977.

Mahar, J. Michal (ed.), *The Untouchables in Contemporary India*, University of Arizona Press, Arizona, 1972.

Mahajan, V.D., *The National Movement in India*, Sterling Publishers, New Delhi, 1989.

Majumdar, R.C., *History of Freedom Movement in India*, Firma KLM, Calcutta, 1962.

Malik, Lokendra and Kusum Lata (eds.), *Role of Babu Jagjivan Ram in Promoting Social Justice in India*, Indian Institute of Public Administration, New Delhi, 2009.

Mandelbaum, David G., *Society in India: Continuity and Change*, Popular Prakashan, Bombay, 1970.

Maurya, O.P., *Babu Jagjivan Ram*, Publication Division, Government of India, New Delhi, 2010.

McLane, J.R., *Indian Nationalism and the Early Congress*, Princeton University Press, New Jersey, 1977.

Mendelsohn, Oliver and Marika Vicziany, *The Untouchables*, Cambridge University Press, Cambridge, 1998.

Moffatt, Michael, *An Untouchable Community in South India: Structure and Conscience,* Princeton University Press, Princeton, 1979.

Moon, Vasant (compiled), *Dr. Babasaheb Ambedkar: Writings and Speeches*, vol. 1, Dr. Ambedkar Foundation, Government of India, 2019.

________, *Dr. Babasaheb Ambedkar Writings and Speeches*, vol. 2, Dr. Ambedkar Foundation, Government of India, 2019

Mukerji, A.B., *The Chamars of UP: A Study in Social Geography,* Inter India Publishers, New Delhi, 1980.

Murphy, G., 'Tensions Affecting International Understanding: A Survey of Research', vol. IV, Social Science Research Council Bulletin, New York, 1950.

Murugkar, Lata, *Dalit Panther Movement in Maharashtra: A Sociological Appraisal*, Popular Publication, Mumbai, 1991.

Mukherjee, G.K., *History of Indian National Congress*, Meenakshi Prakashan, Meerut, 1974.

Narayan, Badri, *Kanshiram: Leader of the Dalits,* Penguin Books, New Delhi, 2014.

Naidu, R.V.K., *Empowerment of Scheduled Caste*, Kalpaz Publication, New Delhi, 2004.

Naikar, Lohit, *Basava and Human Rights*, Basava Samiti, Bengaluru, 2012.

Narake, H. et al. (eds.), *Dr. Babasaheb Ambedkar: Writings and Speeches*, vol. 17 part I, Dr. Ambedkar Foundation, Government of India, 2020.

Nagaraj, D.R., *The Flaming Feet and Other Essays: The Dalit Movement in India*, Permanent Black, Ranikhet, 2010.

Narayan, Badri and A.R. Mishra (eds.), *Multiple Marginalities: An Anthology of Identified Dalit Writing*, Manohar, New Delhi, 2004.

———, *Women Heroes and Dalit Assertion in North India: Culture, Identity and Politics*, Sage, New Delhi, 2007.

———, *Fascinating Hindutva: Saffron Politics and Dalit Mobilisation*, Sage, New Delhi, 2009.

Nath, T., *Politics of the Depressed Classes*, Deputy Publications, Delhi, 1987.

Naimishray, Mohan Dass, *Caste and Race: Comparative Study of B.R. Ambedkar and Martin Luther King*, Rawat Publications, New Delhi, 2003.

Nayar, K., *The Judgement: Inside Story of the Emergency in India*, Vikas Publishing House, New Delhi, 1977.

O'Hanlon, Rosalind, *Caste, Conflict and Ideology: Mahatma Jotirao Phule and Low Caste Protest in Nineteenth Century Western India*, Cambridge University Press, Cambridge, 1985.

Omana, S., *Sree Narayana Guru*, Critical Quest, New Delhi, 2005.

Omvedt, Gail, *Dalits and the Democratic Revolution: Dr. Ambedkar and the Dalit Movement in Colonial India*, Sage, New Delhi, 1994.

———, *Seeking Begumpura: The Social Vision of Anticaste Intellectuals*, Navayana Publishing, New Delhi, 2008.

———, *Dalit Visions: The Anti-Caste Movement and the Construction of an Indian Identity*, Orient Longman, New Delhi, 1995.

——— (ed.), *Land, Caste, and Politics in Indian States*, Authors Guild Publication, Delhi, 1982.

Pai, Sudha and Kumar Sajjan, *Maya, Modi, Azad: Dalit Politics in the Time of Hindutva*, Harper Collins, New Delhi, 2023.

Patankar, Bharat and Gail Omvedt, *The Dalit Liberation Movement in Colonial Period*, Critical Quest, New Delhi, 2007.

Paswan, Sanjay and Pramanshi Jaideva, *Encyclopedia of Dalits in India*, vol. 11, Kalpaz Publications, New Delhi, 2002.

Prasad, Baleshwar, *Four Decades of Jagjivan Ram's Parliamentary Career*, S. Chand & Company, New Delhi, 1977.

Prasad, Chandra Bhanu, *Dalit Diary, 1999-2003: Reflections on Apartheid in India*, Navayana, New Delhi, 2004.

Prasad, Vijay, *Untouchable Freedom: A Social History of Dalit Community*, Oxford University Press, New Delhi, 2000.

Rajashekhar, H.M., *Understanding the Indian Constitution*, Prabodha Publishers, Mysore, 2005.

Rajawat, M., *Encyclopedia of Dalits in India*, Kalpaz Publications, New Delhi, 2004.

Ram, Kanshi, *The Chamcha Age: An Era of the Stooges*, Vedic Mudranalaya, New Delhi, 1982.

Ram, Jagjivan, *Caste Challenge in India*, Vision Books, New Delhi, 1980.

Ram, Indrani Jagjivan, *Milestones: A Memoir*, Penguin India, New Delhi. 2010.

Ram, Nandu, *Beyond Ambedkar: Essays on Dalits in India*, Har Anand Publications, Delhi, 1995.

Rao, Anupama, *The Caste Question: Dalits and the Politics of Modern India*, Permanent Black, Ranikhet, 2010.

Rao, M.S.A., *Social Movements in India*, vol. I, Manohar, New Delhi, 1978.

Rawat, Ram Narayan, *Reconsidering Untouchability: Chamar and Dalit History in North India*, Permanent Black, Ranikhet, 2012.

Roy, Arundhati, *The Doctor and the Saint: Caste, Race, and the Annihilation of Caste, The Debate between B.R. Ambedkar and M.K. Gandhi*, Haymarket Books, Chicago, 2017.

Sadashiva, K., *Babu Jagjivan Ram—Jeevana Mattu Vyaktitva*, Priyadarshini Prakashana, Mysore, 2015.

Sang Wan, O.P., *Social System and the Dalit Identity*, Commonwealth Publishers, New Delhi, 1996.

Saran, S., *Babu Jagjivan Ram Aur Dalit Andolan*, Vani Prakashan, New Delhi, 2017.

Sarkar, Jayabrata, 'NMML Occasional Paper Perspectives in Indian Development', New Series-3, Nehru Memorial Museum and Library, 2012, p. 1.

Sarma, S.K., *The Chamar Artisian: Industrialisation, Skills and Social Mobility*, B.R. Publication, New Delhi, 1986.

Sharma, Nalin Vilochan, *Jagjivan Ram: A Biography*, Sanjeev Press, Patna, 1975.

Saxena, Gulshan Swarup, *Arya Samaj Movement in India 1857-1947*, New Delhi, Commonwealth Publishers, New Delhi, 1994.

Shah, Ghanshyam, *Social Movements in India: A Review of the Literature*, Sage, New Delhi, 1990.

Sharan, D.K., *Scheduled Castes in Freedom Struggle in India*, Classical Publishing Company, New Delhi, 1999.

Sharma, Devendra Prasad *Jagajivan Ram: The Man and the Times*, Indian Book Company, New Delhi, 1974.

Sharma, Sanjay Prakash (ed.), *Dalit Society and Upliftment*, Mohit Publications, New Delhi, 2004.

Sharma, S.R., *Life and Works of Babu Jagjivan Ram*, Sublime Publishers, New Delhi, 2005.

Sharma, R., *Who After Morarji?*, Pankaj Publications, New Delhi, 1978.

Shubha, J., *Glimpses of Freedom Struggle*, Dutta Sons Publishers, Nagpur, 1997.

Singh, D., *Jagjivan Ram—Success Story*, Caxton Press, New Delhi, 2003.

Singh, M.P. and Rekha Saxena, *Indian Politics: Contemporary Issues and Concerns*, Prentice-Hall of India, New Delhi, 2008.

Singh, N.N., *Jagjivan Ram: Symbol of Social Change*, Sandeep Prakashan, New Delhi, 1977.

Singh, Jagpal, *Capitalism and Dependence: Agrarian Politics in Western Uttar Pradesh 1951-1991*, Manohar, New Delhi, 1992.

Singh, Buta, *Dalit and Dalit Awakening in India*, Gyan Publications, Delhi, 2004.

Singh, Manohar, *The Depressed Classes: The Economics and Social Condition*, Hind Kitab Ltd., Bombay, 1947.

Sinha, A.C., *Struggle and Achievements: Babu Jagjivan Ram Commemoration Volume*, Alka Prakashan, New Delhi, 1973.

Sinha, Anil Kumar, *Jagjivan Ram: The Enlightened Spirit*, Aniket Seva, Patna, 2005.

Srinivas M.N., *Social Change in Modern India,* Orient BlackSwan, New Delhi, 1996.

Turadagi, B.M., *Dr. Jagjivan Ram's Life and Achievements: A Critical Analysis,* unpublished PhD thesis, Department of Political Science, Karnataka University, 2018.

Upadhyay, S.B., *Historiography in the Modern World: Western and Indian Perspectives*, Oxford University Press, New Delhi, 2004.

Yengde, Suraj, *Caste Matters,* Penguin Viking, Gurgaon, 2009.

Wilson, H.H., *Siva Narayanis: In Sketch of the Religious Sects of the Hindus*, Trubner & Company, London, 1861.

Zelliot, Eleanor, *From Untouchables on to Dalits,* Manohar, New Delhi, 1996.

Zelliot, Eleanor and Rohini Mokashi-Punekar (eds.), *Untouchable Saints: An Indian Phenomenon*, Manohar, New Delhi, 2005.

JOURNALS/BOOK CHAPTERS

Chandra, Kanchan, 'The Transformation of Ethnic Politics in India: The Decline of Congress and the Rise of the Bahujan Samaj Party in Hoshiarpur', *The Journal of Asian Studies,* vol. 59, no. 1, February 2000, pp. 26-61.

Chatterji, Rakhahari, 'Class Conflict and Nation Building: Gandhi and the Indian Labour Movement', *The Indian Journal of Political Science*, vol. 37, no. 4, 1976, pp. 42-57.

Cybil, K.V., 'Narayan Guru and Formation of Political Society in Kerala', in Simhadri Somanaboina and Akhileshwari Ramagoud (eds.), *The Routledge Handbook of the Other Backward Classes in India*, Routledge, London, 2022, pp. 100-11.

Edinger, Lewis J., 'Political Science and Political Biography: Reflections on the Study of Leadership (I)', *The Journal of Politics*, vol. 26, no. 2, 1964, pp. 423-39.

Friedlander, Peter, 'Reassessing Religion and Politics in the Life of Jagjivan Ram', *MDPI Journals*, 2020, pp. 1-18.

Gandhi, Rajmohan, 'Response to Arundhati Roy', *EPW,* vol. 50, no. 30, 2015, pp. 83-5.

Ghose, Sagarika, 'The Dalit in India', *Social Research*, vol. 70, no. 1, 2003, pp. 83-109.

Ghurye, G.S., 'Caste and British Rule', in Ishita Banerjee-Dube (ed.), *Caste in History*, Oxford University Press, London, 2008, pp. 40-5.

Guru, Gopal, 'Mahatma Jotirao Phule and Reservation', paper presented at the seminar on Phule at the Centre for Social Studies, Surat, 9-11 January 1991, pp. 70-85

Hogan, R. and R.B. Kaiser, 'What we know about leadership', *Review of General Psychology,* vol. 9, pp. 169-80.

Jaffrelot, Christophe, 'The Bahujan Samaj Party in North India: No Longer Just a Dalit Party?', *Comparative Studies of South Asia, Africa and the Middle East,* Duke University Press, vol. XVIII, no. 1, 1998, pp. 35-51.

Javed, Rimsha, 'The Caste System in India during British Raj (1872-1941)', *International Journal of Development Research*, vol. 11, issue 12, December 2021, pp. 526-79.

Jeffrey, Craig, Patricia Jeffrey and Roger Jeffrey, 'When schooling fails: Young men, education and low-caste Politics in rural North India,' *Contributions to Indian Sociology*, n.s., vol. 39, no. 1, 2005, pp. 1-38.

Jeffrey, Robin, 'Temple-Entry Movement in Travancore, 1860-1940', *Social Scientist*, vol. 4, no. 8, 1976, pp. 3-27.

Kumar, Vivek, 'BSP and Dalit Aspirations', *Economic and Political Weekly*, vol. 39, no. 18, 1 May 2004, pp. 1778-81.

Mallavarapu, Ram Babu, 'Transformation of Dalit Politics from Bahujan Samaj to Sarvajan Samaj in Uttar Pradesh State: A Successful Model to Achieve the Political Power by the Deprived Communities in India', *European Journal of Social Sciences,* vol. 6, no. 2, 2008, pp. 277-9.

Mendelsohn, Oliver. '"A Harijan Elite?": The Lives of Some Untouchable Politician', *EPW*, vol. 21, no. 12, 1986, pp. 501-9.

Menon, Dilip, 'Intimations of Equality: Shrines and Politics in Malabar, 1900-1924', in Sumit Sarkar and Tanika Sarkar (eds.), *Caste in Modern India: A Reader*, vol. I, Permanent Black, Ranikhet, pp. 474-510.

Omvedt, Gail, 'The Anti-Caste Movement and the Discourse of Power', *Race and Class*, vol. 33, issue 2, Sage Journal, 1991, pp. 15-27.

________, 'Gandhi and the Pacification of the Indian National Revolution', *Bulletin of Concerned Asian Scholars*, vol. 5, no. 1, 1973, pp. 2-9.

O'Brien, Patrick K., 'Political Biography: A Polemical Review of the Genre', *Biography*, vol. 21, no. 1, 1998, pp. 50-1.

Patel, Hitendra K., 'Aspects of Mobilizations of Dalits in Bihar (1913-1952)', *Contemporary Voice of Dalit*, 9, 2017, pp. 63-72.

Raja, Ramiz, 'Dalit Political Consciousness and the Emergence of Bahujan Samaj Party in Uttar Pradesh', in Nityanand Tiwari (ed.), *Society and Politics*, January-June 2014, vol. 4, no. 1, VL Media Solutions, p. 144.

Rawat, Ramnarayan S., 'Making Claims for Power: A New Agenda in Dalit Politics of Uttar Pradesh: 1946-48', *Modern Asian Studies*, vol. 37, no. 3, 2003, pp. 585-612.

Roy, Bhaskar, 'Paradoxes of Dalit Politics in Uttar Pradesh', *India International Centre Quarterly*, Monsoon 2002, vol. 29, no. 2, pp. 107-16

Saklatvala, Shapurji, 'Who is this Gandhi?', *Labour Monthly*, July 1930, vol. 12, no. 7, pp. 1-49.

Samarendra, Padmanabh, 'Between Number and Knowledge: Career of Caste in Colonial Census', in Ishita Banerjee, Dube (ed.), *Caste in History*, Oxford University Press, London, 2008, pp. 46-66.

Shah, Ghanshyam, 'Anti-Untouchability Movements', in Vimal Shah (ed.), *Removal of Untouchability: Proceedings of a Seminar*, Department of Sociology, Gujarat University, 1980, pp. 110-50.

Singh, Jagpal, 'Ambedkarisation and Assertion of Dalit Identity Socio-Cultural Protest in Meerut District of Western Uttar Pradesh', *Economic and Political Weekly*, vol. 33, no. 40, 3 October 1998, pp. 2611-12.

Zelliot, Eleanor, 'Learning the Use of Political Means: The Mahars of Maharashtra', in Rajni Kothari (ed.), *Caste in Indian Politics*, Orient Longman, New Delhi, pp. 29-69.

Periodicals

Aaj (Hindi daily, Benares).

Calcutta Review (English monthly, Calcutta).

Dawn (English daily, Lahore).
Frontline (English Fortnightly, Madras).
Hindustan Times (English daily, Delhi).
India Today (New Delhi).
Leader (English daily, Allahabad).
National Herald (English daily, Lucknow).
National Mail.
Pioneer (English daily, Lucknow).
The Economic Times (New Delhi).
The Indian Express (New Delhi).
The Times of India (English daily, Lucknow).
The Bombay Chronicle.

Index

Affirmative Action, 17, 59, 61
All-India Depressed Classes League, 17, 27 85, 160, 168, 171, 174, 186, 188, 198, 199
Ambedkar, B.R. 10, 15, 31, 32, 34, 40, 41, 42, 43, 44, 45, 46, 47, 48, 49, 50, 51, 52, 53, 54, 55, 57, 58, 59, 62, 63, 64, 65, 67, 68, 69, 85, 86, 137, 155, 156, 157, 167, 169, 170, 171, 172, 173, 174, 178, 191, 192, 193, 217, 233, 234, 235, 236, 237, 238, 239, 240, 243
Asian, 69, 70, 144, 145, 146, 192, 193, 241, 243
Assembly, 17, 33, 61, 62, 63, 85, 116, 124, 129, 137, 145, 153, 158, 165, 171, 178, 188, 199, 237

Backward, 51, 52, 54, 56, 57, 59, 189, 192, 234, 242
Bahujan Politics, 31, 57, 58
Bahujan Samaj Party (BSP) 31, 57, 58, 60
Bahujan Samaj, 50, 54, 59, 60
Bakshi, S.R. 22
Bengal, 37, 80, 98, 101, 103, 120, 140, 152, 161, 185, 206, 234
Bihar 11, 22, 51, 62, 65, 73, 81, 83, 84, 85, 86, 89, 96, 101, 116, 124, 125, 126, 160, 165, 167, 168, 175, 177, 194, 197, 198, 199, 210, 217, 223, 224, 235, 243; Politics, 83-5
Bombay, 39, 43, 44, 45, 49, 50, 66, 67, 90, 99, 120, 129, 140, 149, 150, 152, 153, 154, 161, 163, 166, 167, 170, 186, 191, 194, 195, 196, 205, 234, 235, 236, 237, 238, 241, 244
Brahmin, 34, 43, 49, 50, 52, 53, 58, 60, 166, 205, 229
British, 34, 35, 36, 37, 46, 47, 49, 50, 64, 66, 68, 73, 84, 89, 90, 91, 119, 120, 121, 161, 168, 172, 220, 234, 242

Cabinet, 21, 27, 32, 63, 65, 66, 87, 94, 107, 172, 200, 201, 206, 207, 208, 211
Cahn, Edmund 16
Calcutta, 77, 79, 80, 81, 82, 99, 109, 123, 148, 152, 160, 162, 163, 165, 174, 175, 197, 198, 236, 238, 243
Caste System, 15, 17, 21, 24, 28, 32, 33, 34, 35, 36, 40, 55, 66,

72, 79, 156, 180, 181, 188, 195, 197, 199, 215, 217, 218, 219, 220, 221, 222, 223, 224, 226, 231, 242
Caste-free Hindu society, 158-60
Casteism, 15, 17, 22
Chanchreek, K.L. 12, 18, 21
Civil Rights, 16, 84
Class, 34, 43, 44, 67, 68, 69, 99, 152, 180, 234, 242, 243
Commission, 45, 60, 83, 89, 100, 150, 151, 168, 174, 177, 179, 233
Committee, 41, 42, 45, 86, 112, 114, 125, 137, 138, 143, 147, 191, 198, 200, 202, 204, 208
Company, 89, 154, 193, 195, 214, 233, 234, 237, 239, 240, 241
Conference, 27, 44, 46, 48, 49, 89, 124, 129, 134, 143, 144, 145, 149, 154, 160, 169, 170, 175
Congress for Democracy (CFD), 209-10
Congress Party, 15, 21, 22, 23, 31, 32, 50, 51, 52, 55, 56, 58, 60, 61, 63, 64, 65, 85, 125, 159, 172, 174, 198, 199, 200, 201, 202, 203, 204, 205, 206, 207, 209, 210, 212
Constituent Assembly, 17, 24, 158-60
Constitution, 17, 25, 33, 47, 52, 53, 83, 84, 121, 124, 141, 148, 158, 159, 175, 176, 178, 179, 184, 185, 186, 188, 204, 216, 225, 227, 230, 234, 237, 239
Council, 29, 43, 50, 85, 108, 147, 154, 171, 172, 199, 238

Dalit Identity, 17, 58
Dalit leader, 33, 34, 58
Dalit Mobilization, 57, 58
Dalit Oppression, 15, 46
Defence, 20, 33, 54, 129, 130, 132, 205, 206, 211
Delhi, 29, 58, 60, 61, 62, 66, 67, 69, 92, 93, 102, 116, 145, 149, 151, 152, 153, 154, 184, 189, 190, 191, 192, 193, 194, 195, 196, 209, 213, 214, 233, 234, 235, 236, 237, 238, 239, 240, 241, 243, 244
Democracy, 14, 21, 23, 24, 26, 66, 72, 77, 83, 84, 91, 127, 156, 157, 168, 177, 180, 193, 207, 208, 209, 210, 214, 221, 222, 224, 234, 237
Democratic Socialism, 16, 210
Discrimination, 61, 72, 74, 78, 79, 85, 92, 119, 163, 164, 165, 169, 170, 175, 178, 181, 186, 189, 215, 225, 226, 230

Economic Inequality, 15, 16
Emancipation, 12, 23, 27, 49, 50, 53, 58, 145, 161, 169, 190, 194, 224, 234
Emergency, 11, 66, 104, 129, 130, 207, 209, 210, 211, 239
Equality, 14, 15, 25, 32, 33, 34, 40, 41, 72, 79, 116, 127, 128, 148, 156, 157, 159, 161, 164, 167, 173, 177, 178, 182, 186, 187, 192, 193, 198, 217, 219, 220, 221, 226, 237, 243

Gandhi, Indira 11, 21, 179, 195, 200, 201, 202, 206
Gandhi, Mahatma, 11, 12, 16, 17, 21, 22, 23, 24, 27, 28, 32, 33,

46, 48, 49, 57, 58, 64, 65, 68, 71, 77, 78, 79, 81, 84, 121, 122, 123, 125, 127, 128, 131, 152, 155, 156, 158, 167, 168, 169, 170, 171, 172, 174, 179, 187, 189, 190, 191, 192, 193, 198, 199, 200, 201, 202, 203, 204, 205, 206, 209, 210, 212, 213, 218, 220, 222, 223, 224, 226, 234, 236, 237, 240, 242, 243

Government, 29, 46, 47, 67, 68, 83, 87, 89, 92, 98, 105, 110, 116, 119, 121, 128, 129, 130, 133, 134, 135, 137, 139, 140, 141, 142, 143, 145, 146, 147, 149, 150, 153, 159, 172, 188, 190, 191, 195, 202, 208, 213, 233, 235, 236, 237, 238

Green Revolution, 34, 89, 90

Harijan, 13, 16, 22, 29, 32, 34, 49, 51, 57, 63, 64, 65, 74, 81, 83, 84, 85, 86, 88, 92, 125, 152, 155, 157, 159, 160, 161, 163, 165, 167, 168, 169, 171, 173, 175, 176, 177, 179, 180, 181, 183, 184, 185, 186, 187, 188, 189, 190, 191, 193, 195, 199, 215, 217, 224, 234, 243

Hindi, 19, 31, 60, 66, 77, 101, 102, 161, 243

Hindu Orthodoxy, 15, 17

Hindu, 13, 14, 16, 33, 39, 41, 42, 43, 44, 45, 46, 47, 48, 52, 57, 63, 64, 65, 71, 74, 75, 78, 80, 81, 82, 85, 86, 87, 123, 155, 158, 160, 161, 162, 164, 167, 168, 169, 170, 171, 177, 178, 182, 183, 185, 186, 189, 190, 191, 192, 199, 205, 215, 220, 221, 224, 226, 229, 236

History, 37, 66, 67, 152, 194, 234, 235, 236, 237, 238, 239, 240, 242, 243

Indian National Congress, 33, 46, 81, 84, 85, 90, 121, 125, 127, 150, 169, 198, 199, 234, 238

Indo-Pak War (1971), 206, 207

International Labour Organization (ILO), 14, 15, 19, 21, 22, 34, 35, 36, 40, 41, 70, 106, 121, 125, 128, 131, 134, 144, 145, 146, 157, 158, 170, 174, 194, 240

Janata Dal, 11, 174

Janata Party 21, 61, 207, 209, 210, 211, 212

Kanshi Ram, 34, 53, 54, 55, 58, 59, 60, 61, 62, 155, 156, 173, 174, 191, 217,

Kumar, Meira 19, 62, 163, 168, 177, 201

Labour Reforms, 90, 118-20, 151-52, 158-60

Labour, 50, 87, 119, 121, 126, 127, 129, 130, 139, 140, 141, 142, 143, 144, 145, 146, 147, 149, 150, 151, 152, 153, 154, 186, 187, 188, 191, 236, 242, 243

Legislative, 43, 50, 62, 63, 85, 116, 137, 153, 199

Lok Sabha, 11, 19, 29, 88, 93, 96, 101, 117, 153, 193, 194, 195, 196, 203, 204, 205, 212, 233, 236; Debates, 118-119

London, 46, 48
Lucknow, 27, 31, 84, 100, 146, 147, 154, 161, 237, 244

Madras, 99, 101, 102, 140, 187, 188, 189, 190, 244
Maharashtra, 37, 40, 50, 54, 67, 177, 192, 236, 237, 238, 243
Marginalized Communities, 15-17
Mayawati, 57, 59, 61, 62
Minority Rights, 84-85
Mukherjee, Pranab 19
Muslim, 39, 64, 65, 123, 162, 167, 189, 220

Narayan, Jayaprakash (JP) 20, 31, 66, 103, 156, 164, 165, 173, 187, 192, 195, 209, 233, 236, 238, 239, 240, 242
Nationalism, 14, 82, 122, 151, 164, 223, 224, 238
Nehru, Jawaharlal 13, 78, 84, 116, 126, 127, 145, 187, 200

Omvedt, Gail, 40, 52, 67, 68, 69, 155, 164, 191, 192, 194, 239, 243
Opposition Politics, 210

Parliament, 19, 20, 29, 32, 62, 66, 77, 84, 93, 94, 95, 104, 107, 108, 109, 110, 134, 138, 139, 153, 173, 191, 193, 195, 196, 197, 202, 203, 211, 212, 213, 234, 235, 236, 239
Parliamentary, 93, 107, 139, 191, 195, 211, 234, 235, 239
Paswan, Ram Vilas, 62 174
Patriotism, 14, 88
Phule, Jyotirao 39, 40, 49, 53, 60, 69, 156, 192, 235, 237, 239, 242
Poona Pact, 58
Power, 67, 68, 69, 70, 193, 235, 236, 237, 242, 243
Prasad, Bimal 18
Prasad, Rajendra 20, 21, 78, 81, 167, 170, 199, 221, 224
President, 19, 20, 21, 27, 83, 90, 168, 171, 176, 177, 179, 186, 188, 191, 200, 202, 203, 204, 207, 208, 212, 217, 221
Press, 66, 68, 69, 70, 117, 151, 152, 191, 192, 193, 195, 234, 235, 236, 237, 238, 239, 240, 241, 242, 243
Prime Minister, 12, 29, 32, 71, 73, 116, 145, 179, 197, 200, 201, 202, 205, 207, 210, 211, 212
Public Distribution System (PDS), 89, 90

Rawls, John 15-16
Religious Conversion, 17
Resignation Letter, 209

Scheduled Castes, 17
Singh, Nau Nihal, 14, 18, 153, 154, 165, 174, 194, 195
Social Democracy, 16, 210
Social Justice, 15-17, 84, 151-52
social reformers 119, 166, 225, 229,

Untouchability, 15, 45-46, 181

Voting Rights, 84-85

Women Workers, 118, 120
Working Class, 118-22